AN
AMERICAN SOLDIER

An American Soldier and Diplomat

HORACE PORTER AT SIXTY

AN AMERICAN SOLDIER AND DIPLOMAT

Horace Porter

BY

ELSIE PORTER MENDE

IN COLLABORATION WITH

HENRY GREENLEAF PEARSON

ILLUSTRATED

NEW YORK : : FREDERICK A.
STOKES COMPANY : : MCMXXVII

PREFACE

My father, Horace Porter, in the course of his more than fourscore years, was soldier, business man, active citizen, writer, orator, and diplomat. He was constantly associated with men of distinction and in each field achieved distinction himself. His career thus calls for a biographical treatment that shall show how it was interwoven with the times in which he lived. To this end I have called Professor Pearson to my assistance.

It happens that I myself am able to present my father's life from another point of view. From my earliest years I had the benefit of his gift for story-telling, and I soon began to store in my memory pictures of scenes in which he had taken part. Then, too, he knew how to make a companion of me, and so, during the years of my girlhood, I was with him a great deal, met many of his friends, and was continually in touch with his interests. By the time he went to Paris, I was able to share his life on terms of real helpfulness.

Although in his day my father had a considerable reputation as a speaker, both on after-dinner occasions and at gatherings of a more serious nature, it has seemed to me that after this lapse of time the value of these speeches was not sufficient to justify quotation from them to any considerable extent. Two of the more important ones, however, are printed in the Appendix.

My father was primarily a man of action: he enjoyed putting his hand to large undertakings and getting things done, often effacing himself and letting the credit go to others. Even with me he was reticent about his motives and what he had accomplished. Thus the reader will have

v

to interpret the nature of the man largely from his deeds as they are here set forth.

The main source of material has been my father's papers. The most important of these are his home letters, written during the time of his service in the army, and the letter-press books covering the years in New York and Paris. With a few exceptions the letters addressed to him he evidently destroyed. For the chapters dealing with the Civil War I have made free use of his *Campaigning with Grant,* in which he retold for the public the stories which, as a child, I heard again and again from his lips. The copy which he gave me, with an inscription, has, indeed, been my guide and inspiration in writing this book of my own.

In the chapters dealing with our social life in Paris and our travels, I have relied on my journal kept during those years. This record, it must be remembered, was made by a very young woman, upon whom the unusual experiences that fell to her lot made a vivid impression; it supplies, as it were, snap-shot glimpses of the scenes and people in the midst of which my father was moving. Moreover, not only have these incidents and these personages, then so notable, receded into the past, but in many cases their like will never be seen again. Their very type is gone forever.

I am under especial obligation to the State Department at Washington, through the courtesy of the Honorable William Phillips, now our Minister to Canada, for permission to use confidential dispatches written by my father while Ambassador. I also wish to make acknowledgment of assistance rendered by the American embassies at Paris and Berlin, and by the American and the German legations at Berne. I am especially indebted to M. Gabriel Hanotaux for help on the chapter dealing with the Spanish-American war. He has been most kind in preparing for me and permitting me to use an interpretation of the position of the French Government at that time. I am grateful also for help from M. Henry Allizé, formerly French

Ambassador to Switzerland; from Peter Augustus Jay, recently American Ambassador to Argentina; from the late Colonel Bailly-Blanchard, my father's devoted friend at the Paris Embassy; from James Brown Scott; from Major Fehr von Ernst; from the late Henry W. Hayden of New York; from the late Albert J. Beveridge; from Mrs. Willis Sparks, of Macon, Georgia; and from Miss Emma Foster, a member of my father's household during his last years. Two of my girlhood friends, Mrs. Beveridge (Catherine Eddy) and Mrs. Frank Griswold (Alice Littleton) have given me advice on many parts of the book.

ELSIE PORTER MENDE.

CONTENTS

ix

Contents

BOOK IV

LAST YEARS—1905-1921

ILLUSTRATIONS

INTRODUCTION

FATHER AND DAUGHTER

On a bitterly cold morning in February, 1921, I sailed out of New York harbor to return to my home in Switzerland. I stood on the deck of the *Rotterdam* and watched the tall sky-scrapers become specks on the horizon. As I saw vanish one by one all the old landmarks of the city in which I had spent the early years of my life, my heart was full of misgiving. I had left behind me, in the big, old-fashioned New York house, the one person who still linked me to my native land,—my father,—who had been my favorite companion and best friend ever since the earliest days of my childhood. Would he still be there to meet me at the top of the staircase when I returned in the early summer? I had come to him so many times across the three thousand miles of water, each year finding him slightly older, but always the same devoted friend. Would this time be the last?

The old familiar setting of the different rooms in the house came vividly to my mind,—the paneled oak hall, the two drawing-rooms with their fine old tapestries and furniture and my father's favorite painting, a gorgeous Vanloo. In the library stood the cabinet containing his decorations and medals, and on the walls hung his portrait and that of my grandfather, together with a picture of the "Battle of the Serapis and the Bonhomme Richard." In the corner under this last stood a fine bronze copy of Houdon's bust of John Paul Jones.[1] The dining-room came distinctly before me, with its crystal and silver, the winter sun warming the oak paneling and showing the clock made from an unexploded shell. Upstairs in the front corner room were my mother's portrait, mementoes of my two brothers and myself, photographs of my children. I saw again the old mahogany chest of drawers, pieces of rare porcelain, the large Empire book-case with gilt wire-work, the comfortable red sofa, the delicately made Louis XVI cabinet, the big, important-looking mahogany table with finely chiseled bronzes of the same period, the shaded lamps, the fireplace. Near one of the three windows stood my father's old rocking-chair. It had belonged to his mother,[2] and I had spent many a happy hour in it on his knee, listening to his stories.

I remember him at first with thick black hair and slightly gray mustache, tall, erect, and slender. The weight of his years had now turned his hair to an iron gray, leaving it as thick as when he was a boy; the tall figure had become a little bent, and he walked with a cane, only at times pulling himself up into soldierly posture. The keen blue eyes were still full of vigor and life. Little in his bearing and looks betokened his eighty-four years. A certain peace and gentleness had come into his face,—the look of a man who had finished with life, who had fought a good fight, who was at peace with the world. Rocking gently backward and forward in his chair, his hands interlocked, he had said to me in his low, melodious voice, the evening before my departure: "Never mind about me. Go back to the children, and come again later. Don't let any one here scare you with a foolish telegram. My time has come. I am all right. I am only sitting here waiting for 'taps.'"

Would he have followed the clear notes of the bugle before I could see him again? The good-by said at the top of the staircase only a few hours before—was that truly to be the last? He had been so full of life I had longed to stay with him; yet I knew it was necessary for me to return at least for a few months to my home and family. Such was the trend of my thoughts as, from the deck of the *Rotterdam,* in the blustering February wind, I watched the great metropolis sink slowly into oblivion.

On a hot June day a few months later, I stood on the deck of the *Aquitania* and saw, with eyes dimmed by tears, the great city again loom up before me. I had come too late: for the old soldier "taps" had suddenly sounded, and he had followed peacefully and quietly the notes of the eternal bugle. The great house mocked me with its emptiness as slowly I mounted the stairs. The old familiar objects were in their accustomed places—nothing was changed; only the tall figure had vanished, and had left for me, as a blessed inheritance, the happy memories of our long years of close companionship. In every room the strong personality of my father rose before me; each object had its tale to tell, and all had as their center his long and varied life.

All these treasures, doubly valuable to me in their associations, I had now to start for their new home in Switzerland; in the course of a few weeks the house, despoiled of its furniture, became a huge, empty shell, and only the beautiful woodwork remained to remind one of what it had once been. Then, one suffocating August day, when the fierce, hot wind was rattling at the windows and sweeping through the gaunt rooms, raising little whirlwinds of dust where the windows were open in a vain attempt to cool the heavy atmosphere, I mounted the carpetless stairs to perform one long task still remaining,—the sorting of my father's papers. I knew there was much to destroy, but also many interesting documents to be found. Chests and cupboards in one of the upper rooms were packed with boxes and bundles and files; and with willing hands to aid me for days I worked,—sorted, read, put aside, and burned. So much of my father's life was revealed in those many closely written sheets of paper! Carefully tied together and marked in my mother's writing, "for Elsie," were all his letters to her. There were the earliest ones, full of nothing but love and happiness; others, hurriedly written on scraps of paper before a camp fire on the eve of battle,

the writer trying to instill courage and a sense of security
in the heart of the anxious girl so many miles away,—
hoping, too, for a short leave of absence. One letter gave
his detailed plans for their wedding. Another described
Lincoln's visit to Grant. A third was brimming over with
joy and happiness at the news of the birth of his little son.
Other letters were written at different periods of his life,
from Washington, New York, London. Each one, no
matter how hastily penned, showed his strong affection and
solicitude for his wife and his boys, and in the later letters
there was always an extra message for his one wee girl.

My father's war letters to his mother and sister,—letters
yellow with age, the ink faded to a dull brown,—were carefully folded in an old linen bag, and had evidently been
passed from hand to hand to be read by different members
of the family. They proved to be a fund of information,
giving details, anecdotes, and graphic descriptions of a
young officer's life at the front. His deep affection for his
mother showed on every page. He begs her not to worry,
not to believe the newspaper accounts of the desperate
fighting. The danger is exaggerated. Yes, he had had a
touch of fever, but he was all right again. He was wounded,
but only a scratch. He is in excellent health. He thanks
her for the warm socks knitted by her own dear hands.
No boy ever had a better, kinder mother. He only regrets
that he can do so little to repay her devotion.

On a shelf in one of the deep cupboards were packages
of other letters, which I opened one by one. At the end
of four carefully written pages I read the signature of
Joseph Choate. The big sprawling autograph attached to
the letters of William McKinley caught my eye, and also
a long letter in the slightly pointed, running hand of Benjamin Harrison. I recognized the scholarly writing of John
Hay, the almost unreadable signature of Joe Jefferson, the
hieroglyphics of Henry Irving, a letter in Mark Twain's
distinct writing, and a hasty note penned in the nervous,

trembling hand of Edwin Booth. Other letters I found from John Sherman, General W. T. Sherman, General Sheridan, Robert Lincoln, Admiral Dewey, and Theodore Roosevelt; some letters from General Grant were in a package by themselves. There were numerous newspaper clippings, in English and French; and a bundle of letters from my father's French friends,—Jules Cambon, Ambassador to the United States, Delcassé, Minister of Foreign Affairs, the Marquis de Lasteyrie, Baron d'Estournelles, and the artist, Benjamin Constant. I read each one and put it aside.

Among the rough drafts of my father's speeches was a large photograph of Li Hung Chang, the great Chinese statesman, with a long inscription in Chinese, which literally surrounded the likeness. Another photograph was in a blue leather frame mounted with the royal lilies of France and bore the legend, "A mon ami le Général Horace Porter," signed "Philippe, Comte de Paris." [3] In a heavily sealed box I found the large cross set in diamonds of the Légion d'Honneur, the highest decoration given by the French Government. I well remember the day that Delcassé, then Minister of Foreign Affairs, brought it to my father, who was the first American to receive it. Continuing to unpack the box, I found a gaudy-looking order, given by the murdered Sultan, Abdul Hamid, the orders of the Loyal Legion and of the Sons of the American Revolution, the insignia of the Army of the Potomac, of the Army of the Cumberland, and of the Navy League. A heavy gold medal beautifully chiseled with the head of John Paul Jones showed on the reverse side the battle of the *Serapis* and the *Bonhomme Richard*. There were also Grant and Franklin medals; others, of silver or gold, with inscriptions in French or in English, had been given to my father to commemorate important anniversaries in the celebration of which he had taken part. On a chair beside me I laid the heavy black robe and the hoods of a Doctor of Letters:

one was the brilliant crimson of Harvard, the other the deep orange of the House of Nassau. Both universities claimed him, and both had honored him.

One small medal lying at the bottom of the package containing the decorations had been almost overlooked. I picked it up; it was of bronze, with the American coat of arms indifferently chiseled on one side and at the top the word VALOR. Turning it over I read, "To Captain Horace Porter, U.S.A., Chickamauga, Sept. 20, 1864. For conspicuous gallantry on the field of battle." This was the medal of honor, the highest decoration that America can give her soldiers and sailors, and my father treasured it as he did his swords. A gold medal, with the same inscription but of beautiful design and execution,* I had seen hanging at his neck, above his other decorations, on the rare occasions when he wore his uniform. This simple medal was for him a reminder of four years of hardship and self-sacrifice,—the years which had most influenced his life and of which the memories were the most vivid and poignant.

Another remembrance of those years I found in my father's desk in an envelope enclosed in a small box and marked "Lee's Pencil." When I opened the envelope there rolled out on my knees a medium-sized, brownish pencil, the blunt end of which bore the marks of a child's teeth. Instantly I recalled that summer afternoon at Elberon, years and years ago, when, drawing pictures at Father's desk, I broke my point by the weight of my talent and helped myself to this very pencil in this very box. It is true Father had forbidden me to touch it, but being unable to read the inscription I saw no value in the pencil. As I drew, suffering the while from two very imminent front teeth, I chewed the top of it, actually at last cutting the teeth in the process. Then I was conscience-stricken. Mother entered the room, and there was a scene; but matters became still worse when my father was called in. He never punished us, but he had

* See page 286.

such a way of saying things in a few words that they remained forever in one's memory. He was distressed, which to me was worse than all the punishments in the world. I was moved to tears, and promised never again to touch that pencil. When I found it again now, after thirty years, I realized that its preservation was due to the fact that it had been lent by my father to General Lee to make an alteration in the terms of surrender at Appomattox Courthouse.[4]

Surrounded thus by the mementoes of my father's life and of his services to the nation, I forgot for a time my sorrow and the big, lonely house, and fell to meditating on the days when, a very young child, I had heard from his lips the stories of his boyhood and the heroic days of the Civil War. My first clear recollections of him went back to the early eighties, when he was established in New York. I was very young but, because I was his only daughter and my brothers were already at school and college, my father made me his companion.

It was in the sitting-room of our apartment at 10 West Thirtieth Street, as he sat with me in his mother's big chair, that he told and retold me the tales which have remained so fresh in my memory. In those hours the reticence that usually covered his deep vein of sentiment was broken. On the other hand, I had the full benefit of his keenness to see and appreciate the comic side of life. He never missed a joke.

When he talked about the Harrisburg days, he loved to speak of his mother, of her goodness and kindness to all about her, her understanding, her keen, dry humor, her devotion to her boys. There was his father, the Governor of Pennsylvania, a brilliant, clever man, with a determined character, but rather a terror to his boys when his quick Irish temper got the better of him. The stories made me see with my own eyes these two figures moving among their many guests, and even more vividly the boy Horace, as he grew up: his first journey, his first attempt at engineering, his father's despair at his backwardness in learning to talk, his dog Veto and horses, his long talks and labors with the old shoemaker, his afternoons at the iron furnace. There were stories, too, of life at West Point, wherein I saw him kicking the interloper out of his tent, or, in very different mood, dancing with a certain slender girl; but West Point was to my mind always connected with the Civil War. My father graduated and within a year was precipitated into the heart of the struggle. His anecdotes of its leaders and his personal experiences interested me at first more than the actual war itself.

The stories of certain battles with the horrors effaced and deeds of heroism accentuated appealed greatly to my imagination. One told of a fight against terrible odds, in a place with the queer name of Chickamauga, led by a young officer,—a friend of Father's, so he said, but he never could recall his name; another was of his own escape from the pursuing Rebels; then there was the story of Sheridan on Rienzi; stories of Lincoln at Grant's camp,—Lincoln on Cincinnati, Lincoln with the negro troops, Lincoln with the kittens,—surely inexhaustible subjects with which to entertain a child. But the figure that was most real to me of all was Father's old Commander-in-Chief, General Grant. This was partly because there were a hundred more stories about him than about any one else, partly because I knew General Grant myself, and partly, no doubt, because my father talked to me so earnestly of what the great soldier had done for America.

It was through Grant's energy, foresight, and brilliant military strategy that the Union had been saved. The Union saved meant everything to my father. It was the realization of the principle for which he had fought during four long years. He saw before him the future prosperity of generations of his countrymen living under a united government in the great rich land that he had helped to win for them. It had been saved from the disaster of division into small squabbling republics. Grant and Lincoln had firmly cemented the foundations laid down by Washington. Therefore my father never allowed any criticism of General Grant. Grant and Lincoln stood at the head of the list of heroes, and we children were taught to respect and honor them. Their faults were easily forgotten and covered up; we were told to remember only the great services rendered to our country in its hour of need. A child's mind could hardly take in the full significance of these statements, but I grasped enough to feel greatly impressed when shaking hands with Lincoln's son. And the first time I spoke to General Grant my hands became quite cold and my tongue literally clove to the roof of my mouth. More clearly than Father could tell me through stories or through explanation, I knew that Grant was the man who stood above all others in his affection and devotion. And I appreciated this regard more and more keenly as through the years of my girlhood I saw the time and energy that he devoted to preserving, by means of the great monument on Riverside Drive, the memory of his Chief.

Thus from my father's lips I learned in my early years the story of that portion of his life when he saw and took part in heroic deeds and received at first hand the inspiration of heroic men. The characters in his stories were so real and his narratives were so vivid that I, as it were, lived through the past with him. Eager that others should know and cherish these memories as I did, I used to exclaim, "Father, what a wonderful story-book you could write!" He answered, "I may write a book some day, but not about myself; there's enough of that sort of book on the market now." When again urged, in later life, to write his memoirs, he always refused, saying, "The best part of my life was spent with General Grant, and I have written enough about myself in my book on his campaigns." *

* *Campaigning with Grant.*

Although the repeated demands of his friends had not shaken him from this decision, I myself had never quite given up the idea, conceived in my early childhood, of taking Father's stories and putting them into a book. Later, when he was Ambassador in Paris, the share that I had in his life made me realize that his devotion to his country and his labors for her good were no less whole-hearted and effective when he was sixty than when he was twenty-five.

Now his life was ended. As I sat alone in the deserted room and saw that life as a whole, with all its varied activities and distinguished achievements, what had once been a vague wish began to take shape as a definite plan. In the manuscripts, letters, and folios which littered the bare floor was material to help me build my monument to Horace Porter. The task which I set myself then has been a labor of love: I have been living with happy and inspiring memories. May some of the happiness and inspiration that have been mine be granted to those who read these pages.

An American Soldier and Diplomat

BOOK I
THE SOLDIER
1837-1865

AN AMERICAN SOLDIER AND DIPLOMAT

CHAPTER I

ANCESTRY, BOYHOOD, YOUTH

HORACE PORTER came of a family which played an important part in the history of Pennsylvania from the time of the Revolutionary War. Some of its members stood high in their chosen professions; others were noted for their sense of public duty. Among these both his father and his grandfather stood out as men of marked personality.

Robert Porter, with whom the story of the family in America begins, a man of good Scotch-Irish stock, came to this country in 1720, and acquired considerable land in Norristown, near Philadelphia. His son Andrew (1743-1813) grandfather of Horace Porter, was as a youth so much interested in study, particularly in mathematics and science, that he determined to support himself by teaching. Abandoning any attempt to help his father in the management of his lands, he opened a school in Norristown. Later, on the advice of David Rittenhouse, a warm friend of the family, he taught in Philadelphia. At the outbreak of the Revolution, leaving five motherless children at home,[1] he joined the Continental forces, his first rank being that of captain. At Germantown, his gallant conduct in fighting on with a handful of men when the rest of his command had been killed or captured was commended by Washington, who later appointed him a member of his staff and selected him to superintend the making of munitions for

3

the army. After the war he refused an offer of the chair
of mathematics at the University of Pennsylvania. Although he established himself at Norristown, where he had
built himself a house (still standing, a beautiful example of
Colonial architecture), he was not content merely to be a
gentleman farmer. Thus he undertook the work of survey-
ing the boundary lines of Pennsylvania, which occupied him
for some years, and from 1809 until his death in 1813 he
was surveyor-general of the state. He also held the rank
of major-general in the state militia. During these years
he was offered two appointments by his friend President
Madison,—that of brigadier-general in the army and that
of secretary of war; but these he felt obliged to decline on
account of his age.

In 1777 Andrew Porter had married as his second wife
Elizabeth Parker, and it was the sixth child of this marriage, born in 1788 and named after David Rittenhouse,
who was Horace Porter's father. David Porter had both
ability and force of character, and his work under his father
in the surveyor-general's office gave a direction to his
powers that determined his career. He became interested
in the State of Pennsylvania at a period when it was about
to develop rapidly. He studied its mineral resources and
engaged in the manufacture of pig-iron at Huntingdon, in
the central part of the state; he advocated the building of
roads and canals. He also saw the need of a public school
system and worked unremittingly for its establishment.

These interests, together with the fact that David Porter
was full of energy and enthusiasm and possessed unusual
ability as a speaker, took him into public life. He served
in both the Assembly and the Senate, and by the time he
was fifty was so well known and highly regarded that he
was nominated by the Democratic party as its candidate
for governor, and elected. Having been chosen for a second
term, he held the office for six years, from 1839 to 1845.

Pennsylvania was fortunate in having at its head during

GENERAL ANDREW PORTER
In Independence Hall, Philadelphia

this period a man with a vision of a great future for the state and with courage to stand by his guns on a matter of conviction. Perhaps Porter's most important act in this respect was his determined fight to insure the payment of interest on the public debt at a time when the repudiation fever was strong in various states of the Union; but no less striking was his course, when an anti-Catholic riot broke out in Philadelphia, in going to the scene of the trouble and taking command of the situation in person. His opposition to capital punishment won for him the nickname of "Pardon Porter," and he was also the subject of much ridicule for suggesting that the transportation facilities of the state needed for their proper development a railroad running from Pittsburgh to the Mississippi River.[2]

On matters of national policy, Governor Porter's opinions were, as may be imagined, clear-cut and vigorous. Although a sturdy Democrat and a friend of James Buchanan, he was strongly opposed to slavery and followed with deep concern the steps by which the questions of slavery and disunion became the dominant issues in our public life. It was no little surprise to him to see the Illinois lawyer whom one of his Kentucky cousins had married[3] emerge from obscurity and finally become the standard-bearer of the new party opposed to the extension of slavery; but he could not overcome the party allegiance of a life-time to vote for Abraham Lincoln in 1860.

After his retirement from office at the end of 1844 Porter continued to live in Harrisburg; he devoted himself to his iron furnaces there and at Reading and Lancaster, and on his farm outside the city he raised Durham cattle and Kentucky horses. He invested some money in railroads (and lost it in the panic of '57), and in 1859 he traveled to Texas to advise his friend Houston, the new Governor, about building a Pacific railroad through that state. The Civil War, however, upset all his projects; many of his investments became worthless, and at the time of his death in 1867 a great part of his large fortune had disappeared.

In 1820, when he was thirty-two years of age, David Porter had married Josephine McDermott, the seventeen-year-old daughter of William McDermott of Spruce Creek, owner of one of the first iron furnaces in Pennsylvania. Her mind was more profound than that of her brilliant husband, and in spite of the fact that she bore him nine children and had the management of a large household she continued to cultivate it by reading and study. Generous and kind, she possessed a Scotch shrewdness and self-control which somewhat tempered the Governor's impulsiveness. Her good deeds were done without ostentation: if a basket of food was to go to some one in need, she did not give it to a servant, but carried it herself, well hidden under her cloak. Her charity and kindness to the poor and sick were not limited by convenience: she did not hesitate at such acts of devotion as nursing a negro servant through the small-pox.

All her life she was her husband's right-hand man. She copied and wrote for him, entertained his guests, and by her wit and charm made the Governor's house a center of hospitality. She accepted his high position and large fortune with the same even spirit in which she accepted his retirement from public life and the loss of that fortune. Of her it can truly be said that she cared little for the treasures of this world, "where moth and rust doth corrupt and where thieves break through and steal."

Horace Porter, the seventh child and sixth son of David and Josephine Porter, was born at Huntingdon on April 15, 1837; his name he owed to his oldest brother, William,[4] who at the time was engaged in reading the Odes of Horace. As the two children afterward born to his parents died in infancy, he grew up the youngest member of the family.

At the age of three he took his first journey,—from Huntingdon to Harrisburg. The family traveled by canal-boat, the only other means of conveyance being the stage-coach over bad roads. The bridges across the canal were very low, and a man was always stationed at the bow of the boat to call out, "Low bridge!" The sight of ladies in crinolines suddenly flopping down on the deck of the boat, bobbing their heads, occasionally with a bonnet on one ear, evidently greatly impressed the small boy. The next day he was discovered in the garden under an old tree. He had dug out the earth under the roots and made a little canal. A negro servant was pouring in water, and Horace was manipulating a piece of wood with a pebble on it up and down the canal. When the piece of wood passed under one of the roots, he called out, "B'idge!" and when the pebble was knocked off he was delighted. This was his first attempt at engineering.

Almost as early in his life occurred the "Veto" episode. One day the Governor came home in a state of wrath: he would "veto" something, and emphasized the fact with even more than his usual violence. Horace, now aged four, deciding that if the Governor used the word so much it must be something good, immediately christened his new puppy "Veto." Veto was a true story-book dog and did wonderful things: he helped drive the Governor's pedigree cows from the farm back to the stables at evening. When the railroad track was to be crossed, Veto ran ahead, looked up and down the track, ran back to the cows, barked at them and nipped them in their hind legs to hurry them out of danger.

As Horace grew older he showed a practical aptitude which first expressed itself in his learning enough of shoe-making to resole the family's shoes and even to make a pair for his sister. The old man who taught him the art had come to America in his youth to begin life again in a young and free country; he used to tell the boy tales of the old world, monarchical governments, enormous standing armies, wars and revolutions. He talked about the new invention

of the "riggleway"—a danger to the health and lives of the
population and a detriment to the beauty of the country.
This was the railroad which had just been completed between Harrisburg and Philadelphia, a journey of eight
hours!

Governor Porter's iron furnace near Harrisburg supplied another outlet for the boy's practical energy. He
made friends with the workmen, studied the different parts
of the machinery, and was constantly trying to think out
improvements. Indeed, at the age of twelve he invented
a gauge to indicate the supply of water in the tanks that
fed the steam-boilers. Every day after school, with his dog
Rover at his heels (Veto at a ripe old age had gone where
all good dogs go), he walked out to the furnace and worked
until evening. The hours spent there undoubtedly helped
him in his after-life. He first of all learned to work and to
think while working, to work systematically and to achieve
an object. He was thrown with men much older than himself who held entirely different views of life from his own.
First they tolerated him, then they liked him, and in the end
admired and respected him. A rather silent boy,—he had
been very slow in learning to talk,—he had a quiet, dignified
bearing which was never haughty but compelled a certain
esteem from all those, young and old, who came in contact
with him.

In the Governor's hospitable house people were constantly coming and going and they were a source of great
interest to the eager boy; in later years he would recount
innumerable stories of them. "One old man," he used to
say, "especially amused me; he was a State Senator and
came every year from his farm when the Legislature met.
He declared he had never indulged in the luxury of a bed;
that was all right for city folks, but the floor and a blanket
were good enough for him. My mother tried to persuade
him to use one of the guest rooms, but he refused, saying
he preferred the drawing-room, provided he could keep the

MRS. PORTER

GOVERNOR PORTER

fire up all night. He would roll himself in his blanket, lie down in front of the fire, and snore peacefully until morning. He was not exactly a welcome guest; but then, as my mother said, 'It takes all sorts of people to make a world.' She was always kind to the old man, and I liked him because he had killed buffaloes and seen Indians."

The visitor in whom Horace especially delighted was General Sam Houston, later Governor of Texas, a hero just returned from the Mexican War. The boy would creep in noiselessly to his father's study and listen with bated breath to the General's stories of the war. On the subject of railroads Houston was also intensely interesting: unlike the old shoemaker, he considered that in this new invention lay the wealth and future of America. Then he talked of the Army; his disapproval of West Point was sure to arouse the Pennsylvanian's opposition. Another point of controversy between the two men was slavery: it came up again and again, and the only way of pouring oil on the troubled waters was to change the subject to politics in general, and particularly America's foreign policy. This topic, on which the two gentlemen were eloquent, became still more interesting to the boy a few years later, when James Buchanan was Minister at the Court of St. James. Governor Porter often read aloud letters from him, and Horace used to listen absorbed, all the time forming his own picture of the court of Victoria. In this way he had his first glimpse of that European world to the problems of which he was later to give so much thought.

As for the more conventional side of his education, that, too, was a field in which, as in practical matters, he showed ability to take hold of things for himself. His sister, Elizabeth, was his favorite companion; she read aloud to him and together they learned by heart a good part of the English translation of *Wilhelm Tell*. Later came *Tales from Shakespeare;* for fairy tales he never had much use. The old Governor was a strong believer in learning languages, and he had his younger children taught French,—an almost unheard-of accomplishment in those days. Horace's first taste of music was a concert given by Christine Nilsson, and after hearing Jenny Lind's rendering of the mad scene in *Lucia* he bought himself a flute, and in the evenings got the old flutist of the town band to give him lessons. He worked away until he, too, could "do" the mad scene.

At the age of thirteen he was sent to school at Lawrenceville, where he formed a friendship with the headmaster, Dr. Samuel Hamill, which remained a strong influence all his life; another life-long friendship made at this time was with his classmate, Alfred Woodhull.[5] During those four years at Lawrenceville the quiet boy with the "iron will," as his father characterized him, naturally developed fast in his relations with other people. He proved to have an ever-ready laugh and the capacity for making others laugh; to a still greater degree he had the capacity for making others do as he wished. He built a house in the grove, he got up a boat company and went to Philadelphia to buy a boat for it, he organized a military company and drilled it with the wooden guns he had made. At the same time his scholarship put him among the best students in his class. When he discovered in himself a strong desire to go to West Point, Dr. Hamill, by way of endorsing his application for an appointment, wrote of him to Jefferson Davis, then Secretary of War: "He is well formed and of fine appearance, healthy and energetic, standing at the head of his class in Latin, French, and Mathematics. His talents are of a superior order. If his life is spared, he is destined to be a man of commanding influence and to make his mark in whatever sphere Providence may place him."

This first application Governor Porter insisted on making to President Pierce, though his son objected on the ground that these appointments "at large" were intended for the sons of army officers. When the Congressman of the Harrisburg district, Nerr Middlesworth, interviewed

Pierce, he was met by the statement that the President preferred appointing sons of veterans of the Mexican War.
Middlesworth parried this remark with the argument that
Porter's grandfather had been an officer of high standing
in the Revolution and commended for his courage by Washington. It was all to no purpose. Horace Porter's name
was not on the list of the President's appointments for the
year 1854.

Disappointed but not in the least discouraged, the boy
enrolled for a year in the Lawrence Scientific School at
Harvard; in one of the debates there he took the stand
that a soldier fights better under a republican form of government than under a monarchy. As soon as the midwinter
vacation gave him a chance, he went straight to Washington
to see Middlesworth and ask for a Congressional appointment to West Point. Apparently he had not cared to request his father to finance the trip, and he was so hard up
that he was forced to spend the night on a park bench.
Middlesworth said that he was tired of appointing boys to
West Point because they "never wanted to stick."

"I'll stick if you give me a chance," replied the applicant.

"Well," said the Congressman, "you do sorter look that
way to me, and I guess I will give you the chance."

Old Middlesworth was a man to be trusted, and Horace
went back for his last term at Harvard with a happy heart.
In due season Governor Porter was informed by the authorities at Washington that his son had passed his preliminary
examinations and was to enter the United States Military
Academy as a cadet on July 1, 1855.[6]

Two decisions were uppermost in Horace Porter's mind
when he reached West Point: first, to be a good scholar and,
second, not to be hazed. His high standing in his class[7]
varied very little during the whole five years he spent at
West Point. He was especially proficient in English, mathematics, French, chemistry, engineering, ethics and philosophy, and the science of war, his standing in his class in

these branches varying from first to eighth. Of French,
which he had begun early and pursued with steady interest,
he had obtained a very good mastery; much of his progress
was due to the habit which he formed at school of reading
aloud to himself, slowly and distinctly, with his French dic-
tionary always at hand.

As for hazing, one or two incidents occurred which put
young Porter on his guard and showed him that, although
most of the upper classmen had decided to leave him alone,
one man was determined to get him into trouble. The
cadets all went into camp during part of the summer. Sleeping practically in the open air and getting used to the early
drills in extreme heat or rain and mud was more difficult for
a Plebe than for an upper classman, especially as, in spite of
drills, fatigue, and bad weather, the equipment was supposed to be kept in perfect condition. Tents were provided
for the cadets, and they very often slept in their trousers,
removing their coats and shoes. One of the favorite hazing
tricks was to open the flap of the tent, seize the unsuspecting
Plebe by the legs, and pull him out into the mud. Of
course adhered to his old party, the candidate of which was
his trousers, and if he appeared at early morning drill in
such a condition it meant several demerits. Some of the
upper classmen had been caught and were reprimanded; so
for a time the Plebes had been spared a good deal of hazing.

One night, however, after a heavy rain, as the cadets were
about to turn in, young Porter's suspicions were aroused,
and, before rolling himself in his blanket, he removed his
trousers but kept on his shoes, which were nailed; then he
stayed awake and waited. By the dim light he saw the flap
of his tent open and the figure of a cadet appear, groping
in the dark for the feet of his victim. Porter pulled up his
legs, braced himself, and then struck out with both his
nailed boots. There was a slight exclamation, the figure
suddenly disappeared, and the tent-flap fell. The next
morning the upper classman, who proved to be Porter's

determined enemy, had a very badly scarred face; the heels of a pair of nailed boots had left an indentation on his forehead which lasted for many days. After that the young Plebe from Harrisburg was left severely alone.

Except that the cadets of to-day are more comfortably housed, their life is probably not very different from that of their predecessors in the fifties. Politics, however, played then a tremendous part, and feeling ran so high that cadets from different sections of the country were assigned to different barracks—Northerners in the East wing, Southerners in the West and South wings. The presidential campaign of 1856 was very bitter, and the recently formed Republican party was the cause of division in many Northern families. Ex-Governor Porter, as has been said, of course adhered to his old party, the candidate of which was his friend, Buchanan; but Cadet Porter was drawn to the new party, which to him stood for what was just and right. He had many friends among the cadets from the South, the sons of large land- and slave-owners, well-born and well-bred, and he saw their point of view; it was not in his make-up to be blinded by party politics; moreover, he had no especial sympathy for the negro as a race. But he felt with many others that in a country like America, which was expanding and developing and was supposed to uphold liberty, justice, and the rights of man, slavery as an institution had no reason to exist. He thoroughly disapproved of it in any form or manner.

In this atmosphere it was not strange that the disputants should sometimes come to blows. Since dueling was forbidden, the two belligerents would go out at night and fight their battles with their fists. Porter frequently acted as second to some friend in these contests, which usually resulted in bruised faces and black eyes and more bitterness than before.

These unpleasantnesses were momentarily forgotten in the enjoyment of the greater liberty afforded the cadets as upperclassmen. Porter was made a member of the color-guard, "which consists," he wrote in a letter to his sister, "of non-commissioned officers who march beside the colors and take care of it. We are also excused from marching to church." He wrote long letters to his father, with always a turn to politics. He waxed indignant at Governor Houston's ignorance in regard to the Army. "The rank and file have scarcely been increased any for years, while from thirty to forty graduates enter the Army every spring. It takes this number and several citizen appointments besides to fill up the vacancies which occur from different casualties. The question is, shall this number be graduates of the Military Academy, educated soldiers by profession, or citizens?"

On one occasion during Porter's last year, when he was Adjutant of the corps, a great stir was created by the arrival of a Russian general, a prince with an unpronounceable name. To do him honor, the cadets were ordered out in full marching equipment, with their winter overcoats carefully rolled. Since it was a very hot July day, they naturally resented the order. One youth had the ingenious idea of taking a plain piece of extra cloth or trouser-leg or sleeve of an old uniform and stuffing it out with straw. It would look like a well-rolled coat, be much lighter, and no one would ever know the difference. This notion was adopted by some; others, conscientious for the moment at least, chose to carry the extra weight of the overcoat.

The review was nearly ended, the Russian General politely enthusiastic. The Commandant, wishing in a hapless moment to impress still further upon the guest the merits of the American soldier, ordered the Adjutant to command the troops to unroll their overcoats and march back to barracks with them on. Porter tried to turn the Commandant's mind to other things; but the officer was not to be diverted. With a thumping heart the Adjutant gave the order. Great consternation among the cadets; those with overcoats put them on, others couldn't undo the fastenings, others tried to drape over one shoulder a bit of cloth, some put on one sleeve. The straw came out and blew over the parade-ground. The Adjutant, not daring to look at the officers, hustled his men to barracks. The offending cadets were reprimanded; no fault could be laid on the Adjutant, because he had his overcoat; what he knew about the doings of the cadets he refused to reveal. The Commandant fumed and scolded; every one at the Point was highly indignant, or pretended to be. The Russian General remained politely enthusiastic. As for the Adjutant, this episode in his West Point life became later one of his most delightful stories.

Another distinguished visitor was Albert Edward, Prince of Wales (the late King Edward), accompanied by the Duke of Newcastle. Cadet Porter was singled out to attend the Prince during his stay at West Point. The Prince was shy, diffident in his manner, and although he played his part bravely in attending all the balls, festivities, extra drills, and full-dress parades got up for his benefit, he was evidently glad when they were over. Turning to the Adjutant, he said, "Don't you think we could get out of this and have a quiet game of billiards?" By leading the Prince out a side door and down the back staircase, Porter managed to conduct him to the billiard-room unobserved. The Prince then became quite talkative and amusing and enjoyed his game. The next meeting of the two was when one was King of England and the other Ambassador to France.

The humors of West Point life as observed by this young cadet were recorded in rhyme, with clever caricatures in pen-and-ink, also done by himself. The poem was originally read before the Dialectic Society, but in 1866 it was published anonymously in New York and achieved a certain amount of success. The author narrates the life of a cadet from entrance to graduation, and in his drawings and verses spares neither himself, his comrades, nor his superiors. He takes them all as a joke, draws an exaggerated picture of himself as Adjutant heading the dress-parade, and shows the fond relatives gaping in admiration at the wonders of military life.

West Point Life is not the only surviving testimony to Cadet Porter's sense of fun. One of his note-books owes its continued existence to the fact that its latter pages were used for jotting down jokes on students and professors, puns, verses, quotations, ideas for speeches, and what not; some of the quotations are serious, too. At this early age, it seems, he had formed the habit of preserving in black-and-white scraps of material that struck his fancy—especially material likely to serve him in his communications with other people.

Summer was the season of romance. The old stage-coach labored up the hill to the hotel and deposited its daily load of mothers, sisters, cousins, and "sisters' friends" on the steps of the piazza. The piazza, encumbered with countless rocking-chairs, was the summer rendezvous of all polite West Point society. Here were lovely ladies in skirts of immeasurable width, with tiny waists, and slender feet encased in little square-toed slippers or boots of bright-colored leather laced at the side. If the day was sunny they carried ridiculous little parasols, all ruffles and lace, which they cocked at any angle. Here, too, came the cadets in uniforms as tight as the ladies' skirts were large, their waists comparing very favorably in dimensions with those of the fair sex. Supper parties were arranged for six o'clock, semiweekly hops took place at eight and ended at the late hour of ten. Long walks around "Flirtation" were the fashion; sometimes also a ride on horseback. There were suppers at the houses of the Commandant and the most popular professors. It was all gayety and laughter, without a thought of what the next few years were to bring forth.

Among the visitors to West Point at this time was "Mary Custis," who came with her father, Colonel Robert

E. Lee. She pronounced the Adjutant to be the best waltzer in the corps. Young Porter put as much energy into his dancing as he did into everything else he set out to accomplish in life. The steel hoops of the ladies' crinolines hit and rubbed against his ankles until they were chafed and sore. No matter how long the drills, how sore his ankles, nothing damped his ardor.

Another arrival was Clara Louise Kellogg, the first American singer to gain international fame. She charmed the cadets, sang to them, walked with them, danced with them, and frankly liked the high-spirited young Adjutant in his red sash and perfectly fitting gray uniform.[8] He was tall and slender, writes a contemporary, with graceful, distinguished bearing. Dark, thick hair, broad forehead, fair skin, determined chin, rather full, sensitive lips, slightly puckered.

One girl who came to West Point during the summer of '59 soon played an important part in Horace Porter's life. She was Sophie McHarg, daughter of John McHarg of Albany. For Cadet Porter it was love at first sight. He saw her standing with her friend, Mary Satterlee, on the old wooden piazza of the hotel. She was beautiful and charming. By the end of the week he was hopelessly in love. In appearance she was rather small and slight, with black, thick hair, brown eyes, delicate features, and lovely fair skin (which she never exposed to the sun). Her waist was small enough to be the envy of her friends; she had tiny feet and danced to perfection, wore bigger hoops than any other girl, and for each hop had the crinoline recovered with voluminous white tulle. No wonder that more than one cadet was smitten. Her affection for Horace Porter never wavered. She kept her secret, and in the following summer, when Lieutenant Porter was in daily expectation of orders for active service, she gave him her promise. Home on leave, three years later, after his exploit at Chickamauga, he made her his wife.

On July 1, 1860, Horace Porter was graduated third among the five honor men of his class. In his chosen field, ordnance, he had so distinguished himself [9] that he was kept at West Point for three months as instructor in artillery. More than this, he was on terms of real intellectual equality and friendship with the ablest men on the Faculty. If ever there was a man made ready for precisely what next awaited him, it was he.

SOPHIE McHARG

CADET PORTER

CHAPTER II

IN the Fall of 1860, Lieutenant Porter, after his service as instructor at West Point and a brief period in Washington, received orders to report at Watervliet Arsenal, at Troy on the Hudson. Nothing could have pleased him better. Watervliet had large stores of ammunition under the charge of Major Thornton, but the reason first and foremost for his joy in being appointed to Watervliet was that it was near Albany, where lived Miss Sophie McHarg.

Two letters written during this winter throw light on the thoughts and occupations of a young officer of the regular army in the face of impending war.

To His Father

> Watervliet Arsenal,
> West Troy, N. Y.,
> January 28, 1861.

Our class is now scattered far and wide, only about 12 out of the forty-one are East of the Mississippi. Six men of my class have already been married, which beats anything on record. They seem to be contradicting the old adage which says: "Our duty is to make widows, not wives."

I was very fortunate in getting this post. It is just across the river from Troy and six miles from Albany, with cars and omnibusses running to the latter place every half-hour. I have made many pleasant acquaintances in both cities. The winter has been very gay. I receive an invitation to a party every few nights. General Wool has his headquarters in Troy with two officers on his staff; as there are four officers at the Arsenal and a recruiting officer in

Albany, we have quite a little army society in the vicinity.

I find the weather colder than at West Point. Heavy teams have been crossing the river and we have had continuous sleighing since early in December. I have gone regularly to housekeeping in true bachelor style. I have for quarters a house with eight rooms and nobody to put in it but myself. I have a garden of more than an acre and can raise all my own vegetables.

We have been very busy lately. General Scott is determined to have troops enough in Washington to suppress any disturbance at the inauguration ceremonies and the companies are already moving. We have sent tons and tons of ammunition from here and are putting everything on a war footing, though we still hope these preparations will not be necessary and the States may yet come to some amicable adjustment.

The state of affairs is truly alarming and I fear we may soon see the worst. True, the South had every reason to complain; her protecting clause in the constitution had been violated, Northern fanatics had waged continual war against her institutions, and the border states have lost much property; yet in my mind nothing can justify the acts of states that in the most precipitate manner pass an act of secession, seize government property, fire on government vessels, annul acts of congress, strike the fourth of July from their list of holidays, and do a thousand unpatriotic and treasonable acts just when peace negociations were commenced, when northern states were repealing obnoxious bills, and before the Republican administration even went into power, and particularly when these states were so far removed from the border that they had never lost a slave by desertion.

The army feels the present crisis more keenly than any other class of men; they are more thoroughly national men and less identified with particular states. They have lived in both sections of the country and have friends and classmates in every state and territory. Two of my classmates have resigned and joined the South Carolinian army, but comparatively few officers have left the army thus far. Some manufacturers near here commenced making arms and putting up ammunition for some of the seceding states, but the state of New York declared it treason and prevented it.

Such has been the state of the treasury that the army has not been paid for two months and there is great dissatisfaction. Time alone can tell us the result of the present deplorable state of affairs.

Write soon, Father, and let me know how you are getting along and how your health is. The Porters are not very demonstrative; they often think more than they express, and I feel very anxious about you so many miles away. Who has a better right to do so, than the

"Son of your old age,"

HORACE PORTER.

To His Mother

Watervliet Arsenal,
West Troy, N. Y.,
April 11, 1861.

A week ago Lieutenant Balch was ordered off, we think to Fort Pickens, no one knows. Major Mordecai was then ordered for two weeks to Fort Monroe. Strong and I were the only officers left. Just at this state of affairs the most enormous orders for supplies came from General Winfield Scott, in command of the United States Army. For thirty-six hours no one put his head on a pillow, and more was accomplished in a short time than was ever heard of here before. We did in that time the work of two weeks. We had barges at the wharf, men running and teams galloping in every direction. Since then we have been working half of every night, sometimes the whole night and Sundays. The Major will be back next Tuesday and this rush will be over by that time. Strong and I have laboured pretty faithfully. You have probably seen our names mentioned in the New York Herald and The Times. We send all the ammunition to Governor's Island; where it will go from there I cannot yet tell. You need not be at all alarmed at the war news; as long as there are so few of us here I cannot get away from the Arsenal.

The day after this letter was written Porter was attending a ball in Albany, in the midst of which, as in the famous scene in *Vanity Fair*, came the summons to battle: the Confederates had fired on Fort Sumter. On the day on which Porter was twenty-four the President's call for volunteers was issued. Suspense was at an end. This was War.

Almost immediately, he was sent by General Wool with important dispatches to Washington, communication with which by ordinary means had been cut off by the rising in Baltimore. Wearing citizen's clothes with the dispatches sewed inside his coat, and feeling himself "clothed with the importance of an envoy extraordinary and veiled in the mystery of a Russian diplomat," [1] Porter went to New York. There he embarked in the small steamer *Daylight*, which was carrying a portion of the Seventh Regiment to join the companies which had already left for the capital. Into this craft, normally holding one hundred men, were crowded twice that number, besides a large amount of supplies and ammunition, the officer in charge exhibiting "a degree of compressive skill that would have done honor to a professional sardine packer." For Porter the trip was a painful initiation into the woes of seasickness.

On the evening of the second day the *Daylight* reached Hampton Roads and anchored at Fortress Monroe, where the passengers learned that the Seventh Regiment had landed at Annapolis and was marching to Washington. Although points on the Virginia shore of the Potomac were known to be held by the enemy, it was decided to risk a trip up the river; otherwise the supplies with which the steamer was loaded would reach their destination only after long delay. Borrowing two howitzers from a United States vessel lying off Fortress Monroe and mounting them on the forward deck of the *Daylight*, Lieutenant Porter proceeded to drill a detail of recruits in artillery service.

As the boat approached the capital and came within what

they believed to be the zone of danger, all were on the alert. "Everything from a cornstalk to a church-steeple now became an object of close examination, and even a water-snipe could not disport itself along the river shore without having the lookout's glass ranged on it with the scrutiny of a searchlight, and its movements promptly reported to the commanding officer." When, at dusk, the *Daylight* reached Fort Washington, a gun was fired across her bows. In order to ascertain whether or not the enemy had seized the fort, Porter and a small detachment of men, each armed with a revolver, rowed toward the shore with oars and tiller muffled. By the light of a campfire he recognized Lieutenant Perkins, a Connecticut man, and one of his instructors at West Point. Leaving the boat, Porter scrambled up the bank and stepped into the firelight. On recovering from his astonishment Lieutenant Perkins told him that though the Confederates were in possession of Alexandria, the boat might still be allowed to pass. The only thing to do was to try. The guns on the *Daylight* were accordingly put in position ready for action, an extra drill was held, and the little boat continued her course up the river. Nothing happened. The *Daylight* steamed by Alexandria as if out for a pleasure cruise, and soon sighted the capital.

When, an hour later, the boat made fast in the rain at the Arsenal Dock, a carriage was seen driving rapidly toward the landing. Two gentlemen descended who, as soon as they were recognized, were greeted by loud cheers. One was William H. Seward, the Secretary of State; the long, thin, bony man with a high hat—"the longest and ugliest man that ever lived"—was President Lincoln. "Half a dozen of the boys seized a piece of canvas and held it over the heads of the illustrious visitors to protect them from the rain while they stood upon the deck. The President expressed a wish to take by the hand every member of the ship's company and thank him personally for the service he had rendered." The last man to come up to Lincoln was a fireman in his shirtsleeves and with his face and hands begrimed with coal-dust. He drew back the hand which the President tried to grasp and said, "My hand isn't fit to give you, sir, but there's not a man aboard as loves you more than I do." "Put that hand in mine," cried Lincoln; "it has been blackened by making fires for the Union."

Meeting their President for the first time at this tense moment of the outbreak of war and seeing him deeply moved, it is not strange that the men were shaken, too, or that they never forgot the scene. The personality of the great President, however, seems to have made little impression on Porter at this first glimpse; it was not till three years later, when he had a chance to see and talk with Lincoln constantly for several days, that he realized what manner of man he was.

Having disburdened himself of his precious dispatches, the young lieutenant now returned to Troy, from which he had been absent about three weeks.

The summer at Watervliet was naturally a busy one; at one time Porter found himself in command of the Arsenal, and he quotes to his mother the jocular remark of a brother officer that he was going up as fast as a "monkey climbs a ladder." This sort of advance, however, was little to his mind; active service was what he longed for, and he was not content till he received orders assigning him to the expedition sailing late in October against Hilton Head. This was one of a series of combined army and navy ventures organized during the first year of the war for the purpose of obtaining suitable harbors along the coasts of North and South Carolina. They were needed to serve as bases of operations, both for the fleets that were blockading the Southern ports and for expeditions into the interior. An extract from a letter written soon after Porter's arrival describes his first experience of actual warfare.

To His Mother

Fort Walker, Port Royal, S. C.,
November 8, 1861.

On the 7th, yesterday, all our vessels except the lost ones having arrived, the attack commenced. Thinking I would not have a very active time with the General, I got him to let me take charge of a light battery which we had brought with us. Two companies of the third Rhode Island served with it. At ten o'clock all the naval vessels opened fire upon a Fort on Hilton's Head, the end of a long Island running from here down to the Savannah River. They rained into it a most terrible fire till two o'clock, when the Rebels retreated. It was a beautiful sight as we watched it through our glasses. They had twenty-four hundred men in the work and a very strong one.

In the evening all the troops commenced landing. I landed my battery with ammunition, implements, equipments, etc., complete in three hours. We had to put the guns on small boats, run them as near shore as possible, then jump into the water and pull them ashore. I had it in position by ten o'clock that night. General Stevens, who was anxiously awaiting it, was greatly pleased. The only other light battery is Hamilton's; it did not get ashore till daylight. I then took a detachment of men and after hunting for ammunition some time at last found plenty in the Fort, and prepared the guns they had left to repel any attack that might be made that night, for we greatly feared they would return when only a small portion of our force had landed. This they did not do. I had been working all night, with my boots full of water and was pretty well worn out.

Before daylight I made my way to a house pretty well riddled with shot, where General [H. G.] Wright had made his headquarters. I found him up and he complimented me on what I had done and gave me some bread and meat, which he had had foresight to take ashore. . . . I then found an old candle and went up to an empty room and lay down on the floor in my wet clothes and got a few hours sleep. . . .

The energy and resourcefulness that had attracted General Wright's attention soon brought Porter an important assignment in connection with the preparations for the reduction of Fort Pulaski, at the mouth of the Savannah River. The conditions which he found at his new post of duty were by no means promising.

To His Mother

Tybee Island, Georgia,
December 26, 1861.

I came here last Monday week, with Tardy of my class. The Island had been taken possession of, and a German regiment, the New York 46th, stationed here. Large batteries were to be erected and a great number of guns put in them, ordnance stores collected, etc. I was appointed chief of ordnance for these operations. Fort Pulaski, one of the strongest works in possession of the enemy, stands opposite to us, at a distance from the nearest point of the Island of less than a mile. General Wright is in command, a very fine officer, formerly of the Engineer Corps.

I found when I landed that this Dutch regiment, consisting of only six hundred men, were at the mercy of two thousand Rebels, who had nothing to do but cross a creek at a point we could not protect. We had not a piece of Artillery ashore. The vessels (two) could not shell the Island without shelling us more effectually than the enemy. In the morning I saw the Rebels put their troops in two steamboats, and the pickets in the evening reported persons on the Island. At these reports the Dutch Colonel only laughed and smoked away at his pipe. I went on board the Savannah at 12 o'clock that night, and arranged a system of signals with the Captain; seeing no one took any interest in the matter, tried to get two howitzers, but could not, came ashore, and awaited the attack. It did not take place, but a deserter the next day said the troops had been put aboard the boats to attack us (2000), and when they were on the way the order was suddenly countermanded for some unknown reason.

I wrote to General Sherman and the next day another regiment was sent with General Wright to command.

General Wright took at once active measures for defence. We worked day and night, Sundays and weekdays, and only now feel ourselves perfectly secure, having erected a strong Fort and armed it with the heaviest guns. I had to get guns hauled up and mounted by day and as fast as one was placed in position prepare ammunition for it, which sometimes took half the night, had to get old sails off the vessels to make an arab tent to protect the ordnance stores. Then I had to drill the Dutchmen to have some men to work the guns after they were in position. We erected one battery of rifled guns right under the enemy's fire, and had to do all the work silently by night. We have it covered by bushes and they do not yet know it is there.

I attended a little council of war in General Wright's tent last night and protested against besieging Fort Pulaski. We can get to Savannah the back way and save lives and time; the Fort will then fall of itself. It has but two months' provision. General Wright also stated this as his view of the matter. He has been very kind to me, and as Tardy and I are the only Graduates on the Island he never does anything without consulting us. If we attack the Fort I will have charge of all the siege armament and remain here, but this I think they will not do. If not, we will finish one more battery to command another channel, and in about three weeks I will return to Hilton Head.*

The German regiment was one of Porter's constant cares: in spite of the fact that they did excellent work, they talked too much, ate too much—three day's rations in one day— and always wanted beer. From this latter circumstance he found a way to make some of them useful. A large cargo of beer had arrived, and after its distribution the Germans became more garrulous than ever. Lieutenant Porter heard one man say to his comrade: "I visch sum of our Kamaraden ofer dere could haf sum of dis." On Porter's asking the

*In this letter I found a dried spray of lilac which he had picked and sent to his mother instead of mistletoe at Christmas time.

man what he meant, he explained that there was quite a settlement of Germans in and around Savannah, and that they were enlisted in the Confederate army and surely some must be in the garrison at Fort Pulaski.

This statement put Lieutenant Porter's mind again at work upon something he had been thinking about for several days. If he could only ascertain in some way the exact position of the powder magazine in the fort, the task of reducing the fort would be much easier. He went back to his "Dutch" regiment, and said to some of the men:

"You fellows are all strong for the Union, are you not? And do you think your Kamaraden over there are for the Union, too, and were only forced into the Rebel army because they happened to be living in the South?"

"Sure we are for the Union, and if our Kamaraden over there knew we were here and had such beer they would desert somehow and come right over."

"Well," answered the Lieutenant, "don't drink up all your beer, and some of you fellows who can blow a horn go down to the edge of the Island under those bushes and play *Die Wacht am Rhein* as loud as you can, and some of you watch out for any deserter who swims over to-night and bring him straight to me, and you can give him all the beer he wants afterwards."

The men did as they were told; they played *Die Wacht am Rhein* as if their lives depended upon it, to the amusement and astonishment of the other troops. Lieutenant Porter waited after dark at the edge of the water. About midnight he heard some splashing and a voice calling softly. Porter waited until the man was nearer, then spoke to him and helped pull him out of the water. He was "a huge fellow who looked as if he were a lineal descendant of Frederick the Great's Potsdam Guards." He said he had lived in Savannah, and although his sympathies were with the Union, he had been forced into the Southern army. When he heard *Die Wacht am Rhein,* he said, nothing could

have kept him any longer; he knew some of his compatriots
in the Union army were near.   He waited until dark when
the tide was coming in, and then floated across on a log from
Cockspur to Tybee Island.   His information proved to be
very useful.²

The plan for taking Savannah "by the back way" had
been abandoned; instead, Fort Pulaski was to be attacked,
and by March 1 preparations had entered upon their final
stage.   Mortars weighing 8½ tons, and columbiads weighing only a little less, had to be moved by night along a
narrow causeway for nearly a mile to a position in the
swamp where, to prevent their sinking into the mud, foundations of logs had been prepared.   All through this period
Porter's advice concerning the position of the batteries was
followed, and he himself worked indefatigably in getting
the guns into place; when all was ready for the attack, the
eleven batteries, comprising thirty-six guns, were put under
his command.   As he made his final rounds to ascertain
whether everything was in readiness, he found that at one
mortar battery fuse-plugs were lacking.   Remembering that
there was a Connecticut regiment on the Island, and knowing that all Yankees are whittlers, he dashed off in the
darkness, to find them and set them to work.³

Of the attack on the fort and its surrender, Porter gives
a vivid account in a letter to his sister written on April 17,
1862.

> I received your long and interesting letter and in reply
> must tell you first how Fort Pulaski was taken. A day
> or two before we opened fire, Generals Hunter and Ben-
> ham, our new stars, arrived on Tybee and were as impatient
> for the fray as Roman ladies for the commencement of a
> gladiatorial combat. The surgeons of the division came in
> scores, with a broad grin on their faces at the idea of having
> a job!
> All being ready, on Thursday morning we determined to
> open. I fired the first gun. I took my station at daylight

in the nearest mortar battery and pointed a thirteen-inch mortar upon the Fort. O'Rorke, acting as aide, rode up to me and said: "The General sends his compliments and desires you to open the ball at once." Away went the shell, bursting over the Fort and scattering the fragments about the Rebel gunners. This was the signal gun for our batteries to open.

The Fort replied actively and the noise of about fifty pieces made the ground fairly rock. For a long time the Rebels devoted all their energy to the battery which opened, and the shells flew about our ears, like a swarm of bees. I next started for a battery of heavy guns; to reach it it was necessary to cross a hundred and fifty yards of open space under the direct fire of the Fort. I got over this in safety, but thought several times I was a goner. It is remarkable how much nearer a ball always appears to one's ear than it really is.

The most unfortunate affair of the morning was the up-setting of our six ten-inch columbiads which were fired with very heavy charges, but the other guns hammered away and destroyed a great portion of the masonry of the Fort. About noon down came their flag. We thought for a moment they had surrendered, jumped up upon the parapets and gave three cheers; but a volley from the Fort told us such was not at present their intention, and we got down into the batteries and went to work again at the guns. The Rebels put up a temporary flag staff on the side of the Fort.

I promised the General I would have the columbiads in working order by morning, and spent the night with a large party setting them up again. By morning they opened fire and told a terrible tale. Great pieces of masonry commenced falling out and we knew the Fort would soon be ours. We had fired one shot every five minutes during the night just to keep the garrison awake. At two o'clock someone removed the Rebel flag and we saw him trying to put something up in its place. It was the white flag and all firing at once ceased.* But we stood to our guns for fear it might be a ruse.

* When the fort surrendered, the powder magazine was in danger of being exploded at any moment.

General Gillmore went over in person and received from Colonel Olmstead the articles of capitulation signed in due form.

I at once got something to eat and a good sleep, and the next morning went to the Fort to take an inventory of the captured ordnance. There were forty-eight pieces taken and four hundred barrels of powder, with an abundance of shot and shells. There were about three hundred and eighty prisoners; you would never have imagined us foes. Officers on both sides asking about their friends and relations North and South. One officer was speaking of the accuracy of our fire, and mentioned that he replied to it by firing the first gun with his own hands. I told him I had had the honor of doing the same on our side. He at once seized me by the hand, remarked, "What a strange coincidence," invited me into his quarters, and told me his name was Freeman. He was a Union man and heartily wished the war was over, but that the best blood of the South had been spilled and he would fight the thing to the end. The Fort is all knocked to pieces, our guns worked beautifully and our firing was much better than that of the Rebels.

The reduction of Fort Pulaski demonstrated the power and effectiveness of rifled cannon for breaching at distances hitherto considered impracticable, and so Porter played an important part in an operation which opened a new era in this type of warfare.[4] He had also had plenty of opportunity to show the thoroughness of his training, his initiative, his courage and coolness under fire, and his ability to command men. In one of his letters he refers jestingly to the praises which he received,—"It is the first time, I believe, I have ever been congratulated for doing my duty,"—and to General Gillmore's speech "about gallantry, etc., which would have made a capital Fourth of July oration"; but he treasured the sword which accompanied the speech.[5] He had fairly won his spurs. His commission as brevet captain was dated April 11, 1862, the day of the capture of the fort.

During the next few weeks Porter reports himself as busy "undoing what we did"—that is, removing the mortars and columbiads from the Island. In order that he might carry out the work, he was given the authority of a brigadier general. Of the colonels of the regiment under his charge he remarked that it was well that they were not regulars; if they had been, they would have made a great outcry at being put on such duty and under such orders.

After the completion of this work, he was employed in preparing heavy artillery stores for the James Island expedition; on June 16 he took part in the battle of Secessionville, an attack on a small fort that served as part of the defenses of Charleston.

In the hot summer days that followed the battle Porter found himself physically in poor condition and uneasy in mind over his prospects for the future. The campaign in the Carolinas had come to a standstill, and the thoughts of the impatient young officer turned to the possibility of obtaining the command of a volunteer regiment.

"It would be better," he wrote his mother, "to serve my country usefully as a colonel than to die a lieutenant on a Carolina sandhill." At the end of June, when sixty sick men were to be sent to New York, General Hunter considered his state of health sufficient justification for a leave. There was no colonelcy forthcoming, but promotion in his own arm of the service followed speedily, as the following letter makes clear.

To His Father

Ordnance Office,
War Department,
Washington, July 24, 1862.

I am at last in luck. After I had put my baggage aboard the steamer to return to Port Royal, I got a telegram to report here. I find the following to be the state of affairs. Gen. McClellan has become greatly dissatisfied with Col.

Kingsbury, his chief of ordnance, and through him with the the whole corps. He has finally asked to have him relieved, and the most competent officer of the corps sent in his place. Gen. Ripley, Chief of Ordnance, said he was going to send Capt. Balch, who is one of the first officers in the corps, but he said I had had more experience in active operations in the field; and he has selected me and appointed me Chief of Ordnance of the armies of Virginia, and a member of Gen. McClellan's staff. He said I could have anything I desired in the way of stores, and all officers would receive orders to furnish everything I required to keep these troops in the field. You see this is the greatest position a young man has ever held in this country, and I am very much gratified, but I will have an immense amount of work.

Not only, as the General says, to furnish and advise upon the subject of ordnance but to conciliate those who are in opposition to our corps. I will join the Army at McClellan's headquarters to-morrow. I am busy now arranging affairs with the different departments to facilitate future operations. I find my report upon the bombardment of Pulaski has been well received here, and every one has something to say about it. I do not care now to serve with volunteers.

I have only time to tell you this much, knowing it will gratify you to know that I have at last got a position in the war. Give my love to all at home. Direct to me,

"Chief of Ordnance,
Gen. McClellan's Headquarters,
James River, Va."

Your affec. son,
HORACE PORTER.

When the new Chief of Ordnance reached General McClellan's headquarters at Harrison's Landing on the James River, the Army was lying idle after the Seven Days' battle, and the air was full of controversy as to what should be the next move. Under Porter's management the confusion and lack of system which he found in his department were soon remedied. Later, when the transfer of the Army to Washington was decided upon, he superintended the removal of ordnance stores, and when McClellan followed Lee into Maryland he had entire charge of the artillery transfer. He had good opportunity to observe the prevailing demoralization, and his criticisms of General McClellan written just before the battle of Antietam are of still further interest because they represent the point of view of an officer of the Regular Army.

To His Father

Ordnance Department,
Washington, D. C.,
Sept. 13, 1862.

It would be an act of madness for the Rebels to attempt to reach our town [Harrisburg] with an army as large as their own in their rear. Provisions they can get, but ammunition they *cannot*. Their supply would run short in a couple of well fought battles. The movements of our army have no doubt greatly encouraged them. It has been just *one* week moving thirty miles. It seems totally without organization. McClellan has taken the armies of Burnside and the Army of the Potomac and combined them into one. The officers take rank according to seniority. The Ordnance officers are Shunk, myself, Flagler, Harris, and Parker. Shunk consequently becomes Chief of Ordnance. Gen. Ripley swore and tore when he heard this, said the Ordnance Corps was ruined by an imbecile like Kingsbury, and now McClellan had chosen a drunkard who would ruin everything again. Gen. Ripley said if I wished he would make me Chief of Ordnance to Maj. Gen. Wright at Cincinnati. I told him I would neither solicit a position nor shrink from performing its duties. I was perfectly satisfied to be thrown out of a position by accident, since I had the satisfaction of knowing I had been chosen for it through merit. The oldest and generally the most *inefficient* officers fall in at the top of the list and become chief. *McClellan* is so terribly afraid of hurting anyone's feelings that he lets affairs go on in this way for fear of offending some old fogy by promoting a younger one over him. Do not mention this state of affairs outside the family. *Let all* people have perfect faith in the army who *can.*

I am sending 440 wagons of ammunition to the army, enough to last it all year if not wasted. Shunk is at Frederick to receive it. If he is up to his old Port Royal tricks the army will never get a round of it.

I cannot tell what will become of us if this state of things continue much longer without any organization. *McClellan* leaves everything to Marcy; the poor old man is now deaf and hasn't an idea left. If we can drive the Rebels back, secure our defence, and get time to organize a new army upon some system or other, *we may come out all right yet.* At present Marcy [6] gives one order, McClellan another, Halleck another, and Stanton another. The feeling here is one of deep depression.

CHAPTER III

CHICKAMAUGA

IT will be remembered that when Porter brought his battery ashore at Hilton Head he was complimented by General Wright, who commanded the landing force. In September, 1862, General Wright had recently been appointed to the command of the Department of the Ohio, and he now sent Porter the welcome invitation to serve as chief of ordnance on his staff. A few months of busy and pleasant life in Cincinnati were followed by transfer to the Army of the Cumberland, then in winter quarters at Murfreesboro, Tennessee. Here as ordnance officer on the staff of General Rosecrans he began that notable portion of his military career which culminated in the battle of Chickamauga and his meeting with Grant.

The late winter and early spring were spent in preparations for the campaigns against the Confederate Army commanded by General Bragg. Weeks went by, however, and, notwithstanding urgent messages from Washington and from Grant at Vicksburg, it was not till June 24 that the advance actually began. In spite of the heavy rains at the start and the increasing difficulties of the country, Rosecrans maneuvered his antagonist further and further South and on September 9 reached Chattanooga.

But the Confederates were not retreating through Georgia, as the Federal commander had at first believed; it soon became evident that it was Bragg's purpose to turn and fight. Hastily Rosecrans recalled his scattered corps, and by September 18 had them assembled at Chickamauga, twelve miles south of Chattanooga. On the nineteenth and twentieth was fought the battle of Chickamauga, well justi-

36

fying the Indian name, "the river of death." It was marked by many deeds of heroism, among which Horace Porter's shine brightly. His letters give clearly the salient points of the struggle and throw light on some of its most dramatic moments.

To His Mother

Chattanooga, Tennessee,
September 20, 1863,
Night.

We have been fighting the great battle of "Chickamauga," as it will probably be called, for the last two days. Yesterday we repulsed the enemy at all points against fearful odds, but to-day have been driven back twelve miles. The battle has ceased, we hold Chattanooga firmly. I escaped without a scratch, but my horse was struck with a shell while I was vainly trying to rally our broken troops. Will Jones, my classmate, is killed and many of my friends. I will give you an account of it when I get time. I have been in the saddle for two days and am dying for some sleep. This is the bloodiest battle of the war. We have lost in all probably 15,000 men.

To His Sister

Chattanooga, Tennessee,
October 3, 1863.

Your letter arrived yesterday; you have received my letter of the 20th before this, and learned that I am safe and sound. Since the battle we have been busy day and night in doing all a small force can to protect itself against a larger one, and until now [have] not had a breathing spell. I suppose you have read all sorts of accounts of the battle in the papers, but no true ones, for the first retrograde movement occurred among that lying body of men, called the "reportorial corps," and men when scared see things in a very absurd light.

The facts of the whole thing are these: We started out
to have a big fight and liberate Tennessee, get Chattanooga
and hold it. We had a big fight, liberated Tennessee, got
Chattanooga and intended to keep it. To outflank Bragg,
Rosecrans had to throw his forces over almost impassable
mountains. The Rebel government thought they had him
in a trap, and sent every available man against him. By
the most remarkable marches our troops were concentrated
in time to meet Bragg's increased army. The Rebels had
collected 82,000 men, [1] and though we had but 38,000 [2]
on the Chickamauga, Rosecrans determined to fight as long
as a man was left to save Chattanooga.

We rose at three o'clock Saturday morning the 19th and
waited for the enemy to attack. He did so at quarter past
seven. The whole day's fighting consisted in his making
the most desperate assaults on different points of our line
with immense columns. But our reserves, which were
judiciously posted, reinforced every point in time to drive
him back all along our line. Our troops fell back rapidly
and lost a battery. Soon our whole line turned around,
apparently without any command, and drove the Rebels
back at the point of the bayonet, recapturing the battery.
It was the fiercest day's fight of the war, but we were pretty
successful at every point. Most of the fight occurred in
dense woods. The roar of artillery and musketry and
shouting of the men, the shrieking of a high wind through
the trees made it a place to try the strongest nerves. We
had had nothing to eat since morning.

At night the General and staff assembled in a log house
to make preparations for the next day. We all knew the
fearful odds we were fighting, and our men had had no rest
for a week. Besides, we had no water in the valley, the
enemy holding the creek. Horses were suffering as well as
the men. The dead and wounded were lying all around our
house.[3] The wounded suffered greatly. Orders were given
for a new line of battle which caused our men to march
half the night again, and at daylight we were in the saddle
once more. In carrying a message for the General [4] I saw
two soldiers on a by-road with a kettle of coffee. They
offered me some, which I enjoyed more than any beverage

that ever went down my throat. I shall never speak slightingly of coffee again.

About ten o'clock the battle was renewed by the enemy's coming down on the left with half his army. It took all our reserves to repulse him, but they did it handsomely. About eleven o'clock they came down on our centre. McCook had not posted his troops as the General had directed,[5] and as all hands were trying to rectify his mistake on came this avalanche! There were no more reserves to put through into the gap. Gordon Granger was hurrying 5,000 men from the rear, but they did not reach us. Our centre came rolling back and the shells and bullets were sweeping everything from the earth. We had dismounted for safety. The General soon cried: "To horse, gentlemen," but before we could get our feet in the stirrups, he dashed down the line between our troops and the enemy, every Rebel taking a shot at him. His powerful gray horse ran off, and no one could keep up with him. Horses were falling at every point. Mine suddenly was going on three legs; I jumped off to see what was the matter and found he was not shot, but had run a nail in his foot. I worked it out with my sabre and found fortunately he was not lame. There was no time to lose, I assure you.

Getting to the crest of the hill, I met Drouillard, who had been with me at West Point. I told him I was going no farther, as long as we could hold ten men together. He joined me, and by urging and threats we formed nearly a hundred men. Soon after a Rebel battery opened on our right, one of the shells exploded close to me, striking my horse but not wounding him very seriously. Our line vanished in an instant.

The enemy came on and on, but their advance soon ended. General Thomas had posted his corps in a good position and about two o'clock Granger came up. The whole Rebel army fought then till night, but did not drive them an inch. Our broken divisions rallied behind these fresh troops, and everything looked well again except the loss of thirty pieces of artillery in the centre.

Fearing reinforcements would cut him off from Chattanooga, the General drew his troops into a strong position outside the town and intrenched himself. The General and the staff came on to Chattanooga that night, to make arrangements for the new line and sending transportation across the river, etc. I was at work all night getting safe places for the ammunition trains to park, and having cartridges issued to the men in case of another battle the next day, which we expected. No one had slept for two nights, and we were very glad to get something to eat and some rest.

So you see our reverse is not a serious one. Nothing could exceed the bravery of our troops. Their endurance and courage alone saved our army and Chattanooga. Burnside was sent to for troops, but some of the couriers were captured, and he could not send troops in time to do us any good, though he is not to blame. He will now have his hands full in holding East Tennessee. Our reinforcements are arriving daily and we are safe.

The Rebels acknowledge a fearful loss of officers. We are in a terribly mountainous country, but manage to feed the army. The great blow of the war will be struck here, and if our men fight as well as they did on the Chickamauga, there will be no doubt as to the result. I never was in better health and spirits in my life. Do not believe any newspaper rumors about us. We are all right now. Give my love to all at home.

Your affectionate brother,
Horace Porter.

P. S. There must be some great changes made amongst our general officers before another battle.

Something needs to be added to Porter's simple account of his doings to make clear his own heroic part in the action. When the fatal moment came his instinct was not to go with his General—indeed, Rosecrans' runaway horse carried him into a ravine, whither none of his staff followed him—but to rally enough fugitives to hold a small crest of the field near at hand so that numerous wagon trains and batteries on the right and in the rear, which were in danger of being cut off, might escape. The crest, partly covered with trees and underbrush, was occupied by a Federal battery (probably the 8th Indiana) which had now been abandoned.

Out of the hundred or more men whom he collected, Porter formed a thin, irregular line, which, keeping up a steady fire, caused the enemy to believe that reënforcements had arrived. They halted, reformed the lines broken by their rapid and exciting advance, and began to throw out skirmishers. In the meantime, Porter, assisted by Captain Drouillard and several company officers, gathered in more fugitives, and awaited the enemy's attack. Simultaneously with their advance, a Confederate battery opened on the group. Under this fire, and the vigor of the attack, the fragments on the crest became demoralized. As soon as a group could be got together, most of the men would be swept away by the shot and shell, and the rest would flee in panic.

In his efforts to hold them—by appeals to pride and sense of duty, by threats with the pistol and blows with the saber—Porter was twice attacked by men with bayonets, and it was with difficulty that he escaped being disabled by them. Finally, when the enemy were so near that the commands of their officers could be heard, and when the men on the hill were all either killed or wounded, Porter decided to retire. He had been struck on the hand and the leg by fragments of shell, but he was able to get his frightened horse under control and ride down behind the hill, being the last man to leave. Not only had the enemy been delayed some twenty minutes; he henceforward advanced less impetuously, and thus the troops, wagons, and batteries were enabled to make their escape before the Confederates gained possession of the roads in the rear.

Mr. Charles A. Dana, Assistant Secretary of War used the following words [6] in his description of this scene at the battle of Chickamauga. "I was on the right of General Rosecrans, the commanding officer. I was asleep on the ground, having been up all the night before, and was awakened by the terrific roar of musketry and cannon. It seemed as though hell was all loose. I arose and got on my horse and then saw all the lines between us and the enemy break and disappear and the men flee into the woods. Rosecrans went off, I don't know where; and the first sight that had any consolation in it was an officer with his sword drawn halting the fugitive soldiers of our army. He would halt them and form them into line and when he got twelve or twenty men together, a cannon-ball would come into the group right over our heads and they would fall. As soon as he would get another lot together, they would be swept down in the same manner. That man, gentlemen, was General Horace Porter."

Captain Porter's conduct on this occasion was spoken of as "conspicuous gallantry" on the field of battle. He was no braver than many others, but by his initiative and his tenacity in holding the enemy at bay even for a short time he actually effected an important saving to the army. Thus dramatically and thus early in life he discovered the power of these faculties within him.

CHAPTER IV

GRANT'S AIDE

THE month following the battle of Chickamauga was full of discouragement and privations for the Army of the Cumberland. Shut up in the town of Chattanooga, with Confederates in possession of the heights, receiving its meager supplies by a circuitous route over almost impassable mountain roads, it stood in sore need of help. The daily rations for officers and privates alike were half an onion and a potato, generally served in the form of soup; the men tried to cheat hunger by sleeping as much as possible; ten thousand horses died of starvation. Soon, however, the broken Rosecrans was replaced by Thomas, "the rock of Chickamauga," and presently news was received of the coming of Grant, fresh from his triumph at Vicksburg and now in command of the newly created Military Division of the Mississippi. The tide was about to turn, and with it came a surprising and momentous turn in the fortunes of Horace Porter.

One evening, late in October, Porter was summoned to General Thomas' headquarters. Besides the usual company in the room, Porter found several strangers, among them a general officer seated in an armchair facing the fireplace. His clothes were wet and his trousers and topboots bespattered with mud. He was a man of slight frame, and as he sat with his head bent slightly forward his whole expression was one of weariness. Thomas, turning to the young captain, said, "I want to present you to General Grant." The latter's "How do you do?" spoken slowly, with his arm extended at full length to shake hands, completed the introduction.

43

That Grant appreciated the critical situation of the army was plain from his prompt arrival. No one had expected him so soon, on account of the condition of the roads; besides, he was known to be still suffering from an injured leg. His determination to lose no time in righting matters was further evident in the conference on this first evening. Though he had had to be lifted from his horse, he had refused to change his wet clothes; and while he dried himself by the fire and smoked a cigar, he listened intently to the report of General Thomas and his chief engineer, General W. F. Smith. Then he suddenly straightened himself up and began asking questions. In reply to his inquiry of Porter as to ammunition, he learned that in Chattanooga there was barely enough for one day's battle; at Bridgeport, however, the end of the railroad, there was an ample supply. And so he went from one member of the group to another.

Needless to say, the officers of Thomas' staff followed eagerly the course of the discussion, hoping to find in these first hours some clue that would tell them whether or not Grant would prove a true leader. To men who had been besieged for a month, it was an unspeakable relief to comprehend from his questions that his mind was dwelling not only upon the prompt opening of a line of supplies but also upon plans for taking the offensive against the enemy. "I cannot dwell too forcibly," wrote Porter, many years later,[1] "on the deep impression made upon those who had come in contact for the first time with the new commander by the exhibition they witnessed of his singular mental powers and his rare military qualities." Not all that they had heard about this man had prepared them or could prepare them for what he was.

In appearance, too, Grant was quite different from the extraordinary pseudo-photographs published in the newspapers, which represented him as a burly beef-contractor with robust features, his hat on one side, striding about in

approved swashbuckler manner. He proved to be a slender man of medium height, slightly bent, weighing not over a hundred and thirty-five pounds, gentle and modest in his manner, a man of few words and a good listener. Porter was especially impressed with his eyes: they were the only feature that gave any indication of his thoughts. His voice was exceedingly musical, clear in sound and distinct in utterance, with a singular power of penetration. His brow was high and square and creased with horizontal wrinkles which added to his careworn, serious expression. His features in repose gave the impression of great will-power and force of character, suggesting little of the unfailing buoyancy and cheerfulness of nature which Porter later came to know so well. Apparently he never carried his body erect, and his movements were often slow, but somehow one guessed that when roused to activity he was quick in motion and could work with marvelous rapidity. It was plain that he was always civil to those with whom he came in contact, regardless of their rank or position.

On the next day Grant gave Porter an even better opportunity to study the workings of his mind. Returning from a tour of inspection of the Federal position, he sent for the chief of ordnance, said bluntly but politely, "Sit down," and then started asking a series of questions as to the character and location of the guns and the amount and kind of artillery ammunition needed. Satisfied with the Captain's answers, he then began writing dispatches, telling the Captain, who arose to leave, to "sit still." The young officer watched the older man, seated at the table, writing swiftly and uninterruptedly, without any marked display of nervous energy. He seemed never at a loss for an expression and seldom made a correction. He sat with his head bent low over the table, getting up from time to time to search for another paper. He would glide quietly across the room without straightening himself and return to his seat with his body still bent and continue his correspondence. Suddenly looking up, he remarked, "Perhaps you might like to read what I am sending," and gave the Captain the dispatches. As he read, Porter found that the General was ordering up Sherman's entire force to be within supporting distance, informing Halleck of the dispositions he had decided upon to open up the line of supplies—"the cracker line"—and assuring him of immediate relief for General Burnside in East Tennessee.

It did not take long for the new commander to gain completely the admiration and confidence of his subordinate, and Grant, on his side, was not slow to realize the young captain's worth. Only later and by degrees came the deep and lasting friendship which linked together for over twenty years the lives of these two men, so different in antecedents and in character.

Grant's leadership showed itself first in the immediate carrying out of his plans for opening up the line of communication between Bridgeport and Chattanooga. There was a short, hard fight, and the work was done. He then was free to develop his purpose of attacking the enemy.

In the events that culminated in the battle of Chattanooga it was ordained that Porter should have no part: fate intervened in the shape of orders from Washington. In *Campaigning with Grant,* he rarely mentions his own personal fortunes. In this instance, however, he has made an exception which is all the more welcome because it shows how quickly the young chief of ordnance had won the confidence of his general.

> Early in November [he writes] instructions came from the Secretary of War calling me to Washington, and in accordance therewith General Thomas issued an order relieving me from duty with his army.[2]
>
> I had heard through personal letters that the Secretary wished to reorganize the Ordnance Bureau at Washington, and wished my services in that connection on account of my long experience in that department in the field. The

order was interpreted as a compliment, but was distasteful to me for many reasons, although I understood that the assignment was to be only temporary, and it was at a season when active operations in the field were usually suspended. It was a subject of much regret to leave General Thomas, for I had become greatly attached to him, and had acquired that respect and admiration for the character of this distinguished soldier which was felt by all who had ever come in contact with him. "Old Pap Thomas," as we all loved to call him, was more of a father than a commander to the younger officers who served under his immediate command, and he possessed their warmest affections. He and his corps commanders now made a written appeal to General Grant, requesting him to intercede and endeavor to retain me in the command.

In the evening of the 5th of November I was sent for by General Grant to come to his headquarters. On my arrival, he requested me to be seated at the opposite side of the table at which he sat smoking, offered me a cigar, and said: "I was sorry to see the order of the Secretary of War calling you to Washington. I have had some other views in mind regarding your services, and I still hope that I may be able to secure the recall of the order, and to have you assigned to duty with me, if that would be agreeable to you." I replied eagerly, "Nothing could possibly be more agreeable, and I should feel most highly honored by such an assignment." He went on to say, "With this step in view, I have just written a letter to the general-in-chief," which he then handed me to read.

Chattanooga, Tenn., Nov. 5, 1863.

Maj. Gen. H. W. Halleck,
General-in-Chief of the Army.

Capt. Horace Porter, who is now being relieved as chief ordnance officer in the Department of the Cumberland, is represented by all officers who know him as one of the most meritorious and valuable young officers in the service. So far as I have heard from general officers there is a universal desire to see him promoted to the rank of brigadier-general and retained here.   I feel no hesitation in joining in the recommendation, and ask that he may be assigned for duty with me.   I feel the necessity for just such an officer as Captain Porter is described to be, at headquarters, and, if permitted, will retain him with me if assigned here for duty. I am etc.,

U. S. Grant, *Major-General.*

Hardly allowing me to finish my expressions of surprise and gratification, he continued: "Of course, you will have to obey your present orders and proceed to Washington.   I want you to take this letter with you, and see that it is put into the hands of General Halleck; perhaps you will soon be able to rejoin me here.   My requests are not always complied with at headquarters, but I have written pretty strongly in this case, and I hope favorable action may be taken."   I replied that I would make my preparations at once to start East, and then withdrew.   The next day I called to bid the General good-by, and, after taking leave of General Thomas and my comrades on the staff, set out for the capital by way of the new line of communication which had just been opened." [3]

Arrived in Washington, Porter tried to get an interview with General Halleck in order that he might present Grant's letter in person.   Finding this impossible, he left the communication with Halleck's adjutant.   It was pigeon-holed, along with other similar requests.

Of Porter's duties in Washington during the winter of 1863-4 little need be said.   He had charge of the issue of ordnance to all the Federal armies; he was busy and did his work well.   The main event of the period was his marriage at Albany on December 23 to the girl whom he had met and wooed three years before at West Point.

All through the winter Porter continued to cherish hopes that something might yet come of Grant's proposal of an appointment on his staff.   With the passage of the bill creating the grade of Lieutenant-General, the nomination of Grant to the position, and his arrival at the capital early in March, these hopes brightened. Nevertheless, Grant's influence was not strong enough to enable him to obtain the officers that he wanted for his staff; Secretary Stanton made it plain to Porter that the request would be refused: he was needed where he was. "I certainly received a very cold bath at his hands," he wrote to his mother. "I was promoted, but told to stay in Washington."

The coming of "U. S. Grant and son, Galena, Ill.," as he described himself on the hotel register, was the event of the hour; its climax was his meeting with Lincoln at a reception at the White House. Captain Porter, who had come with his wife early in the evening, describes the President as he stood in the Blue Room. "His manners, in spite of his ungainly form and awkward movements, were extremely easy and winning." [4] His face wore a general expression of sadness, but at times his features lighted up with a broad smile, and there was a merry twinkle in his gray eyes as he greeted an old acquaintance.

When the President, looking over the heads of his visitors, caught sight of Grant modestly advancing with the rest of the crowd, he strode out to meet him, his face radiant, and held the General's hand long in his, shaking it with great vigor.

The large crowd of invited guests were determined to see Grant. They called, they shouted, in their enthusiasm surging around him. Mr. Seward, the Secretary of State, persuaded Grant to stand upon a sofa, as the crowd was becoming unmanageable. On catching sight of him they started cheering and made a wild rush to shake his hand. It was fully an hour, and then only with the aid of several officers, before Grant could retire and join the President in one of the smaller drawing-rooms.

The new Lieutenant-General, now at the head of all the Federal forces, was anxious to leave Washington as quickly as possible and push with all vigor his plans for the spring campaign. He had many recommendations concerning promotions and appointments, and was at last able to make his authority effective. Although in the case of Captain Porter Secretary Stanton did not yield at once, he finally "climbed down," and on April 27 Porter's appointment as aide-de-camp on Grant's personal staff, with the rank of Lieutenant-Colonel of Volunteers, was officially announced. Two days later he arrived at Culpeper, Virginia, Grant's headquarters, and reported for duty.[5]

The next morning Captain Porter was sent for by his Chief to accompany him to the headquarters of General Meade, commanding the Army of the Potomac. Grant's purpose in selecting the new aide for this journey was evidently that each might become better acquainted with the other; hitherto their intercourse had been almost purely official. It was a distance of six miles, and as the two men rode along, Grant on his bay, Cincinnati, the General talked freely of the things on which his mind was dwelling in connection with the approaching campaign. He was particularly outspoken as to his relations with Lincoln and with Meade. In great detail he told of his conversation with the President—a memorable interview in which Lincoln defended his course in dealing with other commanders and showed his confidence in the new leader by refraining from inquiry about his plans. For Meade, Grant expressed the greatest admiration and respect: he was not only an able leader but a man of unselfish patriotism. What the day's experience revealed to Porter was his Chief's power as a conversationalist. In private talk, far from being reticent, he "had the ability to impart a peculiar charm to almost any topic." As they jogged along over the roads, this power of holding and fascinating the listener became more and more pronounced.

May 4 was the day set for the advance of all the armies under Grant's command. On the night preceding, the senior members of his staff assembled for their final instructions.

For the first time since the beginning of the war the movement of the Union forces was to be coördinated. Sherman in Tennessee, Banks in Arkansas, Sigel in the Shenandoah, Butler on the James, Burnside close at hand, with the Army of the Potomac, were to advance simultaneously against the opposing forces of the enemy. With these plans the staff were, of course, familiar; but on this occasion what Grant wished to impress upon them was his purpose in regard to the impending movement against Lee and their duties as staff officers in connection with the movements of Meade's army.

"I expect to send you to the critical points of the lines," so Porter reports Grant's instructions, "to keep me promptly advised of what is taking place, and in cases of great emergency, when new dispositions have to be made on the instant, or it becomes suddenly necessary to reënforce one command by sending to its aid troops from another, and there is not time to communicate with headquarters, I want you to explain my views to commanders, without waiting for specific orders, from me." [6]

Obviously, in performing such work there was danger of confusion between them and the officers of Meade's staff; to reduce such danger to a minimum, Grant proposed to establish his headquarters in close proximity to those of Meade and to communicate his instructions for the Army of the Potomac through Meade.

When the conference broke up at long past midnight, all was in readiness for the start. Horace Porter was about to enter upon his experience of Campaigning with Grant.

CHAPTER V

THE BATTLES OF 1864

IN spite of the discrepancy in numbers (101,000 effectives against 61,000) [1] between the armies of Grant and Lee, there were other circumstances which tended to minimize the difference in this respect. Lee was familiar with every inch of the ground and was operating on interior lines; the men in his well-disciplined army were fighting for their homes; above all, he had the confidence of the government and the people of the Confederacy. The Northern army, on the other hand, was operating in an unfamiliar and unfriendly country, with inaccurate maps and untrustworthy guides; large bodies of troops had to be detached to guard the long lines of communication, protect the supply trains, and conduct the wounded to points of safety. Moreover, in the North opinion as to the war was sharply divided, and Grant, as Commander-in-Chief, was still on trial. Nevertheless, to those in the army who had come in contact with him, his self-reliance in perfecting his plans and his absolute belief in their success were good omens. His own confidence communicated itself to all who listened to him.

The advance of the Army of the Potomac on the morning of May 4, 1864, was a memorable picture of brilliancy and splendor. In the ten months since the battle of Gettysburg, it had lain practically inactive; it was about to enter upon a month of conflict waged on a scale hitherto unknown in the history of war. Crossing the Rapidan, it plunged into the Wilderness, a region of forest through which it was to penetrate as rapidly as possible. If Lee chose to attack there,—well and good. Grant instructed Meade to lose no time in "pitching into him." At the very outset the armies of both Meade and Lee were to learn that Grant was a man willing to fight and, once he had begun, of extraordinary tenacity.

Attack Lee did, on the morning of the fifth, and for two days the contest raged. The horrors of that battle never lost their reality in Porter's memory. In the gloom of a cloudy day under thick trees the smoke made it almost impossible for officers to see their troops at any distance; every movement was through tangles of underbrush in which progress was slow and one's sense of direction was soon lost. Two armies, bewildered in a vast forest, were trying to find and fight each other. The climax of the horrors came at the end of the second day when a part of the forest caught fire. The dead were roasted in the conflagration; the wounded, in desperation, tried to drag themselves toward safety only to fall back into the flames, their cries mingling with the hoarse shouts of command and the rattle of musketry.[2]

In the midst of all this carnage and confusion Captain Porter spent hour after hour making his way, as best he could, from one commander to another, now carrying his Chief's messages and now hurrying back to report the position of the troops and the progress of the fighting in different parts of the forest. This duty, needless to say, was difficult and hazardous. Often he found himself in the midst of a skirmish in which he himself took part. Thus he was in the attack made by General Hancock, and again in one made by General Burnside. In working his way back to the Commander-in-Chief he was an easy target for sharpshooters, who were concealed in the trees and underbrush and were delighted to get a shot at a Yankee staff officer. That Grant was pleased with his work is evident from a recommendation for promotion to the brevet rank of major in the regular army "for gallant and meritorious services."

Almost every time that Porter went back to General Grant during the course of the battle, he found him on the top of a knoll near the deserted Wilderness Tavern, the only place from which he could survey even to a slight extent the surrounding country. He had taken his position here early in the day, and here he waited for the beginning of the attack. Lighting one of his innumerable cigars, he sat down on a tree-stump, took out his penknife, and began whittling a stick. Later in the day he was sitting on the ground with his back to a tree, still whittling. Once or twice he rode out to important points of the line in company with General Meade, followed by Colonel Porter. The observant member of the staff noted that Grant was plainly affected by the sight of the wounded, and that in the evening, when the firing had died out, he immediately issued orders to succor them—a task almost impossible to perform in the entanglement of underbrush and in such close proximity to the enemy.

During the most critical moments of the battle Grant showed no perceptible anxiety, writes Porter. He gave his orders, sent and received communications with a coolness and deliberation which made a marked impression on those who had been brought into contact with him for the first time on the field of battle. His speech was never hurried, and his manner betrayed no trace of excitement or even impatience. On one occasion, while waiting for the notoriously slow Burnside to get into position, he remarked to Porter: "The only time I ever feel impatient is when I give an order for an important movement of troops in the presence of the enemy, and am waiting for them to reach their destination. Then the minutes seem like hours." On this occasion, as it proved, Grant had good reason for showing his anxiety. Nevertheless, the only sign of it apparent to Porter was his incessant smoking. At the beginning of the day Porter had seen him put twenty-one strong cigars in his pocket. In the evening he had just one left to offer General Hancock.

Another instance of Grant's composure occurred at the

end of the second day, when one officer after another arrived at headquarters, bringing alarming reports of the reverse that had befallen the right wing. "Such tales of disaster," writes Porter, "would have been enough to inspire serious apprehension in daylight and under ordinary circumstances. In the darkness of the night, in the gloom of a tangled forest, and after men's nerves had been racked by the strain of a two days' desperate battle, the most immovable commander might have been shaken. But it was in just such sudden emergencies that General Grant was always at his best." Having convinced himself that the reverse was not serious and having given the necessary orders, he took his seat on a camp-stool, lighted a fresh cigar, and awaited further reports from the right. Still later in the evening, after he had gone to bed, when Porter felt it necessary to awaken him with another alarming message, he dismissed it as an exaggeration and went to sleep again.

But the most striking evidence of his character that Grant gave during the battle of the Wilderness was seen early the next morning, when he issued orders for a night march beyond Lee's right in the direction of Richmond. Having begun, he intended to keep on; there was to be no period of recovery; he proposed "to take no backward steps." The army was quick to sense the significance of this move and, in the evening, as Grant and his staff passed along the road after the march had started, the soldiers of Hancock's corps let themselves go in a fashion which created one of the most memorable scenes of the entire campaign. They cheered Grant as one who was leading them forward, pressing close up to him and calling to him with the familiarity of comrades. Some of them lit pine torches, in the hope of seeing his face. For a moment the General and his staff were caught in the midst of the cheering, excited throng. Even Cincinnati, who was controlled by the slightest word from his master, became restive.

Grant, who was entirely without vanity, thought only of

the success lying within his reach. Fearing that the noise would be heard by the enemy and reveal his movements, he ordered his staff to ride ahead, calm the men, and stop the cheering. But the soldiers, with true American spirit, refused to be silenced; they had a chief who was worth their cheers and they were determined to enforce this opinion. They became less demonstrative, but it was only when Grant was out of sight and the darkness complete that the noise subsided.

A day or so later Porter saw his Chief from still another angle. Sheridan had been brought by Grant from the West to command the cavalry of the Army of the Potomac. He was young,—only thirty-three years old,—aggressive and impetuous, and a soldier of the highest order. It was not strange that he and Meade should clash. On the morning in question they fell into a hot dispute which, as their angry voices rose higher and higher, could be distinctly heard by the Chief and his staff. Meade had lost control of himself and launched out at Sheridan in a towering passion, accusing him of blunders and faulty disposition of his troops on the foregoing day. Sheridan's Irish temper was immediately raised to its highest pitch; he never minced his words, and his language was always spicy. He fired at Meade short, decisive explosives, accusing him of creating the trouble by countermanding his, Sheridan's, orders, and ended his tirade by declaring that he would not command the cavalry any longer under such conditions. The proper way for the cavalry to perform its function, he said, was for it to move against the Rebel cavalry and keep it so busy that it would have no time to attack the Federal trains.

Meade, still furious, rushed over to General Grant's tent to repeat the interview (which was hardly necessary, considering the noise they had been making). When he related Sheridan's boast that he could move out with his cavalry and whip Stuart, the Confederate commander, Grant quietly observed, speaking slowly, "Did Sheridan say that? Well, he generally knows what he's talking about. Let him start right out now and do it." In this way Grant gave the stranger a chance to show his mettle. By one o'clock that same day Sheridan had his written orders from Meade and, mounted on Rienzi,[3] started on his famous cavalry raid to the vicinity of Richmond in the rear of Lee's army, to make good his word.

On his way to Spottsylvania Court House, riding his black pony called "Jeff Davis," on the morning of May 9, the Chief stopped to confer with General Sedgwick, commanding the Sixth Army Corps. Sedgwick was in buoyant spirits. Grant complimented him on his recent services; Sedgwick made light of his difficulties and expressed great confidence in the ability of his troops. The two commanders parted. General Grant, suddenly remembering another important question, sent Colonel Porter back to discuss the matter with Sedgwick. The staff officer followed the road he had seen him take, heard sharp musketry firing, and arrived in time to see Sedgwick's dead body borne from the field. There was nothing to do but retrace his steps and report to the Chief. Grant for a moment seemed dazed, and repeated twice, "Is he really dead?" The shock was so severe that he could not conceal his grief. In the Wilderness, when the report reached him of the death of Hays, he had kept on whittling, speaking in short disjointed sentences of their friendship, their days together at West Point, Hays' many good qualities, seemingly unable to resign himself to the loss of his comrade. On hearing of Sedgwick's death, after the first startled exclamations, he bent his head and rode on in silence, in a vain endeavor to hide his emotion.

An example of his Chief's self-command and supreme indifference to danger was witnessed by Colonel Porter in the fighting around Spottsylvania Court House. Grant was out on the lines supervising an attack. He dismounted and sat down on a fallen tree to write a dispatch. A shell exploded directly in front of him. He looked up from his paper an instant; then, without the slightest change of countenance, went on writing the message. A soldier hurrying past him with his regiment remarked to one of his comrades, "Ulysses don't scare worth a damn."

In the battle of Spottsylvania, memorable for the contest of the "bloody angle," Porter was actively employed. Hancock, commanding the Second Corps, was to carry the intrenchments at that point, and Colonel Porter was sent to him with the Chief's orders. He remained with the Second Corps until long after midnight, helping to direct the movements of the troops and form the assaulting columns. After leaving Hancock he rode through the pitch darkness, losing his way, running against trees and squeezing through the lines of advancing infantry, his horse in the torrential rain constantly slipping in the soft roads churned up by the artillery. In the gray dawn he found Grant sitting wrapped in his greatcoat on a stool before a struggling camp-fire. He offered his hungry, tired aide some coffee and listened attentively to his report. Porter had hardly finished speaking before a rattle of musketry from Hancock's front told the story of the beginning of the assault, and he was immediately on his horse again with the Chief's message to Burnside to "push on with all vigor."

Riding back to Headquarters, Porter found his Chief still sitting on his camp-stool, quite unmoved by the reports of an overwhelming victory for the Union forces. He gave his short, precise orders, the wind blowing the cape of his greatcoat across his face, often cutting off his voice in the middle of a sentence. He made few comments until the reports came in regarding the capture of a large number of prisoners (4,000). Then his face became suddenly animated and he exclaimed, "That's the kind of news I like to hear." His first question after hearing the report of success in any battle was, "Have any prisoners been taken?" This desire to take prisoners arose not from the fact that they added so largely to the trophies of battle, but from his tenderness of heart. He preferred to reduce the enemy's strength by captures rather than by slaughter. It fell to his lot to capture a larger number of prisoners than any other general of modern times, the Great War excepted.

In after years General Porter often spoke of the intense physical and mental strain to which the officers, especially the staff, were subjected during that long and unremitting fighting in the Wilderness, at Spottsylvania, and at Cold Harbor, covering a period of about four weeks. The staff officers rode for hours in heavy rains and under blistering sun, often exposed to the enemy's fire. Since much of their duty consisted in carrying orders at night for the movements of the next day, they had to get their sleep "on the instalment plan." They knew that should their message miscarry, a serious set-back would ensue.

Once, when the advance of the Ninth Corps was all-important to General Grant, he sent off Porter with orders to consult Burnside and then return immediately to Headquarters and report. "But," writes Porter, "the country was so bewildering, and the enemy so completely concealed from view, that it was impossible at the time to know the exact relative positions of the contending forces. . . . I had sent two bulletins to General Grant describing the situation on the left, but the orderly who carried one of the dispatches never arrived, having probably been killed, and the other did not reach the General till quite late. . . . I started for Headquarters that evening, but owing to the intense darkness, the condition of the roads, and the difficulty of finding the way, did not arrive till long after midnight." Then, too, it was often difficult to find General Grant. Unlike the commanders of the Great War, who were stationed in headquarters twenty miles and more to the rear, within reach of the field telephones, Grant used to ride to different parts of the battle-front exposed to the firing and was often surrounded by hurrying troops.[4]

Horace Porter always had a keen eye for traits of character and humorous situations, and during these weeks of hard campaigning he found time to record in his diary much that was not strictly in line with his military activities. These observations and incidents form an important part of his book and were also the foundation of many interesting stories told later to his daughter.

The younger officers, tired and overworked, were delighted to find the slightest relief for their strained nerves. Many smoked, some read. One member of the staff consoled himself by novel-reading: he stuffed out his saddle-bags with the latest publications and sometimes seemed more interested in extricating hero and heroine from the dilemma into which the author had plunged them than in hearing the results of the surrounding battle. He was especially enthusiastic over Victor Hugo's *Les Misérables,* which no one could persuade him to pronounce otherwise than *Lees Miserables*. One day, in passing an old Southern house, he tried to open up a conversation with its pretty but disdainful owner. Dismounting and reaching into his saddle-bags, he produced a book and asked in his best manner if she had ever seen *Lees Miserables*. "Don't talk to me like that!" came the furious reply. "You know they are a good sight better than Grant's miserables, anyway!"

Many a time Porter followed his Chief when he went for a rest up the steps of these houses, and was witness of Grant's uniform courtesy and imperturbability in all his encounters with the excited women who owned them. The house itself the General never went into unless it was to be used for headquarters or for a hospital, and his subordinates had strict orders against taking any liberties. In one house which the General entered just after a battle in order to prepare some dispatches, he found a number of wounded lying about, having "made their way there in accordance with the usual custom of wounded men to seek a house." When Grant and Porter went on into a back room, in the hope of finding some "dry spot" for their maps and papers, a Confederate corporal, whose cheek had been shot to pieces, rose from the only chair and offered it to the General with a bow and a smile. At that Grant bade him sit down again: "You need that chair much more than I." The soldier replied that if "you folks" would let him go back to his own lines he might get home to see his girl— "but I reckon she wouldn't know me now." General Grant had one of the Union surgeons dress the man's wound, and he left him in peace in the little room.[5]

The severe struggle around Spottsylvania was noteworthy as being the last offensive movement on a considerable scale made by Lee during the campaign. Both armies were rapidly learning the protective value of hasty intrenchments, and from this time on the Confederate commander relied on them to offset his disadvantage in numbers. On May 20th Grant ordered another forward movement, in pursuance of his plan of getting round his opponent's right. As he and Meade rode along with their staffs, they were accompanied by a small escort of infantry and cavalry only. Before pitching camp for the night, one of the officers suggested that it would be safer for the Chief not to advance too far with such a small escort, but to move back on the road and await Warren and his troops. The Chief's intense dislike of any manner of retreat, a feeling amounting almost to a superstition, was shown in his answer on this occasion: "I think, instead of our turning back, we had better hurry Warren forward."

The positions which the two armies had now taken at the North Anna River were of such a character that neither side felt it advantageous to attack the other. The fact that Lee was unwilling to move against him Grant thought significant. "Lee's army is really whipped," he wrote to the War Department. "A battle with him outside of intrenchments cannot be had." [6]

The Federal commander accordingly determined on another movement to the left in the direction of Richmond. The possession of Old Cold Harbor was an important part of his plans, and he sent Sheridan with the cavalry to seize and hold it. Colonel Porter, coming with orders for Sheridan, found him mounted on Rienzi, advancing with his little band of cavalry to attack Lee's first intrenchments. They carried the position. The enemy reattacked. Sheridan held his ground, hoping for reënforcements. All night the two officers worked with the men, throwing up breastworks and strengthening their position. "We could distinctly hear the enemy's troops making preparations for the next morning's attack, and could even hear some of the commands given by their officers." At daylight on June 1 the assault began, Sheridan bravely holding his ground until General Wright, with his troops jaded and footsore from an all-night march over unknown roads, moved into line, relieved Sheridan's small force, and secured Old Cold Harbor for Grant.

Again the Northern army faced opponents protected by breastworks so placed that an attack on them must be accompanied by heavy loss. Grave as the risk was, Grant determined to make a direct assault. A scene that Porter witnessed on the evening before the attack indicated that the soldiers realized fully what was before them. "As I came near one of the regiments which was making preparations for the next morning's assault," he writes, "I noticed that many of the soldiers had taken off their coats, and seemed to be engaged in sewing up rents in them. This exhibition of tailoring seemed rather peculiar at such a moment, but upon closer examination it was found that the men were calmly writing their names and home addresses on slips of paper, and pinning them on the backs of their coats, so that their dead bodies might be recognized upon the field, and their fate made known to their families at home. They were veterans who knew well from terrible experience the danger which awaited them, but their minds were occupied not with thoughts of shirking their duty, but with preparation for the desperate work of the coming morning."

The attack made in the early morning of June 3 soon demonstrated its futility and was ordered suspended. The Union forces held the positions that they had gained, in close proximity to the Confederate lines, but their losses had been appalling. The number of killed and wounded was estimated at 12,000;[7] the Confederate loss was very much less.

At Headquarters that evening there was naturally much discussion of the attack. Porter quotes Grant as deprecating it in the following words: "I regret this assault more than any one I have ever ordered. I regarded it as a stern necessity, and believed that it would bring compensating results; but, as it has proved, no advantages have been gained sufficient to justify the heavy losses suffered."

For the next nine days the main portion of Grant's army remained in the positions in which they found themselves when the fighting ceased on June 3. The conditions under which the Army of the Potomac endured and suffered in this period were not unlike life in the trenches during the Great War. Porter had frequent occasion to visit the front during these days. "Between the lines," he writes, "where the heavy assaults had been made there was in some places a distance of thirty or forty yards completely covered by the dead and wounded of both sides. The bodies of the dead were festering in the sun, while the wounded were dying a torturing death from starvation, thirst, and loss of blood. In some places the stench became sickening. Every attempt to make a change in the picket-line brought on heavy firing, as both sides had become nervous from long watchfulness, and the slightest movement on either front led to the belief that it was the beginning of an assault. In the night there was often heavy artillery-firing, sometimes accompanied by musketry, with a view to deterring the other side from attacking, or occasioned by false rumors of an attempt to assault. The men on the advanced lines had to lie close to the ground in narrow trenches, with little water for drinking purposes, except that obtained from surface drainage. They were subjected to the broiling heat by day and the chilling winds and fogs at night, and had to eat rations that could be got to them under the greatest imaginable discomfort."

The main reason why Grant kept the Army of the Potomac so long at Cold Harbor in a position in which it was bound to suffer great deterioration in health and morale was that he desired to hold the Confederates where they were while he was making arrangements for the transfer of the Army to the south side of the James River. By this move he would unite Butler's force at Bermuda Hundred with his own, and the combined armies would approach Petersburg and Richmond from the south. In order to reach its destination, the Army of the Potomac must make a rapid march of fully fifty miles, including the passage of the Chickahominy and the James. Furthermore, these operations must be conducted so swiftly and secretly as to leave the Confederate commander in the dark, lest he should move by shorter roads and so crush Butler before Grant could arrive.

Three days after the battle of Cold Harbor Grant, summoning Porter and Colonel Comstock to his tent, unfolded to them his plan, and instructed them to start at once for General Butler's headquarters and impart it to him. That done, they were to find the best point on the James for the building of a pontoon-bridge. The step was momentous, and Grant's manner in speaking to his aides was unusually impressive.

The two officers left Headquarters the next morning, rode to White House, took a boat to Bermuda Hundred, delivered their orders to Butler, and started down the James, making careful reconnoissances of the banks and approaches on each side. Wilcox's Landing, opposite Fort Powhatan, was selected as being the narrowest point on the river below City Point. Returning to Headquarters on the twelfth, they found the General and the army fully prepared to withdraw from their present position. As he listened to their report, the General turned and twisted his big cigar in his mouth, laid it on the table, let it go out, picked it up, relighted it, asked quick questions, interrupted their narrative with, "Yes, yes," and altogether showed an agitation that was strangely foreign to him.

That same evening the march to the James began. Porter writes of riding all night in the bright moonlight, half suffocated by the dust arising from the tramp of countless feet and the turning of countless wheels. It was so blinding that often the artillerymen had to walk ahead and locate the small bridges along the road by feeling for them. Forced marches brought the army to the James, where the pontoon-bridge, twenty-one hundred feet long, had been thrown across the stream with remarkable speed; by means of this and ferry-boats the transfer of the army was accomplished in three days.

Grant's change of base had been effected successfully; having thus mystified his opponent, all his energies were bent on the capture of Petersburg before Lee could move sufficient forces to it to defend it adequately. A series of mistakes and misunderstandings, however, delayed the attacks while the enemy's lines were still thinly held; and the prize which, if obtained, would have shortened the war by eight or nine months, was lost. Porter speaks of Grant's philosophic resignation at the disappointing news which he brought him after a long day at the front. The General's last chance for success by the method he had hitherto used was gone; but he was not to be turned from his one purpose. "I am perfectly satisfied that all has been done that could be done," he wrote to Meade that evening. "Now we will rest the men, and use the spade for their protection until a new vein can be struck." [8]

Rest, indeed, the men needed sorely. For over six weeks they had marched and fought incessantly. Their losses (64,000) had been staggering; [9] many of their best officers were gone. And while they dug themselves in with the spade, their resourceful commander, whose faith never waned, hunted for the new vein the working of which would revive their confidence in him and in the success of the cause.

CHAPTER VI

AT CITY POINT

CITY POINT, which for the next nine months was to be Grant's headquarters, was the name of a high bluff at the confluence of the Appomattox and the James Rivers. It was well situated for communication with the armies in front of Richmond and Petersburg, and it had easy access to Fortress Monroe and Washington by steamer. The tents of the staff formed a line close to the edge of the bluff, and here the officers quickly made themselves comfortable, welcoming the change from the weeks of hard campaigning which they had just been through. In a short time City Point became an important base of supplies. Wharves and storehouses were constructed at the foot of the bluff, hospitals were erected, and a military railroad was built running to points south of Petersburg and in the rear of the lines of the Army of the Potomac. When cold weather came, log cabins took the place of the tents.[1] Porter's cabin had a floor of boards, a bed with a straw mattress, a table with a wash basin, and a fireplace,—the last a great luxury.

The end of the first stage of the campaign and the beginning of the next with the siege of Petersburg brought President Lincoln to the scene for a conference with Grant. "A few days ago," wrote Colonel Porter to his wife on June 24, "we were sitting in front of the General's tent, when there appeared very suddenly before us a long, lank-looking personage, dressed all in black and looking very much like a boss undertaker. It was the President. He said, after shaking hands with us all: 'I just thought I would jump aboard a boat and come down and see you. I don't expect I can do any good, and in fact I am afraid I may do harm, but I'll put myself under your orders and if you find me doing anything wrong just send me right away.' Gen. Grant informed him bluntly that he certainly would do so. The old fellow remained with us till the next day, and told stories all the time. He did not ask, and said he did not want to know, Grant's plans. On the whole he behaved very well. The black troops received him enthusiastically, grinning from ear to ear, and displaying an amount of ivory terrible to behold."

The summer of 1864 was a time of intense anxiety. Lee, behind the defenses of Petersburg and Richmond, was able to detach troops for offensive purposes elsewhere. "The affairs of the country were now like a prairie in the season of fires: as soon as the conflagration was extinguished in one place it immediately broke out in another." [2] On one raid down the Shenandoah Valley and into Maryland, the Confederates reached the outskirts of Washington. Grant from a distance had to give the orders necessary for meeting such emergencies, and owing to the commanders on whom he must rely the results were not always satisfactory. His remedy for the situation was to keep Lee busy where he was, but even under his own eye his plans were sometimes wrecked by the incompetence of the generals to whom they were entrusted.

One such instance was the famous "mine explosion" of July 30. It was planned, by exploding a large amount of powder in tunnels dug under the enemy's works, to make an opening sufficiently wide for an assaulting column to push through. Partly owing to accident, but mostly owing to bad management, everything went wrong: the explosion was more than an hour late; the attacking troops had difficulty in getting over their own parapets and through the obstructions outside of them; the sides of the crater formed by the explosion were so steep that it was almost impossible for the men to climb out; worst of all, the division commander remained under cover in the rear.

Apprehensive of disaster, Grant started for the front, taking Porter with him. They soon dismounted and pushed their way forward on foot in the midst of the troops of the assaulting columns. Grant's object was to find the corps commander, General Burnside, and bring some measure of control into the disorder before it was too late. Seeing a group of officers at a distance, one of whom he understood to be Burnside, Grant, as the quickest way of reaching him, climbed over the parapet and landed in front of the outer earthworks in direct line of the enemy's fire. This action on the part of the commanding general was so unheard-of that the soldiers did not even recognize him. The heat was intolerable, and the General wore his thin blue blouse and blue trousers, with only his shoulder-straps to distinguish him from the ordinary soldier. The General walked rapidly, sometimes almost running. The enemy's fire was so direct and so intense that the young staff officer following him held his breath in apprehension for his commander's safety. In later years Porter described that walk as the hottest he had ever taken. "The very recollection of it," he declared, "starts the perspiration."

The commanding general and his aide reached comparative safety by climbing over one of the outer earthworks behind which General Burnside was stationed, to the utmost astonishment of that officer. General Grant then ordered the immediate withdrawal of the troops, as he considered the situation nothing less than slaughter, and he and Major Porter joined the staff and rode back to City Point. "The ride," Porter wrote home, "was anything but cheerful"; and yet for him, who had been singled out to accompany the Chief on his dangerous mission, the day had had its compensations.

Less than a fortnight later, Porter was again under fire, at Newmarket Heights. During the engagement he bore himself so well that Grant recommended that he be brevetted a lieutenant-colonel in the regular army "for gallant and meritorious services in action." The nature of the service was never divulged to his family, for Porter was very reticent on such subjects; but it may well have been in connection with it that he had the narrow escape from capture which furnished one of the most thrilling of his stories.

In carrying a message for General Grant he lost his way and ran into a Confederate patrol, which started in pursuit of him. Suddenly his little mare went lame; he dismounted and worked the stone out of her hoof with his sword; the enemy had for a moment disappeared behind a wood, but as he was in the act of mounting they came in sight again. Lying low in his saddle, he put spurs to his mare, which she hardly needed, for, realizing the danger, she galloped madly on, straining every nerve. Then, with his pursuers almost at his heels, he suddenly saw the line of Federal breastworks in front of him. The Union soldiers, not daring to fire, gave vent to their feeling by shouting words of encouragement from behind the intrenchments. Gathering all her strength in one supreme effort, the little mare leaped the intervening breastwork and brought her rider to safety in the midst of the cheering, excited throng.

Whatever the "gallant and meritorious services" may have been on this occasion, it is certain that Grant was eager to show by such promotions his appreciation not only of his aide's work but also of the sacrifice that he made in remaining on the staff, where, as Grant expressed it many years later,[3] he was "lost." "As a commander of troops, Porter would have risen, in my opinion, to a high command." But he was "too useful to be spared."

Grant's calmness in the presence of immediate danger, as during that hot walk along the front after the mine explosion, was shown on several other occasions during the months at City Point. Apparently the purpose in hand filled his mind so completely that the thought of danger to himself had no space to crowd itself in. If a dispatch needed to be written forthwith, he sat down where he was, deaf to the suggestions of his staff that he move to a place of greater safety. With the shells bursting above his head, his pencil continued its even tracings. In one battle, as he was riding forward with General Meade, he came into the direct line of fire. When a shell exploded just in front of his horse, the animal reared, entangled his hoof in some twisted wire, and in trying to extricate himself became unmanageable. The General sat still, endeavoring to calm him, and seemed more occupied in seeing that Babcock, who was trying to uncoil the wire, did not hurt the horse's leg, than in observing the bursting shells. On another occasion, when a barge loaded with ammunition exploded at the wharf close to Headquarters,[4] killing a number of men and dealing destruction in all directions, Grant did not even get up from the camp-stool on which he was sitting. Familiar as this characteristic became to the members of his staff, they never ceased to marvel at each new manifestation of it.

Early in September, 1864, news of the capture of Atlanta reached the headquarters at City Point. Colonel Porter writes to his wife of Sherman's sending the most encouraging dispatches, and "yesterday we got the detailed account of the taking of Atlanta from Sherman himself." The next move had now to be initiated. "On September 12," writes Porter, "General Grant called me into his tent, turned his chair around from the table at which he had been sitting, lighted a fresh cigar, and began a conversation by saying: 'Sherman and I have exchanged ideas regarding his next movement about as far as we can by correspondence, and I have been thinking that it would be well for you to start for Atlanta to-morrow, and talk over with him the whole subject of his next campaign.'" Then followed a long conversation, in the course of which the aide received abundant information for amplifying the brief letter which he was to take to Sherman.

Traveling by way of Cincinnati and Louisville, Porter reached Chattanooga on the nineteenth. The traffic on the railroad was in the congested state which accompanies every war. One train on which he was traveling jumped the track, and there were rumors of guerilla bands attempting to capture or wreck others. The Colonel paid no attention to the rumors and started that same night on a freight-train. As they passed over the battlefield of Chickamauga, exactly a year after that memorable day, all its exciting incidents came vividly back to his mind.

Having reached Atlanta, Porter found General Sherman sitting on the porch of an old-fashioned Southern house, reading a newspaper. "His coat was unbuttoned, his black felt hat slouched over his brow, on his feet were a pair of slippers very much down at the heels." Porter describes him as tall and gaunt, with restless hazel eyes, bronzed face, and crisp beard. Their greetings over, they plunged into an animated discussion of the military situation. Porter's account of his stay in Atlanta shows how keenly he noted the peculiarities of manner that made Sherman one of the most dramatic and picturesque characters of the war. "As he waxed more intense in his manner the nervous energy of his nature soon began to manifest itself. He twice rose from his chair and sat down again, twisted the newspaper into every conceivable shape, and from time to time drew first one foot and then the other out of its slipper, and followed up the movement by shoving out his leg so that the foot could recapture the slipper and thrust itself into it again." He was no less appreciative of Sherman's great qualities of mind and heart, and he quotes at length the warm words about Grant that reveal the comradeship and loyalty existing between the two men.

During the two days that Porter spent in Atlanta the march to the sea was planned. Then he was entrusted with a letter to General Grant, but most of the details of the plan he was to repeat by word of mouth. With a touch of his homely humor Sherman writes in this letter: "I will have a long talk with Colonel Porter and tell him everything that may occur to me of interest to you, etc. If you can whip Lee and I can march to the Atlantic I think Uncle Abe will give us a twenty days' leave of absence to see the young folks." [5]

Grant was evidently well satisfied with the report that was brought back to him, but before he issued any orders to Sherman there was much discussion at Headquarters concerning its merits. The staff turned itself into a small debating society, in which the principal defender of the plan was naturally Porter himself. His opponent was Rawlins, Grant's chief-of-staff, who had only recently returned to camp after an illness of some weeks. No one was more amused by the vehemence of the debaters than the Chief; he sat smoking and listening, which he ordinarily preferred to talking, while Porter argued one point after another and Rawlins steadily disagreed. Finally the General went to bed, leaving the staff still fighting. Rawlins, bawling out one of his most eloquent passages, was suddenly interrupted by the voice of his commander from the tent, "Oh, go to bed all of you. You're keeping the whole camp awake." As the Chief never nagged his officers and seldom reprimanded, the staff realized that their debate was exceeding the limits of his patience. They were soon to learn that he had fully decided on the march to the sea before they began talking.

In the course of the winter the General had many visitors at City Point, and in this connection a passage from *Campaigning with Grant* may be quoted to lay the ghost of one calumny that used to be repeated against Grant as general-in-chief—if it still walks. "He never offered liquor of any kind to visitors at Headquarters. His hospitality consisted in inviting them to meals and to smoke cigars." "It so happened that no one in the mess had any inclination to drink wine or spirits at meals, and none was carried among the mess's supplies. The only beverage ever used at table besides tea and coffee was water, although on the march it was often taken from places which rendered it not the most palatable or healthful of drinks. If a staff-officer wanted anything stronger he would carry some commissary whisky in a canteen. Upon a few occasions, after a hard day's ride in stormy weather, the General joined the officers of the staff in taking a whisky toddy in the evening."

To return to the visitors: their presence gave Porter numerous further opportunities of hearing Grant at his best in conversation. The charm of his sense of fun, his laugh, the twinkle in his eyes when he was about to say something humorous had become familiar; but he frequently astonished his aide by the amount of knowledge that he had acquired, for he was supposed to care for no more learning than was necessary to his profession.

Other visitors besides Lincoln and Seward were the Secretary of War, the Secretary of the Treasury, Major General Doyle, of the British Army, commanding in Nova Scotia and Newfoundland, a jolly old fellow of nearly seventy, and Congressman Elihu B. Washburne of Illinois, Grant's steadfast friend and supporter, who brought with him the medal voted by Congress to the general-in-chief. During Washburne's presentation speech, Porter was reminded how stiff and embarrassed Grant could be on formal occasions. The soldier stood listening, apparently wishing himself anywhere else than in a situation like the present, where a reply was expected from him. His few words of acceptance were uttered in a voice so low that he was hardly audible, and he was not at his ease again till the band burst forth in the first inspiring notes of a waltz. Mrs. Grant and some other ladies had arrived for a short visit at Headquarters; they were determined to dance and urged the General to join them. Now Grant had no ear for music or sense of rhythm: he never kept step with the music of the band and once said that he knew only two tunes. "One is Yankee Doodle, and the other isn't." However, on this occasion, to avoid the impossibility of a waltz, he went through the complicated figures of the lancers in very creditable fashion. Colonel Porter, thinking of the dark-haired girl of West Point days, in her voluminous skirts, waltzed as best he could with other partners, for the first time a little jealous of his Chief.

As the winter wore on and it became evident that the fortunes of the Confederacy were steadily ebbing, it was natural that the possibility of ending the contest by negotiation should be discussed. The Richmond government, anxious to avert the threatening disaster, made the first move, and on the evening of January 31, after receiving permission to cross the Federal lines, a "Peace Commission," consisting of Alexander H. Stephens, Vice-President of the Confederacy, J. A. Campbell, a former Justice of the Supreme Court of the United States, and R. M. T. Hunter, a member of the Confederate Senate, arrived at City Point. General Grant, accompanied by Colonel Porter, after a short conversation conducted the Commissioners to a steamboat lying at the wharf, gave them comfortable quarters in the staterooms, as there were no available houses, and waited for orders from Washington. He felt that they were sincere in their desire for peace and union, and it was at his suggestion that the President himself met them at Fortress Monroe.

Lincoln, however, insisted so emphatically on complete submission and the restoration of the Union that the conference was brought to an abrupt end and the Commissioners were sent back through the lines toward Richmond. It was Porter who escorted them. Stephens, who talked freely to him, discussing Grant and Lincoln and his disappointment at the failure of his own plans, made a great impression on the young man. Ill-favored and small as he was, wrapped up in a coat three sizes too large for him, he had "brains enough for the whole company."

Plainly there was only one way of bringing the contest to a decisive termination. Spring was close at hand and both sides addressed themselves to the task of making the best use of the few weeks remaining before the final struggle should begin.

CHAPTER VII

APPOMATTOX

IN the month of March, 1865, Grant was devoting himself to perfecting the plans for the spring advance which he hoped would crush the Confederacy. Although its strength was fast failing, whereas the Northern armies were never more powerful, the time was none the less one of great anxiety. Porter's statement of the problem facing Grant puts it in the simplest terms. "The movements of armies depend almost entirely on the condition of roads; so when the spring came and the roads began to dry up General Grant became very apprehensive that General Lee might suddenly retreat from his stronghold and throw himself back into the mountains, and that he (Grant) would have to pursue him there and take up a long line forward move from his base of supplies and that the war might be continued for another year, or probably break up into what was most dreaded, a general guerilla warfare. It was important to put a stop to the war as soon as possible, for the expenses of it had then reached to the enormous sum of $4,000,000 a day. The latter part of March General Grant slept with one eye open and one foot out of bed, watching Lee so that he could not give him the slip, for he knew that when the roads got in condition there would be either a fight or a foot race, and probably both." [1]

A memorable episode of this last month of the war was the visit of Lincoln to the Army. Besides his desire to confer with Grant, he was drawn to City Point by the fact that his son Robert had just been appointed to Grant's staff. [2] For six days General * Porter saw the President constantly:

* He was brevetted Brigadier-General, U. S. A., on March 13, 1865.

77

in the daytime he accompanied him and General Grant on their tours of inspection; in the evening he and the rest of the staff sat with him and Grant by the camp-fire and listened almost breathless to their talk.   Under these informal conditions Porter could learn to know and to love the man, at this time a statesman and ruler at the very summit of his career.   From the "kind-hearted old fellow who told amusing stories, rode a horse well, and did not interfere with Grant's methods of fighting," Lincoln rose in the eyes of the young officer to be the embodiment of the nation he was serving.

The conversation was naturally much occupied with discussion of the campaign, and several times, when contemplated battles were spoken of, the President remarked, "I cannot pretend to advise, but I do sincerely hope that all may be accomplished with as little bloodshed as possible." Yet the only way to end the war quickly, he knew, was to push it with vigor.   Then the two men went pretty thoroughly into the internal politics of the country; Lincoln spoke of the course which he thought had better be pursued after the war and expressed his inclination toward a policy of generosity.   Perhaps the most interesting part of the whole discussion was that of America's foreign relations, and particularly her relations with England.   The President admitted that the return of Mason and Slidell had been "a pretty bitter pill to swallow, but I contented myself with believing that England's triumph in the matter would be short-lived, and that after ending our war successfully we would be so powerful that we could call her to account for all the embarrassments she had inflicted upon us." [3]   He made his points by drawing on a far-reaching knowledge of history, politics, and international law, and above all by incomparable anecdotes.   A sentinel on duty near by was heard to say in astonishment: "Well, that man's got a powerful good memory and a mighty poor forgettery."

Of the many incidents of those six days one is almost in

a class by itself. The President found three tiny kittens crawling around his tent; the mother had died, and the little waifs were mewing piteously. Lincoln picked them up and tried to comfort them, and then asked one of the officers to go to the cook of the officers' mess and get a bowl of milk. When Porter arrived at the tent to bring a message from Grant, he found the President seated on a camp-stool, his long legs hunched up almost to his chin, balancing a saucer of milk on his knees; he held the three kittens in his arms and was patiently trying to make them drink.

On the 27th Sherman arrived from the South, having been summoned by Grant to talk over the final plans for the campaign. Naturally the Chief and his staff were most anxious to hear the story of the march through Georgia. The bluff veteran had a strong sense of humor and, seated before the camp-fire, gave a description both graphic and humorous of his famous march from Atlanta to the sea, all without the slightest suggestion of egotism. "Never," writes Porter, "were listeners more enthusiastic, never was speaker more eloquent." He rattled on in his quick, off-hand manner, telling of amusing incidents among his soldiers. Wading a river one day which was bordered by miles of swamp, and seeing no prospect of reaching the other side, one tired soldier remarked to the other, "Say, Tommy, I'm blowed if I don't believe we've struck this river lengthways." He told stories of his "bummers," the foraging parties who gathered enough food for the army from the destitute population and devastated country (a suffering population has never yet won much sympathy from the leaders of an invading army). Then came stories of hard marches and heavy fighting.

On March 28, the day before that set for the advance, occurred the final conference of Grant and Sherman with the President. Admiral David Porter was also present as representative of the navy. In speaking to Horace Porter

of this memorable meeting, General Grant said that when
Sherman talked about acting on the defensive against
Johnston until Grant could encircle the enemy and hold
him in a vise, Mr. Lincoln, full of pity, asked if it were not
possible to end the matter without a pitched battle and the
attendant loss and suffering. As to the Confederate political leaders, the President intimated that it would relieve
the strained situation if they would "escape" after the war
to some foreign country. He spoke more emphatically than
ever of leniency towards the enemy. He wanted to see the
country strong and united again. He believed that a policy
of forgiveness would be more successful than one of punishment, and that through kindness the South would forget
more quickly and be more willingly reunited to the Northern
states.

With these injunctions of Lincoln's still ringing in his
ears, Grant started on March 29 on his last campaign. He
was to go by train with his staff to the Petersburg front.
The President, who preferred to remain for a time at City
Point rather than return to Washington, walked with them
to the train. The lines on his face were more visible than
usual, there were deep rings below the twinkling gray eyes,
and his anxiety was more than ever apparent. Shaking
hands with the General and each member of the staff, he
called to them as they stood on the platform of the car,
"Good-by, gentlemen. God bless you all! Remember, your
success is my success!"—waving to them until a turn of
the track hid him from their sight.

Although the campaign began with a downpour of rain
lasting thirty-six hours, events after that moved with bewildering swiftness, and in eleven days the climax had been
reached. Of all those scenes, momentous in American history and inspiring in their revelation of the character of
great men, Horace Porter was a witness. Sheridan, Grant,
Lee, Lincoln—he saw them at supreme moments in their
lives; thanks to his own greatness of soul, these mighty

GRANT AND HIS STAFF

Left to right: *Leet, Webster, Parker, Bowman, Morgan, Babcock, Williams, Grant, Rawlins, Bowers, Comstock, Porter, Badeau*

events became a part of his own nature, an ideal of heroism and patriotism which he did his best to exemplify throughout his life.

The first major encounter was at Five Forks, on the extreme right of the enemy's line. Finding the Confederates there in force, Sheridan asked urgently for infantry to help him attack. Having brought his message to Headquarters, Porter joined in the task of getting Warren's corps started on its all-night march. It was a night of intense strain and feverish activity. The commanders were writing dispatches and telegraphing from dark to daylight. Staff officers rushed through swamps and over corduroyed roads from one headquarters to another, making every effort to hurry the advancing troops to be massed against the enemy at Five Forks.

Early on the morning of April 1, the Chief ordered Porter to join Sheridan's command and send a bulletin every half-hour or so to report to Headquarters the progress of the fighting. "Tell him," said Grant, "that the contemplated movement is left entirely in his hands, and he must be responsible for its execution. I have every confidence in his judgment and ability."

Followed by half a dozen orderlies, Horace Porter set out and met Sheridan at ten o'clock in the morning on the Five Forks road. Sheridan informed Porter that the enemy force in front of him had fallen back early in the morning, that he had pursued it with his cavalry, and had had several brushes with it. By one o'clock the enemy was retiring to its intrenched position at Five Forks near the White Oak road. Warren, according to Sheridan's ideas, was inexcusably slow in getting his men up. The little Irishman paced up and down, striking his clenched fist on the palm of his hand, and then, remounting Rienzi, sent off another batch of staff officers to hurry the troops, exclaiming, "This battle must be fought and won before the sun goes down. My cavalry are rapidly exhausting their ammunition, and if the attack is delayed much longer they may have none left." So he fumed and fussed and fretted. Rienzi, catching the impatient spirit of his master, was pacing, turning, and pivoting, throwing up his head and looking anxiously for the advancing line of blue.[4]

By four o'clock the formation was complete. Porter rode to the front with Sheridan and Warren. Sheridan, putting spurs to his horse, dashed up to a skirmish line that was beginning to waver. He shouted words of encouragement to the men, riding ahead of them, leading them on, turning again to advance with the front line of each regiment, riding with them into the thick of the fight, urging, shouting, cheering. To one man who had fallen covered with blood and crying, "I'm killed!" he called out, "You're not hurt a bit! Pick up your gun, man, and move right on to the front!" The poor fellow was so electrified that he actually picked up his musket and rushed on a dozen paces, then fell in a heap, never to rise again. On rode Sheridan, closely followed by Porter, over the swampy fields and through the dense underbrush, Rienzi, his black coat shining with sweat, "dashing the foam from his mouth and the mud from his heels." The troops were falling back in confusion under a heavy fire. Sheridan seized his battle-flag from the hands of the sergeant, and, waving it above his head, cheered and threatened and finally forced the men to close up their ranks and follow him. "It would be a sorry soldier who could help following such a leader." "Bullets were now humming like a swarm of bees about our heads, and shells were crashing through the ranks."

The men advanced with fixed bayonets, and with a rousing cheer dashed over the enemy's earthworks, sweeping everything before them. Sheridan never stopped. He spurred Rienzi on to the "angle" (the second line of earthworks); with a bound the animal carried his master over the breastworks and landed in the midst of a line of prisoners who had already thrown down their arms. Seeing the crouching men, Sheridan immediately opened up a running talk with the "Johnnies"; his rage and excitement of a moment before had completely disappeared. "Go right over there," pointing to the rear. "Get right along, now. Oh, drop your guns; you'll never need them any more. You'll all be safe over there. Are there any more of you? We want every one of you fellows." Porter, seated on his panting horse, watched the scene, laughing quietly to himself at Sheridan's sallies, at the same time helping him form the prisoners in line to march to the rear. Fifteen hundred men were taken at the "angle."

His victory complete, Sheridan now turned his energy to protecting his slightly detached command from a possible attack by Lee in the morning. Porter, still in astonishment at the marvel that he had witnessed, remarked to the cavalry leader, "It seems to me that you have exposed yourself to-day in a manner hardly justifiable on the part of a commander of such an important movement." Sheridan's reply gave "the true key to his uniform success on the field": "I have never in my life taken a command into battle and had the slightest desire to come out alive unless I won." And in this culminating battle of the Civil War—also the culminating moment of his own military career—he had won.

Porter was determined to be the first to carry the news of the decisive victory to his Chief. This was by no means an easy matter. The roads were blocked by advancing ammunition trains and ambulances, by prisoners and wounded wandering to the rear, and by troops bivouacking by the roadside, kindling fires and shouting the good news. Some of the men were still skeptical. Porter's orderly, calling out the news as he rode by, received the response from one soldier, "No, you don't! April fool!" After four long years of hard fighting, the men were not of those who believed in the first rumors of an overwhelming victory.

Exalted by the triumph that he had taken part in, and

by the significance of the message that he bore, Porter pushed on over the encumbered roads, reaching Headquarters ahead of the last courier he had dispatched.   At the sight of his beloved Chief in his blue cavalry overcoat, sitting before a blazing camp-fire smoking the inevitable cigar, Porter's joy knew no bounds.   He began to call aloud as soon as he was within shouting distance, and then, throwing himself from his horse, he rushed up to the surprised commander, clasped him by the hand, and so far forgot all propriety that he actually clapped Grant on the back, all the time overpowering him with a torrent of words.   (He writes himself that he was in a condition to poke the Archbishop of Canterbury in the ribs or challenge the Chief Justice of the Supreme Court to a game of leap-frog.) Badeau, one of the military secretaries, who was watching these antics through his gold-rimmed spectacles, wrote afterwards, "The bearer of the good news was Colonel Horace Porter, one of the most abstemious men in the army; but he came up with so much enthusiasm, clapping the General-in-Chief on the back, and otherwise demonstrating his joy, that the officer who shared his tent rebuked him at night for indulging too freely in drink at this critical juncture.   But Porter had tasted neither wine nor spirits that day.   He was only drunk with victory." [5]

Grant's first question to his excited staff officer was the usual one.   "How many prisoners?"   "The estimate is over five thousand," came the prompt reply.   "This was the only part of my recital that seemed to call forth a responsive expression from his impassive features."   The General listened attentively to the recital of Sheridan's achievements and then, with hardly a word of comment, walked to his tent, wrote several dispatches by the light of a flickering candle, and gave the papers to an orderly to be sent over the field telegraph-lines.   Rejoining his staff before the camp-fire he casually remarked, "I have ordered a general assault along the lines."   No other comment on the attack which was to compel Lee to evacuate Richmond and Petersburg. A little after midnight, satisfied with the enthusiastic replies of his corps commanders, he was "sleeping as peacefully as if the next day was to be devoted to a picnic."

Sunday, April 2, was a day of even more wonderful accomplishment. Preceded by prolonged artillery fire from one end of the Union line to the other, the attack on the Confederate works began at daybreak, and in spite of sharp resistance it carried the defenses. In a few hours the Union troops were sweeping everything before them. Some officers, in their eagerness, wished Grant to order an advance on Petersburg, but the General refused. Enough lives had already been lost, and the Chief felt that the city would undoubtedly be evacuated during the night—as it was. He sent a dispatch to City Point, reporting captures of 12,000 men, "since the army started out gunning."

On the evening of the next day, Monday, April 3, Grant and his staff, after a brief visit to Petersburg, went into camp at Sutherland's Station; at three o'clock on the following morning, they were again in the saddle to catch up with Sheridan, who was in advance, thundering along with his cavalry and trying to get ahead of the retreating enemy. The Chief and his staff rode all that day and the next. Just before dark, as they were passing the outskirts of a dense wood, Porter saw some of the headquarters escort dash up to a horseman emerging from the woods in full Confederate uniform and seize him as a prisoner. Porter, on coming closer to the man, discovered him to be the indomitable Campbell, Sheridan's scout, bringing a message from his commander. It concluded with the words, "I wish you were here yourself."

The Chief understood the significance of the appeal. Dismounting from his pony, Jeff Davis, who was tired, he mounted Cincinnati, and calling to Campbell to lead the way followed him towards the trees; it was to be a twenty-mile ride by moonlight through a wooded country and pretty close to the enemy's lines. At one point their camp-fires came into sight; the scout suddenly became confused; his manner seemed to Porter suspicious. After all, Campbell was almost unknown to the General and might, like so many scouts, be playing for the enemy. Porter cocked his pistol and rode beside the boy. But Campbell was loyalty itself; he was only seeking for a short cut through the tangled underbrush to Sheridan's pickets.[6] The tired band of cavalrymen, who were sleeping on their arms, looked up and, recognizing Grant, said to each other: "Great Scott, the old Chief's out here himself! The rebs are going to get busted to-morrow, certain. Uncle Sam's joined the cavalry sure enough. You can bet there'll be lively times here in the morning."

The riders found Sheridan awaiting them, sure that Campbell would reach the Chief and that the Chief would come. The moment was critical. Lee, Sheridan feared, was slipping through their fingers, and the movements ordered by Meade would not meet the situation. Convinced by Sheridan's reasoning, Grant presently went over to the headquarters of the Army of the Potomac, and roused Meade from sleep to give him directions for a change of orders.

The first news of the next day, April 6, proved that Sheridan's theory had been right. Lee's army had been in motion during the night; another attempt must be made to head it off. The battle of Sailor's Creek, resulting in the capture of General Ewell's corps, was a severe blow to the Confederates; it was now apparent to both sides that the end was close at hand.

Forced marching was the order of the day for all; but "straggling had entirely ceased, and every man was now a rival for the front."[7] On the evening of April 7, at Farmville, Porter, standing beside Grant on the little hotel piazza, watched the men of Wright's corps, who, after a long day's march, had been ordered to move at once to the support of Humphreys. They came swinging through the main street, forgetting their fatigue. Bonfires were lighted, straw and pine knots were improvised as torches. Cheers rose from the throats of the marching men, bands played, banners waved, one regiment broke into the song of "John Brown's Body," and in a moment a whole division was shouting the chorus. Assured by the reports reaching him at the end of the day that Lee's situation was hopeless, Grant sent off his first letter proposing surrender, and went to bed.

April 8 was a day of long and hard marching for the men.[8] Grant himself was laid low by a prostrating headache, the result of the uninterrupted strain of the last ten days; he stopped at a farmhouse by the roadside and there submitted to the attempts of his aides at relieving his pain. At last, utterly worn out, he threw himself down on the sofa of the so-called parlor and tried to sleep.

At about midnight a letter from Lee arrived.[9] Rawlins opened the parlor door gently, Porter following with a lighted candle; a tired voice said, "Come in." The little crumpled figure in shirtsleeves and stocking-feet sat up on the sofa and, stretching out a weary hand for the expected letter, read it by the light of Porter's candle. "It looks as if Lee still means to fight," was his comment; "I will reply in the morning," and he rolled himself up again on the sofa, in the hope of a few hours more of sleep. By four in the morning Porter found him pacing up and down in front of the house, his hands to his head, still suffering excruciating pain. When Porter, trying to cheer him, suggested that he might at any time now get good news from Lee, he received the unexpectedly human reply, "The best thing that could happen to me to-day would be to get rid of the pain I am suffering." Presently Grant wrote the Confederate commander another letter, restating the terms on which peace might be had, and then, mounting Cincinnati, started to join Sheridan. Nothing would induce him to avoid the intense heat of the sun by riding in an ambulance.

When he was within nine miles of Appomattox Court House, Lieutenant Pease of Meade's staff rode up with a letter from Lee asking for an interview to ascertain definitely the terms of surrender and another from Meade which announced that he had granted a short truce. On reading these letters Grant dismounted and, seating himself in his accustomed fashion on a grassy bank at the side of the road, as he had done so often among bursting shells, wrote Lee that he was on his way to meet him. The General then rode rapidly forward towards Appomattox Court House, saying, in reply to Porter's question about his state of health, "The pain in my head seemed to leave me the moment I got Lee's letter." Undoubtedly the impassive Grant had nerves!

At about one o'clock the Union commander and his staff were riding into the little village of Appomattox Court House, with its half-dozen houses on a single street. The broad valley beyond was covered with the columns and wagon-trains of the enemy; still farther west and south, on high ground, the Northern troops hemmed them in.

The riders passed a group of officers collected about the stocky little figure of Sheridan.

"Is Lee over there?" asked Grant.

"Yes, he is in that brick house, waiting to surrender to you," was Sheridan's delighted reply.

The commanding general rode on, Sheridan and others following, and the staff bringing up the rear. The cavalcade halted before a two-story brick house which stood a little back from the street and presented a better appearance than the others. It belonged to a Mr. McLean, and General Lee had entered this house about half an hour before to wait for Grant. Colonel Babcock of the staff had ridden in advance, had delivered to Lee Grant's letter, and had then brought him to Appomattox. The Union commander quickly mounted the wooden steps of the porch, passed into the hall, and disappeared into the room on the left, the door of which Babcock had opened for him. The rest of the party contented themselves by wandering around the little garden, watching General Lee's powerful gray crop the short grass in company with Colonel Marshall's brown mare, now and again turning their eyes to the window and wondering what was happening within those four walls.

In a few moments Babcock appeared on the porch and said in a low voice, "The General says come in."

"We walked in softly," writes General Porter, "and ranged ourselves quietly about the sides of the room, very much as people enter a sick-chamber when they expect to find the patient dangerously ill." The Confederate leader was sitting opposite the door, in a plain armchair beside a marble-topped table. Colonel Marshall of his staff was standing beside him, leaning against the mantelpiece. Grant was seated at a short distance in an old office armchair, beside another table. Standing silently against the wall, Porter watched the two commanders. He wished in his heart of hearts that his own adored Chief had been a little more careful of his dress. He looked not even "shabby-genteel": except for the shoulder-straps, his uniform was that of a private; it was unbuttoned and in a thousand creases; his shoulders more bent than usual. His boots and clothing were bespattered with mud, he had neglected to put on his spurs, and his sword had disappeared. The night that he had cut loose from the headquarters trains to find Sheridan under Campbell's guidance, he had left his sword with his baggage; swords he considered useless and cumbersome articles. Lee, on the contrary, was immaculate: his uniform was perfect in every detail, a sword with the hilt studded with jewels hung at his side, large spurs were attached to his fine top-boots. He sat tall, erect, and dignified, an aristocrat to his finger-tips, the embodiment of all that was dear to the chivalrous South. For a moment the scenes of seven years ago at West Point flashed through Porter's mind: the ballroom, the parade-ground, the tall, erect figure of Colonel Lee of Virginia, the officers and cadets vying with each other in paying their respects and dancing with his daughter. Who in those days had ever heard of U. S. Grant?

There was a dead silence in the little parlor. All eyes were turned to the bent figure of Grant writing quietly and swiftly in his manifold order-book. Suddenly he hesitated; Porter saw him look at the glittering sword hanging at Lee's side; then he went on writing.[10]

The terms of surrender finished, Grant handed the manifold writer to Porter, who passed it on to Lee. The Confederate leader, after carefully adjusting his steel-rimmed spectacles, read the draft of the terms slowly and deliberately, looking up from the top of the second page and remarking to Grant, "The word 'exchanged' seems to be omitted. With your permission I will mark where it should be inserted." "Certainly," answered Grant. But Lee had no lead-pencil. He made a futile search of his pockets. Porter, who was taking careful notes of every step in the proceedings, handed General Lee the pencil he was using, and Lee marked the omission. Then, as he read on, he kept twirling the pencil in his fingers and tapping it on the table. Porter realized that his little brown pencil had suddenly burst its way into history. He was only afraid that Lee, in a fit of absent-mindedness, might put it in his own pocket, but the Confederate leader carefully returned it to its owner.

Lee was evidently touched by Grant's act of generosity in permitting the officers to retain their horses, personal baggage, and side-arms. He then asked that similar leniency be shown to the soldiers, to the extent of allowing them to retain their own horses.[11] Realizing the desperate state of the South and knowing that many a soldier depended upon his army horse to till his little farm and save

his family from starvation, Grant immediately acceded to
Lee's request. Colonel Parker, as his hand-writing was considered the best, copied out the terms of surrender in ink
borrowed from Lee's aide, and Colonel Marshall drew up a
letter of acceptance on writing-paper supplied by the
Federals. Lee read the letter carefully, struck out some
words, shortened several sentences, and, when another copy
had been made, signed it.

While the two letters were being copied, Grant introduced
every one present to General Lee. Lee shook hands in
silence with one or two of the Union officers who had extended theirs, speaking affably with General Seth Williams,
who had been his adjutant at West Point, staring in evident
surprise at Colonel Parker, a full-blooded Indian, whom he
probably took for a negro, and bowing formally to the
other members of the staff. Lee's last request to Grant
was that he notify Meade immediately of the surrender, so
that there would be no more useless shedding of blood.
Then he shook hands with Grant, bowed to the other officers, and walked out, followed by Marshall; as he waited
for his horse, he stood a moment, oblivious of the salutes of
the Union officers gathered in the little garden; his gaze
was fixed on the valley, where stretched the long line of
gray. "All appreciated the sadness that overwhelmed him,
and he had the personal sympathy of every one who beheld
him at this supreme moment of trial. The approach of his
horse seemed to recall him from his reverie, and he at once
mounted. General Grant now stepped down from the
porch, moving toward him, and saluted him by raising his
hat. He was followed in this act of courtesy by all our
officers present. Lee raised his hat respectfully, and rode
off at a slow trot to break the sad news to the brave fellows
whom he had so long commanded."

At nine o'clock on the following day, April 10, Grant and
his staff rode out to the enemy's lines, and a final meeting
with Lee took place on a knoll overlooking the two armies;

that afternoon the Union commander returned to City
Point to make rapid preparations for departure.   His
duties in the field were over, and since from now on he and
his staff would occupy quarters at the War Department in
Washington, he gave to Horace Porter the Headquarters
flag. No wonder that it was treasured as one of his most
precious possessions.[12]

During the next day Porter and some other members of
the staff got permission to visit Richmond—a strange and
piteous sight. "The fire which our troops found blazing
when they entered had left a third of the place smoldering
in ashes. The white population were keeping closely to
their houses, while the blacks were running wildly about
the streets in every direction. They had not been able to
persuade the General to go with them: nothing would induce him to play the part of a conqueror entering a fallen
city. His one thought was to wind up his affairs at City
Point so that he might begin the new task of reducing the
army and relieving the appalling burden of expense which
the Government was carrying. On the afternoon of the
twelfth, the party embarked for Washington; they arrived
the next morning and took up their quarters at Willard's
Hotel.

Grant immediately started for the War Department,
thinking to make his way unseen and unnoticed through the
streets on foot. His appearance was the signal for a popular demonstration: shouts rent the air, the people crowded
around him, he could neither advance nor retreat. It looked
at one time as though he would have to take refuge in a
carriage, but the police intervened and he succeeded in
reaching his destination. Next the General went to the
White House, still accompanied by Porter. Lincoln, beaming and happy, was all cordiality and congratulations. He
wanted Grant to come the next day, Friday, to meet all the
Cabinet. After more hand-shaking the General left the
President to return the following morning.

Porter, impatient to set out for Harrisburg, had obtained leave of absence. When the Chief, after his morning with the Cabinet, came back to the hotel to go with Mrs. Grant to Burlington, New Jersey, where their children were,—"Do you know," he remarked to Porter, "the President wanted Mrs. Grant and me to stay until to-morrow and go to the theater with him to-night? He told me to bring you along. But I said we wanted to go home, and that you were probably already on your way to Harrisburg; you were afraid that that boy of yours might be grown up before you saw him." Mrs. Grant assented, saying that when any man had won such a pretty girl for his wife he was sure to start for home as soon as possible, in spite of a President's invitation. She seemed rather agitated, on account of a man who had followed her into the dining-room, seated himself near her table, and was staring at her during lunch. (This man proved to have been Wilkes Booth.) Porter, anxious to catch his train, paid little attention to the remark, attributing it to the overwrought state of the lady's nerves; he hurriedly took his leave, promising to return to duty as soon as his Chief needed him.

"The war is over!" Horace Porter kept repeating the words to himself as if in a dream. Four long, hard years were behind him, and yet he felt as if he had ridden through them at a gallop, so much experience, so much living had been crowded into them. He began going over the different battles and engagements in which he had taken part; twenty-five he counted. Pulaski, Secessionville, Chickamauga, The Wilderness, Petersburg, Spottsylvania, Cold Harbor, The North Anna River, the mine explosion, Fort Harrison, Hatcher's Run, Newmarket Heights. (The train rattled on; counting was difficult when one was so sleepy.) Five Forks— Some unknown voice was shouting the name of Lincoln. It was early morning. The train had stopped at a station, and the newsboys were doing a lively business.

"Dastardly attempt on President's life. Lincoln shot at Ford's Theater. President mortally wounded."

The words danced before Porter's eyes. Only yesterday he had seen and talked to the President and shaken his hand. And he, Horace Porter, had been included in the invitation to the theater; he would have been at the back of the box, near the door. At the risk of his own life perhaps he could have stopped Booth's mad attack on the President. He tried to picture every detail of the assassination. He longed to grip the throat of the miserable murderer. One comforting thought came to him: his Chief at least was safe. Undoubtedly he would have shared Lincoln's fate had he stayed in Washington. . . .

The train pulled in at the Harrisburg station, and as he passed quickly through the old familiar streets, the tragedy at Washington faded from his mind. He was at home; a few steps more brought him before his father's house, small and modest compared to the one he had owned as Governor. His telegram had been delayed, no one was expecting him. He rushed through the garden and up the front steps. Yes, some one was expecting him, some one had seen him. The door was flung wide open by a tall, gentle-faced woman in plum-colored silk and white cap—his mother. Some one else—a slight figure in voluminous skirts was hurrying down the staircase and in her arms she carried his boy, with eyes as blue as his own and a head already covered with a mass of fair curls. Young Horace, aged six months, had, however, no intention of permitting any liberties from the tall, rather dirty-looking man who proclaimed himself his father. The boy resented all caresses and set up such a lusty howl at being kissed that he was speedily put in his nurse's arms and removed to the upper rooms. From the end of the hall came the old Governor, still erect, and wondering what the hubbub was about. As they sat talking, he said little, but listened, his eyes clear and bright, beaming on his youngest son, the pride of his old age.

COLONEL HORACE PORTER

How familiar the room looked! How little his mother had changed! Her hair was still the same dark brown. His young wife was more beautiful than ever: how well it suited her to be a mother! How they talked, how they laughed, how many questions were asked, some of them never answered! How wonderful it was to sit at the old familiar table, shortened to suit the small family! The table linen, the fine silver, and all the delicious dishes prepared for him—how different from the hasty meals snatched here and there, or eaten beside the camp-fire! A marvelous peace and happiness came over him; no more hurrying away to the front, no more good-bys. He was home, he was safe, it was his birthday, and his life stretched before him.

The knocker banged on the door. The colored servant brought in a telegram for "Ginral Porter" from Washington. It read:

The President died this morning. Join me here by end of next week.

U. S. GRANT.

BOOK II
BUSINESS AND PUBLIC AFFAIRS
1865-1897

CHAPTER VIII

AT THE WAR DEPARTMENT

THE years of Horace Porter's early manhood reached their culminating point at Appomattox. The professional training which he had received he had put to immediate and effective use; more than that, his contact with the leaders of the war had given him a vision of greatness of spirit, an inspiration which was to last through his life-time and which he was later to interpret to a younger generation. For more than seven years after the war he remained in the army and in close touch with Grant. Although the work that he was called upon to do during this time became less and less professional in character, it gave him experience and training which were to stand him in good stead. Afterwards business and public affairs occupied him continuously for a quarter of a century. This long middle period of Porter's life, though full of variety and significant achievement, always ranked in his eyes far below the four years of service to his country in time of war.

On his return to Washington after the assassination of Lincoln, Porter found Grant perplexed and anxious. The leaders of the government had barely escaped being the victims of a conspiracy against their lives; as for Stanton, he was in the clutches of a spasm of physical terror. With the guiding hand of Lincoln gone, the counsels at Washington were ruled by wild passion and ignoble fear. These distracted men were in no position to act reasonably when they received the news of the terms which Sherman had conditionally granted to Johnston for the surrender of his army. Following the dictates of a generous heart and undoubtedly guided by his recollection of what he had heard Lincoln say at City Point only a few weeks before, the Union commander innocently gave his opponent terms much beyond his power to offer. President Johnson and Stanton stormed against Sherman, denouncing him as a traitor. Grant, with few friends in Washington, found himself involved, as Sherman's superior in command, and welcomed the arrival of Porter, one man, at least, on whom he could depend. "They want me to go to North Carolina," he explained, "cancel Sherman's terms, and make Johnston accept the same terms I gave Lee."

After a hastily summoned Cabinet meeting, at which Sherman's arrangements were repudiated, Grant started early on April 22 for Raleigh, leaving his staff officer in Washington to watch matters at the War Department and report any new development. Of course Grant had no intention of humiliating Sherman; so he went no farther than Raleigh and let Sherman conduct the new negotiations with Johnston. He was disgusted with Stanton's slanderous hints that Sherman was implicated in a scheme to let Confederate officials get away with plunder from the Richmond banks, and indignant at the vindictive spirit shown by the Secretary toward the conquered enemy. It was not a fortnight since Grant and Lee, equals in authority over their armies and equals in magnanimity, had pledged each other, on behalf of North and South, to peace and forgiveness. Now they were both at the mercy of a panic-stricken civilian authority inflamed with the lust of punishment. How deeply Grant was stirred is evident in the words he wrote to his wife from Raleigh: "People who talk of further retaliation and punishment except of the political leaders either do not conceive of the suffering endured already, or they are heartless and unfeeling, and wish to stay at home

out of danger while the punishment is being inflicted." [1]
This was the soldier's answer to the talk of the windy politi-
cians at the Cabinet meeting three days before.

Again Grant was destined to suffer from Stanton's hys-
teria, when the Secretary proposed to arrest Lee and bring
him to trial. Grant remonstrated at this violation of the
promise which he had given the Confederate general, arguing that so long as Lee kept his parole he could not be tried
for treason.[2] Indeed Grant's own honor as a soldier was so
deeply involved that he carried the case to President Johnson and won his point. "I told him," he said to Porter that
evening as they sat in his hotel room, "that if they touch
Lee I will resign my command to-morrow morning and go
back to Galena." And he meant it. Seldom had Porter
known his Chief to be so wrought up; both men felt that the
incident boded ill for the days to come.

Though in the weeks following the end of the war
Porter's time was spent in office work connected with the
routine duties of demobilization,[3] he was presently to learn,
and in most unexpected fashion, what it was to have the
eyes of the crowd focused upon him. Grant was so persistently urged to give the general American public a chance
of seeing him that early in the summer he made a trip to
New England. It was a triumphal progress. The crowds
everywhere surged around his car to catch a glimpse of the
little man who had saved the Union. At one town where,
not satisfied with seeing him, the people wanted to hear him
also, Porter met his fate. The throng at the station gathered about the rear platform of Grant's car and became
more and more clamorous for a speech. Wholly at a loss,
the hero turned to his ever-resourceful aide, plucked him
by the sleeve, and pushed him forward to the edge of the
platform, exclaiming, "You can talk better than I. Go
ahead and make a speech; otherwise we shall never get
away from this place." Porter stood for a moment non-

plused. His breath failed him, and his collar became suddenly too high and too tight. Every idea he ever had in his head completely vanished. But the crowd demanded a speech. "What I said I don't remember," so he used to tell the story. "I knew I had to say something, so I just started and I just kept on. The crowd seemed pleased, then they applauded, and when I had finished they started cheering. I managed to get behind the Chief, open the door, and slip back into the car; then I closed the door and held it so that he had to stay outside and take the applause."

General Grant had discovered a new talent in Porter and was quick to make use of it. After the success of the first speech, Grant insisted that he should answer for him all the long-winded addresses of welcome composed by the patriotic citizens who received him; and by the time the party returned to Washington Horace Porter was fairly started on a new branch of his many-sided career. It was not many years from the day he lost his breath and found his collar too tight before he held a high place among the speakers of the country.

Grant's headquarters as Commander of the Army during the Johnson administration were in Washington, and there, too, Porter presently established his little family. At first they boarded; then, in August, 1867, we find him writing to his wife in Harrisburg: "We can get the large brown-front house next to the corner of G and 20th Streets for forty dollars a month. It is three stories high and has a good back building." It became their home for the next five years. The war had ruined Mr. McHarg's business, so that, like Governor Porter, he had little of his fortune left. The Horace Porters, entirely dependent, therefore, on a colonel's salary, economized by joining forces with the Babcocks, after the fashion of an army mess, to the satisfaction of all concerned.

The young couple, handsome, friendly, well-bred, amusing, and reflecting doubtless some glory from the General, rapidly made a place for themselves in the capital. As far as their means allowed, they kept open house for their friends and went about indefatigably. Without stopping to lament that they could not afford to hire a carriage, they would start gayly out on foot to an entertainment, she holding her hoops well out of the mud and he carrying her party slippers tucked under his arm, to be exchanged, on arrival at their destination, for her bespattered shoes. The charm of these nocturnal walks was doubtless greatly affected by the state of the weather, but that first winter in their own home remained a bright spot in their lives and helped to minimize the bitterness of the intrigues and jealousies with which they came in contact during the Johnson administration.

Meanwhile Porter's duties on the staff were of many sorts. Perhaps most important and interesting were the inspection trips on which he was sent, usually in company with Babcock. The South, it will be remembered, was divided into military districts, each governed by a general of the army, and the tours that the two aides made through that region were one of the means by which Grant kept in touch with his subordinates at distant points. On one trip Porter investigated the condition of the freedmen, and his suggestions were made use of in drafting the law by which the Freedmen's Bureau was to be administered. In the spring of 1867 he went to Louisiana, where Sheridan, by his action in removing state and city officers, had made himself obnoxious to President Johnson. "Sheridan is liked by all honest men," Porter wrote from New Orleans, and on the basis of his detailed reports Grant sent to Johnson his urgent letters of August 1 and 17, protesting against Sheridan's removal.

An extract from one of Porter's confidential letters to Grant illustrates the atmosphere which he usually found characteristic of the difficult situation in the South.

Horace Porter to U. S. Grant

New Orleans, La.,
March 2, 1868.

I have seen all classes, conditions and colors here, and I think have ascertained the true state of affairs.

The "Conservatives" are rallying for a tremendous effort, and the Unionists are apparently depressed but will lose no opportunities.

There is great poverty, and there have been heavy losses in property, wherever I have been, but all owing to the people attempting to work for a *fortune* instead of a *living*.

I find the mass of the residents are war democrats i.e. in favor of a war upon Congress if it doesn't legislate to suit them. I enclose a few amiable articles to illustrate the beauties of the freedom of the press.[4]

A trip to Arkansas and Louisiana, in the winter of 1868-9, gave Porter firsthand knowledge of the growth and strength of the secret organization known as the Ku Klux Klan. A succession of brutal murders of white men, several of them officials of the state or of the Federal Government, had led the reconstruction governor of Arkansas, Powell Clayton, to declare martial law in the counties where the trouble was greatest. Rejecting the offer of United States troops from the commander of the district, he was endeavoring to maintain order by means of bodies of state militia organized for the purpose. It was a daring experiment, and Grant, in order that he might be fully informed, sent Porter and Babcock to the scene of action.

When they heard from the governor's lips the stories of assassinations and outrages committed by the Klansmen to terrify negroes and such whites as were known to be friendly to the new government, they could well believe that rebellion was again raising its head. A similar tale Porter heard while spending a night at a lonely farmhouse belonging to a poor white. According to the most charitable interpretation, such an organization is a cloak for venting jealousies and stirring up strife, and Porter was never inclined to be very charitable towards men who "sneak out at night to do things they are ashamed or afraid to do by daylight." Once he saw men and horses shrouded in white ride round the house in which he was staying. If such a performance seemed merely a childish device to frighten the inhabitants, it was quite otherwise with later acts that he witnessed: the brutal flogging of a negro, and the tarring and feathering of a white man.

The "carpet-bag" governments against which these excesses were a reaction Porter found sometimes in the hands of bad men; still, the stern measures employed would in the end, he believed, be productive of good. On January 8, 1869, he wrote to his Chief from New Orleans:

> . . . I feel more encouraged than ever before in regard to the success of "Reconstruction."
>
> The present state governments, with proper moral and physical support from the Government, will be able to maintain themselves and build up a permanent loyalty without a doubt. True, there are many bad men among the leaders, but such men have often taken the advance in redeeming new countries. Kansas, now one of the best and most loyal states in the Union, was purged by means of freedom-shriekers, hymn-book-warriors, and jay-hawkers. They were the pioneers who paved the way for better men. Some one must remove the thorns from a path before people will tread it.
>
> These states will, in a measure, have to be "Kansasized." [4] . . .

These trips, particularly a journey across the plains and the Rocky Mountains on his way to the Pacific Coast, supplied Porter with many stories. His descriptions of a small mining town, the shooting, drinking, gambling, fighting, rivaled Bret Harte's stories of "Bloody Gulch." "They were a hard lot, those fellows," he would say. "The only thing they had any respect for was an officer's uniform backed by pistols. I always carried both of mine loaded, and you had to be mighty quick with them, or the other fellow was quicker." At one of the army posts he found "Woody," his schoolmate of Lawrenceville days, and Colonel Cody (Buffalo Bill), and joined a party of officers and their wives in a buffalo hunt.

As a result of the quarrel with Stanton which disgraced the latter part of President's Johnson's administration, Grant for five months acted as Secretary of War, with Porter serving as Assistant Secretary. Brief though it was, the term was long enough to give the younger man experience in the department of the government responsible for the United States Army and to impel him to say, twenty-eight years later, when his name was mentioned as a possible Secretary of War, that nothing would induce him to accept the "African slavery" of such a position.

Official duties, however, could have occupied but little of his thoughts at this critical period of Grant's career. The unhappy course of events was carrying the Chief into political life. Every act of his simple and straightforward nature was being twisted by political friends and enemies, who insisted on giving it a bearing in connection with the coming presidential campaign. Disgusted at the coil in which he found himself, Grant would sometimes speak out to his aide his indignation against the men who, for partisan ends, were willing to denounce him as a liar. Porter, who knew him to be the soul of truth, resented the insult hotly; he was no less incensed at the so-called friends who were making use of Grant for the sake of party or personal success and who could not understand that the nation's hero was a partisan of neither Johnson nor Stanton.* He knew that Grant's one idea since the war had been to reunite the

* Among my father's papers I found the letter written by Stanton in acknowledgment of Grant's nomination of him as a Justice of the Supreme

country; no union could be built upon the bickerings and quarrels of the President, the Cabinet, and Congress. Grant himself had subordinated all personal feelings and interests to bringing peace to his distracted land, but now the hard-won peace was being sacrificed on the altar of party strife, self-interest, and self-advancement. Thus it was that Grant was willing to accept a new call of duty and to strive to prevent as President of the nation the loss of what he had had so glorious a part in winning. In Porter's eyes he could take no other course.

Court. The date is only three days before his death. I print it as evidence of the relations existing between the two men.

> 320 K Street,
> December 21, 1869.

Dear Sir:

I beg you to accept my thanks for your nomination of me as one of the Justices of the Supreme Court of the United States. It is the only public office I ever desired, and I accept it with great pleasure.

The appointment affords the more pleasure as coming from you, with whom for several years I have had personal and official relations, such as seldom exist among men.

It will be my aim, so long as health and life permit, to perform the solemn duties of the office to which you have appointed me, with diligence, impartiality and integrity.

I have the honor to be, truly your friend.

EDWIN M. STANTON.

To the President.

CHAPTER IX

SECRETARY TO THE PRESIDENT

WHEN Grant became President on March 4, 1869, Porter and Babcock, though technically on the staff of the Commander of the Army, now General Sherman, were at Grant's request assigned to duty at the White House as secretaries.[1] Of course the only methods of conducting affairs with which Grant was acquainted were those of a military headquarters: his two secretaries he continued to treat as aides and to call upon for any kind of service. They were practically members of his family, in the White House at all hours of the day and night.

Social life cut little figure with Grant. He wanted his guests properly entertained and was satisfied if things passed off smoothly and without complications. All responsibility he left to his secretaries. During the Johnson régime the Porters had kept away from the White House, but throughout Grant's administration there was hardly a dinner there to which they were not invited, hardly a reception at which Mrs. Grant was not assisted by Mrs. Porter. Many years afterward, a delightful description of those festivities and of the two young people playing their part therein was given to their daughter by old Sir Henry Howard,[2] in Grant's time attaché at the British Legation. "Sophie McHarg," he declared, "was the prettiest young woman in Washington. I never saw any one wear such big white tulle skirts, and how she kept them so fresh was a mystery, for she generally came to parties on foot. I know it was only on rare occasions that the G Street household joined forces to hire a sleigh or carriage. Your father always managed the dinner parties at the White House," he went on, "and what a time he had with the seating problem alone! No protocol in those days! On one occasion the Turk was so angry at the way he was placed that it actually was all your father could do to induce him to stay. Splendid training in tact and patience for any young man; for your father, most valuable experience."

Meanwhile there was the President's correspondence to handle, and his engagements and his innumerable callers; he was accessible to people of every sort. In all this work the secretaries were thrown with him as intimately as ever. He kept steadily at his tasks, attended faithfully to the routine business brought to his attention, and talked over things and people very freely with them. Porter and Babcock, knowing well and thoroughly enjoying the situation exemplified by the staff's discussion of the proposed march from Atlanta to the sea, did their work as loyal subordinates.

In marked contrast to this familiar relationship were the President's dealings with the members of his Cabinet. As one of them, General J. D. Cox, has written, Grant "lacked the faculty of conversational discussion which is the very essence of successful conduct of business where coöperation is necessary." [3] Thus the situation in which Porter and Babcock found themselves was full of peril for both them and their Chief.

Even a subordinate part in large affairs is education for a wide-awake mind. Perhaps Porter had no one chance that seemed to him as interesting as Babcock's trip to San Domingo to bring back the secret treaty which put Senator Sumner into such violent opposition to Grant, but he had lesser ones too numerous to mention. To follow out a single example: on one occasion, while the treaty with Great Britain for the adjustment of the Alabama Claims was under discussion, Porter took from Grant's dictation a

memorandum of his opinions;[4] he was a witness at close
quarters of all the moves in the negotiations which finally
resulted in the signing of the Treaty of Washington in May,
1871. He had heard the American side of the case discussed by Lincoln and by Seward at City Point; he knew the
men, British as well as his own countrymen, who took part
in framing the treaty; as it happened, his oldest brother,
William, of the Superior Court of Pennsylvania, was a
member of the Court of Alabama Claims. Thus Horace
Porter was thoroughly familiar with this most important
episode in our foreign relations. The effect of the experience upon his feelings with regard to England and her
foreign relations is shown in the following passage written
some years later:

"When the war ceased and America emerged from it a
first-class military power, with a million of armed veterans
at her command, she did not employ them to right the
wrongs she believed she had suffered from England, but
patiently claimed redress through peaceful arbitration, even
submitting to arbitration a question upon which she did
have a reasonable doubt—the question as to her right to
claim *consequential* damages arising from the depredations
of cruisers turned loose upon her commerce through the
connivance of England. In consenting to arbitration, to
settle the policy as to the responsibility of neutrals for the
depredations of hostile cruisers sailing from her ports,
America well knew that while a favorable decision might
bring to her a few paltry millions and whatever prestige
might be gained by success, the principle established would
be of incalculable benefit to England in her future wars, she
being the chief maritime nation of the world."[5]

As fate would have it, Porter's name was to be publicly
associated with the Administration only in connection with
business and New York City. He would hardly have
entered so eagerly on his service at the White House if he
could have foreseen the situations, repugnant to his sense

of decency, in which he was to find himself.   But he was still a novice in politics.

His baptism of obloquy came in the very first months of the term.   Babcock had gone to San Domingo, and Porter, left as the only personal attendant on the President, had no reason for expecting anything but an easy summer of routine work in Washington and the duty of accompanying Grant on the trips and visits which he was proposing to make.

In those days a President could go about the country on his personal affairs much like a private citizen.   In August Porter accompanied Grant and his wife to Newport; thence they went to the White Mountains for a few days, riding up to the summit of Mount Washington in the new railway and driving to the Profile House in a coach drawn by eight horses.   Later they were at Saratoga Springs.   In the intervals between these trips, Grant made short visits to Washington to attend to official matters, and also to see his devoted friend, Rawlins, formerly his Chief of Staff, now his Secretary of War, who was in the last stages of consumption and had evidently only a short time to live.   When the party passed through New York, they stayed at the house of Grant's new brother-in-law, Abel Corbin, an elderly business man, now retired and quite willing to magnify his connection with the President.

Among the many callers at the Corbin residence was Jay Gould, the mysterious and powerful man of Wall Street, and when he was present there was much talk concerning the price of gold.   Constantly the argument came back to one point: in order that the Western farmers might get a good return for their crops, it was desirable that gold should rise. If Grant knew anything of Gould's reputation as a speculator, he apparently did not connect it with the suggestion that the Government for the time being suspend its practice of offering for sale each month some $2,000,000 of the gold deposited in the United States Treasury.   If this course were adopted, it was reasoned, gold would rise, the farmer would have money to spend, and business would prosper. Most of the talking that Porter heard was done by Corbin, Gould putting in a word now and then; Grant, after his custom, sat silent. At several times during August and early September such conversations took place; and at last Grant, impressed by the arguments, wrote to the Secretary of the Treasury, Boutwell, saying that in his opinion it was undesirable at this time to force down the price of gold by offering any for sale, but adding explicitly that he had no desire to control the policy of the treasury.[6]

On the occasion of one of these stays in New York, when there had been much talk of business in general, with incidental reference to gold, and when for a few moments Grant and Corbin had left the room, Gould spoke to Porter about his large operations in Wall Street. Suddenly he brought the matter home to his listener by saying,[7] "I purchase and sell immense sums of gold in New York, and I have means of knowing just when gold is going up, and when it is going down, and I sell when it is going down and buy when it is going up. Do you ever purchase or sell gold or stocks?" On Porter's replying in the negative, Gould continued: "You had better let me get you some gold; gold is going to rise before long, and suppose I purchase some for you." Porter replied that he had neither the inclination nor the means of purchasing gold; "and if I had, I am an officer of the Government, and cannot enter into anything that looks like speculation. It may be perfectly proper for you to do it, but it would be manifestly improper for me." Gould's only reply was to begin assuring him that there would be no risk of loss, but the return of the others put an end to the conversation. The chief impression it left on Porter was that Gould's obliging proposal had made clear to him once for all his proper attitude, as an army officer, toward speculation; it hardly occurred to him to connect the incident with his position as private secretary to the President.

Shortly afterwards, the President and Mrs. Grant, accompanied by Porter, went to Washington, Pennsylvania, a small town in the mountains about thirty miles from Pittsburgh. A few days later, on opening a package of the President's mail which had been forwarded from Corbin's, Porter found slipped into it a half-sheet of paper, unaddressed and unsealed, and containing a statement that $500,000 in gold had been purchased at the current rate and placed to his credit.[8] It was signed by Jay Gould. Greatly astonished, and also annoyed that his declaration of a few evenings before had produced so little effect, and fearing that silence would be misinterpreted, Porter at once wrote to Gould that he had never authorized any one to buy gold for him and wished no purchase made. The incident suggested to him that Gould must have some ulterior end in view; but the hamlet of Washington was remote from the excitements and intrigues of Wall Street, and Porter, putting the matter out of his mind, turned his thoughts to the enjoyment of the mountains and—as far as possible—of his games of croquet with the General.

One morning, as they were thus employed, a man drove up to the house with a letter for Porter—merely a line from Corbin asking him to see that another letter brought by the messenger was delivered to the President. This man, it appeared, had come directly from New York and had spent the night driving from Pittsburgh. These unusual circumstances aroused Porter's suspicions, and after the man had been dismissed he opened his mind to the Chief, and Grant showed him Corbin's letter. It was another urgent plea that the Government continue the policy, so favorable to the farmers, of not selling gold. Since the President had already committed himself to this course, there must be some personal motive in Corbin's urgency. It seemed evident that he was speculating; indeed, the newspapers had already hinted that he was a "great bull in gold." Furthermore, considering Gould's attempt to bribe

Porter, it was a fair guess that an operation in gold on the part of the financier was at the bottom of the whole business.

Porter had now the unpleasant task of inspecting with the President and Mrs. Grant a family skeleton; if the letter meant anything, it meant that Corbin was misusing his connection in a manner not only outrageous but full of peril for the chief executive of the nation. The result of the council of three was that Mrs. Grant wrote a letter to Mrs. Corbin, expressing the President's anxiety lest her husband should be speculating and hoping that he would instantly disconnect himself from anything of that sort. The letter was sent off, and the two men could again return to the enjoyment of the mountains and croquet.

Within two days the President's party was back in the capital. The operations in gold were now attracting general attention; the price was mounting so rapidly that the question of action or non-action by the Treasury Department was a matter of the first importance. The argument that the farmer would benefit from the rise in gold was no longer heard; instead, bulls and bears were raving at each other and business was in danger. In the midst of the confusion of charges and counter-charges, it was difficult to know what course the Government should pursue in order to serve the public interest and keep clear of the charge of complicity. On Thursday, September 23, at the end of the day, gold stood at 145.

That evening Secretary Boutwell, just back from New York, where he had been besieged by both factions, called to consult Grant. The President's recommendation of ten days before must be reconsidered. It was now agreed that if on Friday, as seemed probable, gold rose still higher, Boutwell should sell; and the next morning, when the telegraph from hour to hour brought news of the mounting price, together with intimations of general disaster to business, he sent off a telegram ordering the sale of $4,000,000 of gold. Just before the message reached Wall Street, after a morning of frantic excitement, gold had touched 162; then, still in advance of the message, as Washington learned later, the break had begun; in a few minutes gold was at 135. This was "Black Friday," September 24. Trade was paralyzed; ruin spread far and wide.

Meanwhile Grant had received from his brother-in-law a letter containing a solemn assurance that he had no interest whatever in gold, and on Sunday morning, as Porter was sitting at breakfast with the President's family, both the Corbins appeared, having come from New York by the night train. They were plainly fatigued and agitated, but when Corbin began to speak of the nerve-racking experiences of the last few days and to deplore the sufferings of bulls and bears alike, Grant replied bluntly: "I am not at all sorry to hear it; I have no sympathy with gold gamblers." [9] He went on to express his relief at learning from Corbin's letter that he had no part in the "disgraceful speculation." [10] Corbin made no reply.

Alone with the President, as Porter learned later, Corbin broached the purpose of his visit and proved to be the spokesman of the very men with whom he had denied all connection. The losses on both sides had been heavy, he declared. If the Government would suspend the announced sale till November, bulls and bears could get together and arrange a selling price for gold which would involve the least possible loss to all concerned. But Grant was still unmoved by the tale of the gamblers' distress. Probably, too, his suspicions of Corbin were again aroused. "The subject has been concluded," he told the pleader, and he would neither speak on it himself nor permit Corbin to continue.[11]

The crash of Black Friday had been so resounding, and the effects were so far-reaching that the newspapers were noisy with rumors and accusations. The names of both Grant and Porter were brought in, and with the assembling of Congress in December investigation was in order. When the whole story was told, it was revealed that Jay Gould, scheming to bring about a corner in gold, had from the first made a tool of the President's brother-in-law. Corbin's business was to convince Grant that the good of the western farmers required a rise in gold, and that to insure this result the Treasury must forego its usual sale. To make certain of reliable performance on Corbin's part, Gould had credited him with $1,500,000. Thus for every point that gold rose, Corbin stood to win $15,000. The financier used the same inducement with Butterfield, the Assistant Treasurer of the United States Government in New York, and attempted it with Horace Porter. Disgrace overtook the first two; Porter was saved by his honesty and quickness of action. It was Gould who dictated Corbin's letter to Grant at Washington, Pennsylvania. It was Gould and his associate, Jim Fisk, who browbeat the terrified old man into going to Washington. To cap the climax, it was Gould who, guessing from Mrs. Grant's letter to Mrs. Corbin that Grant was no longer in the dark, turned bear and broke the market.

Grant's mortification was extreme. Against the men of Wall Street he should doubtless have been on his guard; but he naturally had no thought that he might be compromised through his sister's husband. The only bright spot in the story was Horace Porter, prompt and wise as an adviser, and mindful of the honor of his Chief.[12] Rawlins was dead, but here was another no less faithful. And Porter, seeing more keenly than ever before the perils of the path in which the President's feet were set, resolved that he should at least receive all the guidance and protection that could be had from devoted service.

Unfortunately, as things turned out, the loyalty of Porter and Babcock had its disadvantages, for it was open to misinterpretation. The President's reticence with the members of his Cabinet had become the talk of Washington. His opponents chose to believe that the intimacy between him and his former associates of the staff had a sinister significance,—that they formed a military clique which dispensed favors and directed policies. Grant's act in sending Babcock to San Domingo at the very beginning of his administration on a diplomatic mission of which the Secretary of State was in complete ignorance was used to give color to this view. Porter's turn as victim of the popular myth came later; before he could vindicate himself and the President he had to wade through the mire of a New York custom-house scandal.

During the last years of the war and in the period following, there was attached to Grant's staff a young man by the name of Leet. Originally a private in a Chicago battery, he had been given a clerk's position under Rawlins in the summer of 1863, and his duties had always been clerical. Desiring to better himself and knowing well where the best opportunity lay, he asked Grant, immediately after his inauguration, for a letter of recommendation to Moses H. Grinnell, the newly appointed Collector of the Port of New York. Grant wrote one in general terms, stressing the young man's ability and integrity, but naturally making no specific request on his behalf. After a short interval of absence, Leet turned up again in Washington, having apparently been unsuccessful in his errand to New York, and continued his work in the War Department, his rank being that of lieutenant-colonel. At this time Porter and Babcock with their wives were living in the house on G Street. As Leet was living alone, they invited him to stay with them; and when the arrangement was continued for a number of months he paid his share of the running expenses. So far as they knew him at this time, he was merely an army officer, having no other occupation than that of arranging the papers accumulated by the headquarters of the army while Grant was its commander.

At the end of a year, however, Leet's desire for a larger opportunity revived. He announced to his messmates that he was resigning from the army, with the intention of bidding for the contract under which labor was supplied for the New York custom-house. Porter remonstrated. He saw plainly that no one who had been personally associated with Grant should try to establish a business connection with a branch of the Government, and after ascertaining that the President was of the same mind he wrote to Leet in energetic fashion.

Horace Porter to George K. Leet

Executive Mansion,
Washington, D. C., May 4, 1870.

My dear Leet:
I do not like to be the bearer of bad news to you, but I think I ought to tell you what the President said when he returned from New York. He remarked that he had heard so much talk about corruption in custom-houses, jobs, the influence brought to bear in getting positions, &c., that he would never appoint any one who had been around him to a position in a custom-house, no matter what his qualifications. In speaking about you he said (I don't know who told him of the offer) that you ought to accept Don Cameron's proposition, for though he believes you to be as pure as any one, yet he would never consent to have you go to a custom-house. He said the attacks would be constant, and injure both you and him. He feels just as I have always felt about such matters. You can now judge of the situation and act accordingly.

Yours in great haste,
HORACE PORTER.
He told me I could say this to you.[13]

From recent experience Porter knew whereof he spoke. He had been publicly accused of controlling jobs in the New York custom-house and had only just returned from New York, where he had talked the matter over thoroughly with the Collector and obtained from him an explicit denial of the charge.   But his letter, instead of deterring Leet, merely angered the young man.   He thought it strange that the fact that he had served faithfully upon General Grant's staff during the war should now prevent him from obtaining business for which any citizen had a right to apply.[14]   Meanwhile, failing to get the labor contract, Leet had been given the "general order" business, that is, the right to store until they were called for goods from transatlantic liners consigned to merchants in New York.

At about the same time Grinnell was succeeded by Thomas Murphy, who in his brief reign of eighteen months proved one of the most objectionable collectors that the port has ever known.   In order to protect the President as well as himself against a repetition of such charges as Grinnell had recently denied on his behalf, Porter immediately wrote to Murphy, adjuring him to pay no attention to applicants who professed to have White House backing.[15]

Nevertheless the rumor connecting Porter with customhouse jobs would not down.   Indeed, it presently became clear that Leet himself was keeping it in circulation.   He and his partner, Stocking, had succeeded in turning their concession into a monopoly, and the importers were at their mercy.   Not only was it necessary to pay a month's storage for goods that remained in the ware-house only twenty-five hours, but other exactions were fully as exasperating.   To maintain themselves against the swelling tide of protest, the greedy grafters needed to claim strong support in Washington.   As one of the custom-house inspectors testified: [16]

> I cannot understand how it is those two men, strangers in this city, should have such a job, without General Porter standing by them.   My idea is that he has an interest in it. I cannot swear to it.   They told me from the start that General Porter was their friend, and would stand by them.
> Q. Did they tell you that?
> A. Yes, sir.   Before I went in I said to them, "Now here is Mr. Grinnell who, by the reports in the papers, will

soon be removed and someone else fill his place. How will
you stand then?" "Why we will go right on to Washington, and get a letter from General Porter to General Grant,
and set it straight in two minutes." That was their language.

The next form which the slander took was an innuendo in
an interview given to the press by Murphy. He intimated
that he had not a free hand in dispensing patronage and
mentioned Leet as a case in point. By Grant's direction,
Porter sent a letter [17] to the Collector which most officials
would consider an incentive to clean house, if not an order,
but nothing was done. The New York merchants groaned
under the extortions of Leet and Stocking; and with every
day they believed more firmly in the sinister power of
Porter.

During the Congressional session of 1870-71 the whole
matter was aired before an investigating committee of the
Senate. The importers, led by A. T. Stewart, voiced their
protests; inspectors dropped dark hints. Some curious facts
came to light: Leet, on his first visit to New York in 1869,
had made such good use of the President's innocent letter
that another man in the general order business had been
willing to pay him at the rate of $5000 a year for his
supposed influence. This money he had been receiving
while he continued his army work in Washington. He had
further alleged the heavy expenses of the G Street mess as
a reason why he must have a more remunerative job. Also,
in corresponding with certain people he had used stationery
of the Executive Mansion, having gone there on Sunday
mornings to write his letters on the plea that the War Department was closed. In short, at Porter's expense, he had
played all the tricks of the grafter. It is no wonder that
the New York *Nation,* when he had continued in power for
another year, paid him a tribute of satirical admiration:

"The young man Leet" seems certainly as lucky and as
mysterious a young man as ever got into the public service.
He got one of the most valuable places in the gift of the

Government, though nobody wanted him to get it, and the President wanted him not to get it. With incessant change going on about him, too, he has proved immovable as a rock. Other officers come and go, but he stays where he is —the storm of public indignation beating on him in vain; and yet everybody, from the President down, denies all interest in him and all desire to keep him in office. The steamboat companies, powerful and wealthy corporations, have tried to uproot him; A. T. Stewart and Co. have tried; one hundred leading commercial houses have tried; and, last of all, a powerful section of the press, headed by the *Tribune,* which bowled over Murphy himself, has assaulted him, and yet this obscure and friendless youth defies them all.[18]

The investigation led to no action, and the slanders against Porter were still afloat. When it was discovered that Leet had recently received an appointment at the custom-house, Grant ordered his removal, but the fact of the appointment only gave more plausibility to the insinuations concerning Porter's influence. The next session led to another investigation, which was carried on with all the elaborateness and partisanship that characterize a congressional inquiry at the session before a presidential election. The feeling against the Administration was high: a movement of "Liberal Republicans" to nominate a candidate in opposition to Grant was under way, with Horace Greeley, of the New York *Tribune,* as one of its leaders. As the investigation of the custom-house dragged on from month to month, the *Tribune* found in the activities of Leet and Stocking and their alleged connection with the White House the political capital that it needed.

At last Porter was given his day in court. He had prepared himself carefully, and had been able to find documentary evidence to refute every charge. Many of the questions were of course trivial and irrelevant, but the main portion of his testimony was exceedingly pertinent and held the attention of all who heard him. It showed not only his own uprightness but the care which he had taken that the White House record should be demonstrably above reproach. The story itself was a sordid one; but the revelation which it gives of honorable conduct in a public servant is as valuable now as it was then.

The investigations proved not only that Grant and Porter were innocent of wrong-doing in connection with the New York custom-house, but that they had striven to prevent it.[19] Meanwhile the new collector, Chester A. Arthur, had made reforms as a result of which the firm of Leet and Stocking ceased to be a public nuisance. The political campaign, however, was now under way: Horace Greeley, nominated by the Liberal Republicans and the Democrats,[20] was running against Grant, and abundant use was made of all the charges that could be raked up to smirch the President. Sumner, in a ponderous speech in the Senate, had denounced the "illegal military ring" at the Executive Mansion, and declared that there existed no necessity for a "levy of soldiers" to perform the duties of secretaries.[21] Unquestionably the status of Babcock and Porter was anomalous, and at that distance of time from the end of the war the use of officers of the army was certainly unacceptable; but only in a campaign remarkable for personal attacks could the accusation have carried much weight.

All this abuse Grant took in the way of duty. From the beginning of his public career he had been subject to detraction on account of personal characteristics, real and alleged, some of which were of the most private nature. His countrified air, his fondness for horses, his strong cigars, his lack of discrimination in the choice of friends, his simplicity, and a dozen such qualities and habits were seized upon for purposes of ridicule; others, like his alleged intemperance, were invented for purposes of vilification. Fundamentally a man of great delicacy and sensitiveness, tender and considerate of others, he suffered intensely from these attacks, but he bore them in silence.[22] He had a task to perform which he could not shirk. These were the disagreeable incidents that went with it.

But if Grant must continue perforce, with Porter the case was entirely different. His record of honorable service to his country measured twelve years; he was under no obligation to continue it to his own disadvantage. In his present position of secretary he was unwilling to keep on; in the army there was no career for him. Moreover, he was a poor man, with constantly increasing family expenses. Since his father's death in 1867 he had contributed to the support of his mother and his sister. He determined, therefore, to look for a place in the business world which would be a sufficient outlet for his energies and would give him a satisfactory income. Fortunately, through his acquaintance with Robert Lincoln, he presently received an offer to be the New York representative of the Pullman Palace Car Company, which had its headquarters in Chicago. He was to have the title of vice-president, and his salary was to be $10,000 a year. The contract was made for five years.

These arrangements were completed late in the fall, and after election day, when Grant received a triumphant vindication at the polls, Horace Porter resigned from the army and from his position as secretary to the President. It was nine years since he had met his hero in the little parlor at Chattanooga. They had been true to each other. If they felt the wrench of this parting, realizing that for each it meant the breaking of another bond with a glorious past, they could not know in what several ways fate was still to test and deepen their affection and finally link their very names.

Here are the formal letters which passed between them:

Horace Porter to U. S. Grant

Washington, D. C.,
Dec. 1, 1872.

My dear General:
The proposition which I recently received to enter into business in civil life is of so advantageous a nature that I

cannot help feeling that in rejecting it I should do a wrong to my family and injustice to myself. I have therefore decided, with your approval, to tender the resignation of my commission. It is not necessary for me to assure you of the extreme reluctance with which I bring my mind to consent to interrupt the personal intimacy and sever the official relations which have so long existed and the memory of which I shall always regard as the most cherished recollection of my life. For many years it has been my privilege to be a daily witness to those transcendent qualities which a grateful people have repeatedly recognized by a bestowal of the highest offices within their gift. I feel confident that a continued exercise of the same qualities cannot fail to render the remaining years of your official life as brilliant in results as your previous achievements have been fraught with advantage to the true interests of the nation.

My best wishes shall always attend you, and your countless acts of kindness shall always be remembered with feelings of the profoundest gratitude and esteem.

I shall always remain
Your obedient servant and devoted friend,
HORACE PORTER.

U. S. Grant to Horace Porter

Executive Mansion,
Washington, D. C.,
Dec. 1, 1872.

My dear General:
Your letter of this date notifying me of your desire to quit the public service to accept a more advantageous position in civil life and expressing regret at severing a connection of such long standing as has existed between us is received. It is with regret on my part also that our official relations have to cease, though I am glad to believe that our personal relations will, through life, remain as in the past. You have my hearty congratulations that you have received so favorable an appointment. Your services in time of war and, since the close of sectional hostilities, your services in

time of peace, both in a military capacity and in a civil capacity, have been of so satisfactory a nature to myself and all coming in official or personal relation with you as to give assurance of your eminent fitness for the new and responsible trust you are about undertaking.

My best wishes go with you for your success in life and for the continued health and happiness of yourself and family.

With great respect

Your obt. svt.,

U. S. GRANT.

General Horace Porter, U. S. A.

The term of Porter's apprenticeship to public life was over. The knowledge that he had acquired in Washington was not idealistic, but it was to help him in the career before him. He had learned that the intentions of some men were in exact opposition to the ideas they expressed, and he could guide himself accordingly. As a boy he had been fearless, honest, and outspoken, and fearless and honest he remained as a man; but his frankness was tempered with wisdom, and from the bitter experiences of his Washington life he acquired the art of curbing his tongue and "letting the other man do the talking"—a favorite expression of his. "During those years," he used to say, "I was thrown with all sorts and kinds of men. It was a hard school, but a good one." He had reason to feel that he was now ready for encounter with the world of business.

CHAPTER X

BUSINESS

THE Pullman Car Company, of which George M. Pullman was the originator and president, was organized not long after the close of the Civil War, and its growth followed the great railroad expansion of that period. In 1872 the business of the company had reached a stage of development such that Mr. Pullman, directing its affairs from Chicago, felt the need of a representative in New York of sufficient judgment, force of character, and general standing to do business effectively with the leaders of railroad finance. It was for this work that Horace Porter was selected. He was of just the right age,—thirty-five years,—young and energetic, and yet, from his experience in the war and at Washington, sufficiently mature. His social standing was a great asset to Mr. Pullman; no less were all those qualities of his which are included in the general word, personality.

The larger problems connected with the management of the company and Porter's responsibility in dealing with them in these first years may be illustrated by the story of his trip to England and the Continent in the early part of 1877. The President of the company, in the true spirit of an American railroad pioneer, had for some time been inspired by a vision of a Pullmanized England and Europe. The torch of progress, illuminating America, should be carried to those backward regions. He had formed a company, the Pullman European Car Associates, of English subscribers, had made frequent visits abroad, and had recently spent a large sum in demonstrating in France, Italy, and elsewhere, the advantages of his product. Up to 1877 the results of his efforts had been meager, being represented by a few cars on the Midland Road in England, one parlor car running between London and Brighton, and an Italian contract which had not been put into effect. The "English subscribers," as they were known, were actively expressing their discontent. They refused to complete their subscriptions, which were considerably overdue, and clamored for relief from liability for possible future loss. Since business matters kept Mr. Pullman in America at the time when the crisis occurred, he selected Porter to go to England to find out the cause of all these woes, and if possible to apply a healing remedy.

Remembering his adventures on the *Daylight* in the year 1861, Porter, a poor sailor at all times, had little relish for a voyage across the Atlantic in the dead of winter, and his fears were rewarded by encountering the worst storm of the season. On board the first *Majestic* the cabins opened directly on the deck; his door got jammed, and he was held a prisoner, with his stateroom floor awash, until the first officer finally came to his rescue. To add to his discomfiture, he was assigned a seat at table at the captain's right.

Upon landing, he went straight to London and plunged into negotiations lasting for weeks with English business men who were apprehensive and therefore even more obstinate than usual. The Midland Road had continued to run first-class carriages in competition with the Pullmans, and as the amount of travel of this class was small at best, the returns for the new type of car were unsatisfactory. The fact that the cars were heated was not attractive, and some of the directors raised objections to the mirrors, which, by showing the landscape in reverse motion, made people car-sick. "I quoted American experience, my own delicacy of stomach under motion, showed that no one looked out a window and into the mirror at the same time." [1] From several such conversations Porter became convinced that the real trouble was that the company was "not giving the cars moral support." As tactfully as he could he suggested more advertising and more satisfactory rates; but he was not at all encouraged by the way in which his proposals were met. "The slowness of everybody in this country grates upon my nerves; but as one can't go at them butt end first, he has to exercise increased patience and be prepared either to stand and take it or run."

On the Continent Porter's luck was no better. His plans for inaugurating a through Pullman service between Calais and Brindisi encountered every imaginable obstacle. In France he found that "the fact of their having all their stations, tracks, &c., arranged for shunting their trains by means of small turn-tables suited only to their small cars, is a drawback to their using our cars, or rather furnishes them with a good excuse to reject them. It is the same policy which kept France without any railways for twenty years because they decided that France, having canals, did not require railways like other less fortunate countries." Again, in Italy the small amount of first and second class travel was done almost entirely by tourists, who traveled in short stages by daylight in order to enjoy the scenery. Most discouraging of all were his dealings with the Italian Government officials, whom he found to be "treacherous, unscrupulous, and unjust." Eventually the Government ordered a few Pullman sleepers to run from Turin to Brindisi, Rome, Naples, and Reggio. The train to which the first of these was attached caught fire; steel cars had not been invented, and the sleeper burned with the rest. Whereupon the Italian Government brought a suit for damages against Pullman because his sleeping-car had caught fire on an Italian train! He paid little attention to this extraordinary claim, and stopped all negotiations for the delivery of the other sleepers. Thus ended the Italian episode.

In England, after the inhabitants had at last overcome their natural prejudice against anything foreign and American, the Pullmans became a great success. General Porter's

contract, which ran for eighteen years, proved very profitable, and at the end of the period fixed, when the English
began building their own cars on a slightly different model,
the parlor cars retained the name of Pullman.

Although this first trip to Europe was for Porter one of
hard work and responsibility, demanding ceaseless tact and
patience, he managed to get a good deal of enjoyment out
of it.² Here again was a source of many stories, of which
a favorite one dealt with his ordering a bath at the Grand
Hotel in Venice. After waiting an hour, he rang the bell.
A few minutes later he heard on the stone corridor outside
his room the rumbling of a large vehicle, accompanied by
the shouts and screams proper to a street fight. Interested
to see what was going on, he put his head out of the door,
and saw advancing slowly down the corridor a huge affair
on wheels about the size of a Roman sarcophagus. It was
being pushed and pulled by several men, all shouting and
perspiring, and at each pull water slopped out; hence the
shrill expostulations of the chambermaid. *"Ecco, Signore!"*
said the triumphant valet, mopping his brow and pointing
to the sarcophagus, which had been finally landed in the
middle of the room. It was the bath!

During his short stay in Vienna the thing that made the
most vivid impression on him was his glimpses of the Empress, whom he always declared to be one of the most beautiful women he had ever seen and the finest horsewoman.
He saw her first on horseback, with her heavy hair in braids
down her back. Later, at a court ball, she was wearing her
emerald and diamond crown and necklace, but her own
beauty outshone their brilliancy. He had his first taste of
English country life on his visit to Lord Leven and Melville.
He went to Edinburgh and then to Abbotsford, where a
nephew of Sir Walter Scott showed him over the historic
old house and invited him to dinner. In London he saw
everything worth seeing, and also got lost in a fog.

Perhaps his most interesting experience was his presentation at the court of Queen Victoria. The pretty princess who had figured in his boyish imaginings, when he listened to Mr. Buchanan's letters from London, vanished before the reality of a short, fat, elderly person with red hands. Beside her stood the slender, beautiful Princess of Wales. But the person who most drew his attention in the royal group was "the Russian bride," as he called her, the only daughter of the Tsar, the young Duchess of Edinburgh and later of Coburg. She was a pretty, blue-eyed girl, wearing extraordinarily large pearls and the Russian half-crown. To him she represented that great mysterious country which had always held a spell for his youthful mind.

In short, Horace Porter returned to his own country with one of his dreams fulfilled. He had seen much of Europe which was worth seeing. He had looked upon the original of many pictures which he knew through copies. Architecture had always interested him: he did not miss a single noted building or church that was accessible to him. But most of his spare time was spent in going through the palaces and monuments which have seen so much history. He went home to work harder than ever, but with a fixed idea that he wanted to return again to the Old World, and, being a good American, he cherished Paris above the rest, as the pearl of great price.

As has already been said, Porter's most important work as representative of the Pullman Company was in connection with various railroad enterprises of the period. For example, his labors in behalf of the Elevated Lines in New York constituted one of the most important contributions of his time to the city's ever-present problem of rapid transit. Mr. Pullman was president of the construction company which was to build the projected road on Sixth Avenue; but as he was in New York only occasionally the real work of managing its affairs fell upon Horace Porter. He it was who conferred with the engineers and the lawyers, arranged the details of contracts, obtained subscriptions and conducted the board meetings, some of which, he wrote to Pullman, were "stormy." There was work enough to occupy a man's full time; there was also reason to worry, for the enterprise, besides being novel, was on a large scale. Skeptics and opponents outnumbered believers; even the believers had an imperfect comprehension of the project as a whole. The board itself was "conservative one day and radical the next." One man there must be who, besides comprehending and believing, had the power of inspiring others with faith and understanding. That one was Porter.

When, after many vicissitudes, the road was opened in June, 1878, it proved successful far beyond the expectations of its promoters. This success was due to the fact that, running through the heart of the retail shopping district, it took people where they wanted to go. Rapid transit for New Yorkers was a reality, and within a short time the Elevated was doing the largest railway business in the world, running 441 trains a day each way.

Porter's connection with the road did not last long; the part he had played was characteristic of the American railroad man of the period: what appealed to his imagination and called forth his energy was the opportunity to break ground in a new field.[3]

The next enterprise in which Pullman and his friends were associated was the construction of a railroad line from the eastern end of Lake Ontario to Weehawken, on the west bank of the Hudson, opposite New York City. Having acquired a broken-down railroad running for a considerable part of the distance, they set to work to raise the funds necessary to complete it. This project very soon led to an expansion in which Porter took the leading part. It was proposed to build from Cornwall-on-Hudson up the west shore of the river and thence through the Mohawk Valley across the state to Buffalo. The new line would thus closely parallel the New York Central and compete for its business, which was large and profitable. The older road was not popular on account of the well-known "the-public-be-damned" attitude of its management, and its service was inferior. From this unpopularity the new road expected to benefit. At any rate, since the region was well settled and prosperous, it was a safe assumption that there was business enough for two roads. As to the traffic on the west bank of the Hudson, the proposed line would naturally have that to itself.

When the company was organized under the name of the New York, West Shore, and Buffalo Railroad Company, Porter was by common consent made President. The ability which he had shown in pushing through the Sixth Avenue Elevated had won the respect of New York business men, and he was as highly regarded for his honesty as for his energy.

That the project of the new road appealed to the investing public and that the management had its confidence was evident when the plans for financing it were made public. The $15,000,000 issue of bonds [4] was, Porter wrote to Pullman, "the greatest success of the season." "After our four years' struggle with the elevated roads, this enterprise seems a very easy and comfortable one, and I am perfectly satisfied with regard to large profits." Other sums supplied by the New York Ontario and Western, which would use the road from Cornwall to Weehawken, and by the construction company, made up a total of $35,000,000, which at that time was the estimate of the cost of construction. Porter's plans called for a double-track road that was to be first-class in every way. They were a sign of a new era in railroading, in that the owners were building not for the purpose of selling to a competitor but with the object of operating the road themselves.

$35,000,000, however, was not enough. As the work proceeded, construction expenses mounted beyond all first calculations; more money had to be raised; and when, on January 1, 1884, the first trains were run through to Buffalo, the road had cost $58,000,000, and had no resources for meeting the interest charges, except what it might be able to earn. The state of the market was bad, and the company was unable to pay all of the January interest on its bonds.

Naturally the enemies of the West Shore were quick to take advantage of this unlucky start. The statements given to the press by Cornelius Vanderbilt, president of the New York Central, showed from what quarter the danger threatened, and the powerful railway magnate soon proceeded from words to deeds.[5] Although the West Shore, according to the arrangement made by the trunk line association, had been allotted a reasonable proportion of the through freight, there was nothing to prevent the New York Central from cutting the local freight rates, and this it did ruthlessly. Porter and his associates, with no large resources to fall back upon, could not hold out against Vanderbilt's determination to control both sides of the Hudson. The succeeding months were the darkest Porter had ever known. Efforts to get the bondholders to agree to measures that would save the situation came to nothing; there was not money enough to pay the employees; a crash was inevitable and immediate.

I well remember the evening when my father came home saying that the West Shore would soon be in the hands of a receiver. The wiping out of nearly all his own fortune troubled him least: what he dwelt on was the loss incurred by the men who had invested in the stock of the road because they believed in him. He felt the blow to his prestige, and his pride was hurt to the quick. I shall never forget his appearance. A very small child, I was terrified to see him so completely crushed.

At the moment when the worry of the West Shore business was never out of his mind, came another blow. The firm of Grant and Ward, betrayed by its junior partner, Ferdinand Ward, failed, and Porter's former Chief stood before the world ruined and, though innocent himself, the cause of ruin to others. The only thing left was his nobility of character. The soldier whose constancy had saved the nation, the President who for eight years had wrought to reunite it, the American who had been welcomed all over the world by other peoples as the embodiment of our finest national qualities, now was publicly humiliated beyond the power of words to express.

If men and women to whom Grant was but a name heard the story with awe and pity, Porter, who knew the sensitiveness of his Chief's nature and whose love for him was as strong as in the days of their campaigns together twenty years since, shared with the victim his suffering as it were on equal terms. He could not even offer to help Grant with money, so deeply involved were his own affairs at the time. Side by side they traversed that dark portion of the business world in which fair play and upright endeavor find themselves at the mercy of scoundrelism and of the spirit which sees in a competitor only a dangerous foe to be crushed at all costs. It was out of these bitter experiences that Porter made the phrase, "Abandon the path of ambition when it becomes too narrow for two to walk abreast." And from this time, too, dates his fondness for the motto, "Live and let live." He was a good hater, none better; but he was guided so consistently by this motto that however much he hated a man he never had any desire to injure him by word or deed. Merely, he was done with him.

Meanwhile, the affairs of the West Shore moved swiftly on to their inevitable conclusion, and in June a receivership was declared. At the same time the construction company, to which it owed money and which was heavily in debt, failed, and the disaster was complete. Porter's resignation as president, which followed in due season, terminated his career in railroad management. The road was eventually bought by the New York Central for $25,000,000, less than half its cost.[6] *

One incident of my father's business life is worth recording before I enter on the story of his other interests and activities. During the course of the great Pullman strike of 1894 he was called to Chicago, and I have vivid recollections of the telegram in the early morning, the hasty packing of his valise, and his hurrying to the Grand Central Station. Mother kept saying, "What are you going to do, Horace? Why doesn't Mr. Pullman go himself? If somebody's got to be killed, I don't see why it should be you!" But of course there was no arguing with Father: he merely muttered that "Pullman thinks I may be able to do something to influence the men." Pullman had always been kind and generous toward his workers and the strike was not directed against him personally. Although it was not broken till after much damage had been done and until after it had raised questions of lasting importance in the struggle between capital and labor, it was always a satisfaction to my father to have gone out among the strikers and talked to them and with them. He found the Americans amenable, the real agitators being mostly foreigners.

A year or so later it was decided to discontinue the New York office of the Company, and in the spring of 1896 my father terminated his connection with Mr. Pullman, after an association of nearly twenty-four years.[7] During this period the company had grown from a corporation with a capital of $5,800,000 and owning 422 cars to one capitalized at $36,000,000 and running over 1,700 cars. Its employees numbered 11,515. In its operation, which was directed from Chicago, Porter had taken almost no part; but as its representative in the financial world of New York he had

* In note 6 to this chapter, the reader will find extracts from my father's letters written at this time which show that the management of the West Shore built the road in good faith and which explain some of the miscalculations and misfortunes that wrecked it so quickly.

served it well and earned for himself an honorable position. When, in the course of years, he occupied himself more and more with other matters, his standing as a business man gave him unique prestige in the new fields.

CHAPTER XI

THE CHIEF

THE story of Horace Porter's life up to this point has shown him as a soldier and a man of affairs, and in both cases circumstances and his own nature combined to confine him strictly to the work in hand. But much as he delighted in action he had no mind for a life given over exclusively to business, and his resolve, after the failure of the West Shore enterprise, never to undertake another such responsibility must have been made with a distinct sense of relief. His plan was to build up a certain fortune, and meanwhile and thereafter to cultivate other interests and follow other pursuits. For the next seven years strict economy was practiced in his household: his family lived comfortably but were not permitted any luxuries. And in the meantime, by keeping clear of enterprises such as those which formerly had drawn upon him so heavily and confining himself for the most part to the routine work of the Pullman Company, he found the time he wanted to turn his thoughts to other matters.

Magazine articles made a modest beginning in the new field, and it was natural that they should deal with aspects and problems of railroading. For example, *Scribner's* magazine for September, 1888, contained an article by him on Railway Passenger Travel. It is a compact and at the same time interesting summary of information on this subject, with copious and quaint illustrations. His discussion of Railway Rates in the *North American Review* for December, 1891, is a clear and able analysis of conditions before and after the passage of the Interstate Commerce law, and his words of prophecy, read to-day, show the soundness of his judgment. Gradually, however, his writing, and also his speech-making, found their inspiration in the historic days of his young manhood. It is as an interpreter of the campaigns and leaders of the Civil War that he did his best work in these fields. And this brings the story back to his hero, General Grant.

After 1872, when Porter left Washington to establish himself in New York, the two men naturally saw little of each other; it was not till 1880, when, after his famous trip around the world, Grant came to New York to live, that their intercourse was renewed. In the meantime, however, there had been a period of coolness between them, caused by the jealous and malicious interference of a man who not only had been one of Porter's closest friends from their days together at West Point but also was under deep obligations to him. This man's insidious slanders Grant had for a time believed, and Porter could not understand the altered behavior of his Chief. When in the end the treachery was revealed, it is not strange that its effect was to draw together the two victims more closely than ever.

I was a tiny child when my father began to give me a share in his feeling for the Chief. Many a Sunday afternoon during the winter and spring of 1883-'84, which is as far back as I can remember, clutching tightly my father's forefinger, I marched with him up Fifth Avenue to a house on East 66th Street. If the weather was bad we scrambled into a noisy, rickety Fifth Avenue stage (the word bus appeared later in the American vocabulary). We buried our feet in the evil-smelling straw and patiently sat for what seemed an eternity, until the tired horses had slipped and stumbled up to the Park. After alighting from the stage we entered a house a short distance from the Avenue. A dark wooden staircase brought us to the door of a good-sized library, lighted by one window. There, in an arm-chair by the fireplace, a cane and a table of papers and magazines at his side, sat an elderly man with head and shoulders drooping a little wearily.

If asked to-day how tall he was or whether his hair and beard were turning gray, I could not answer; I know only that his hair was still thick and grew well on his forehead. What I remember distinctly are his eyes, his voice, and his hands. He had a way of suddenly looking up and fixing his eyes upon you. They were the finest feature he had, true and searching but never hard; they were of a deep gray-blue, and had sometimes a questioning look almost like a boy's. His voice had a clear, carrying quality which was agreeable to hear; it was never loud. He spoke very distinctly, and used such simple words that his talk was easy for me to follow unless it turned on subjects quite incomprehensible to a child. Sometimes he told a story or spoke of the days when he and my father first knew each other; he could be amusing, in his quiet, dry way. More often he listened to my father's talk, leaning forward in his chair, his elbows on the arms, his cane held loosely in his right hand, his eyes fixed intently on Father's face. As he sat thus, I used to watch his hands; they were well-shaped, with fingers somewhat long and tapering, and he had an expressive way of using the index finger of his right hand. Sometimes, in the midst of the conversation, he would draw me gently away from my father and hold me beside him, stroking my hands and hair.

When my first shyness had worn off, the General won his way to my heart by inquiring after my dolls, and the next time I came he even remembered their names. One day, leaning heavily on his cane, he took me to a large glass case and showed me the wonderful swords, medals, and trophies within. At first I did not realize that all these glittering objects had been presented to him personally. Then, on my asking him why those people across the ocean gave him such beautiful things, he laughed, said something about its being a "notion of theirs," and referred me to Father. I was delighted, for of course that meant a new story for me during our walk home down Fifth Avenue. When Father told me that the General had commanded great armies, fought desperate battles, and been President of the United States, a country so big that New York was only a speck on its surface, my awe and admiration increased tenfold.

At Elberon, New Jersey, General Grant's summer place was not a half-mile from ours, and I frequently played there with his grandchildren. To a small piece of land on each side of the entrance from the main road he had given the appropriate name of "the Wilderness." It consisted of a few hardy pine trees which in spite of salt winds and sandy soil had managed to reach a respectable height. The other trees were low and distorted, with branches at all angles and tangled bushes growing around their roots. It was an ideal spot for a firm believer, like myself, in Puck and Titania, Pease Blossom and Mustard-Seed. A small clearing had been made at one end of the wood, where were erected the swing and the seesaw. Here we played for endless joyful hours.

Occasionally the General came down and watched the fun. When one child climbed too adventurously, he or she was peremptorily ordered to a lower branch. We were not to swing too high or to seesaw too hard. He always looked out for the little ones of the party. He made once a remark which immediately aroused my interest. Turning to General Badeau, he spoke about some other Wilderness. I heard my own name: something about Porter's being a surprised man if any one had told him twenty years ago that . . . What followed I didn't understand, a remark about three hard days. "Glad to see it a children's playground." I dropped down from the low branch on which I was sitting and ran after the General's retreating figure. I was no longer quite so afraid of him, and putting my hand in his, keeping well away from his bad leg, I asked, "Was there ever another Wilderness than ours?" An expression half comical, half sad, came into the General's eyes when he heard my question. "Yes," he answered, "There was another Wilderness many years ago. Your Dad had some pretty hard work to do in it. And I was glad he was along. You ask him to tell you the story of 'our Wilderness.' He's a better story-teller than I am."

So it was that my father began to tell me his stories of the war, in which the central figure was always the Chief—in other words, the kindly old man, leaning heavily on his cane, who watched our games and sometimes joined in our fun.

But as the weeks went by I realized that the General was graver and more silent than he used to be in New York and that for days at a time we did not see him at all. He seemed to be always writing; we children were told not to make too much noise. Once I heard him say, "Oh, leave the children alone. Let them have a good time; they can't bother me." General Badeau was with him a great deal, and would often meet Father at the afternoon train, read over with him at our house endless, closely written sheets of paper, and then go off with him to the Chief's cottage. It dawned upon me that all this was connected with an afternoon in the late spring, in New York, when Father had come home in a great state of excitement. I heard him exclaim to my mother, "He's lost everything—gone, wiped away, not a penny left. It's all that scoundrel's fault. He ought to be tarred and feathered. I wish I could wring his neck." Father was walking up and down the room with his arms behind his back, from time to time throwing them out in dramatic gestures. His face was flushed—he kept hunching up and down his left shoulder. I remembered, too, that General Badeau had come, his round red face and short-sighted eyes wearing a troubled expression. Even the gold-rimmed spectacles had a look of despondency and slipped farther than usual down his nose. Then I remembered subsequent conversations between Father and Badeau, in the course of which I heard the words "the Chief," "new memoirs," "fine offer," and "Century." So, by putting two and two together, I gathered that something terrible had happened to General Grant, but that something good had been arranged with somebody by the queer name of Mr. Century, and this something was connected with General Grant's preoccupied air and his continued writing.

The situation which I was too young to understand was this: Shortly before the failure of Grant and Ward, the editor of the *Century Magazine* had urged General Grant to write a series of articles on the battles of the Civil War in which he had been engaged. He had refused, saying that writing was not his line. Nevertheless, he was a good letter writer and an entertaining talker when among his friends and interested in the subject under discussion. So, under pressure of necessity, he reconsidered the *Century's* offer. Into the new task he threw himself with all his energy, and he was astonished to find how quickly and easily he wrote. In preparing the narratives of the campaigns it was of course necessary to consult all possible sources of information, to compare conflicting evidence, and to verify figures and statements.

My father knew the story of the last year of the war almost as well as Grant did; moreover, in his letters sent home and in the notes taken at the time, he had preserved an accurate record of all the significant events that had taken place at Headquarters. On this information, as well as on my father's good literary and military judgment, Badeau had greatly relied in the preparation of his *Military History of Ulysses S. Grant*. Now, in the summer of 1884, Porter and Badeau worked together evening after evening, relieving their Chief, as far as might be, from the drudgery inevitable to his undertaking.

His health already undermined by the terrible disease to which he succumbed, old and penniless, Grant sat stolidly day after day, at his desk or in his armchair on the piazza overlooking the sea (I can see him now as I write), a little huddled figure, his pencil racing over his pad, writing against time. Each sentence meant a further reduction of his debts. But how much longer had he still to write? A few months? A year?

When winter came my father and I continued our usual Sunday afternoon visits to him. The visits were shortened; often I was not allowed in the room—a bitter disappointment. My father, on leaving the General, would take me by the hand and walk down Fifth Avenue without saying a word. He looked so troubled I hadn't the heart to ask for a story. I squeezed his finger to express my sympathy, about what I didn't know. When I again saw General Grant he had aged greatly; the face was utterly weary, and deeply lined. Only the eyes had not changed; they were still young and glad to see us when we entered the room. He made no attempt to rise from his armchair, but his eyes and the warm grasp of his hand told us how welcome we were. He had great difficulty in speaking. Instead of the funny old-fashioned white collar and little black tie which was always crooked, he wore around his neck a silk handkerchief. Sometimes he couldn't raise his voice above a whisper. Father talked about every conceivable thing that he thought might interest him. The Chief listened for a few moments; then his face relaxed, his eyes lost all expression, and he leaned back in his armchair exhausted.

There were days when he was better, his voice clearer; then he would point to the pile of closely written papers lying on his desk or the big table, get up, shoulders and head forward, shuffle the papers until he found what he wanted, and sign to my father to read it. They would comment and talk, the General's face for the time resuming its old expression of interest.

On one of the occasions when I was allowed in his room, he held out his hand to say good-by. I mumbled something, looked up into his clear, kind eyes, tried to speak, and followed my father to the door. Turning round for an instant, I saw him sitting back in his armchair, head bent on his breast, eyes perfectly listless. I never saw him again.

Finally the time came when my father must make the journey to bid his Chief farewell. With the approach of summer Grant had been taken to Mount McGregor, not far from Saratoga. He was growing steadily weaker; though conscious, he could hardly speak; he was in constant pain. All through the night my father sat by his bedside, while Grant tossed and turned and hoped for day. The watcher, his heart wrenched with sympathy, could not help remembering the occasions when, after the strain of a terrific battle, Grant had slept like a child.* The figure of the courageous and determined soldier, of the victorious commander at Appomattox, faded; the real hero was the Grant of the last months—a man prematurely aged, worn and tired, suffering untold agonies, but working to restore his honor and provide for others until death took the pencil from his hand.

A short time after my father's return home the telegram came. My mother cried; my father, as was usual with him when under strong emotion, walked up and down the room, blinking to keep back the tears and exclaiming in short, disjointed sentences. He said something about the Appomattox flag. I knew what that meant. My brothers and I had hung it out on the Fourth of July. This time it was put at half-mast.

The entire country had followed with heart-stricken anxiety the progress of the disease which was slowly conquering Grant; the funeral was a national demonstration in honor of the soldier whose greatest words were "Let us

---

* "Twenty-one years thereafter, as I sat by his death-bed, when his sufferings had become agonizing, and he was racked by the torture of insomnia, I recalled to him that night in the Wilderness. He said: 'Ah, yes; it seems strange that I, who always slept so well in the field, should now pass whole nights in the quiet of this peaceful house without being able to close my eyes.'" *Campaigning with Grant*, p. 71.

have peace." In the procession which accompanied the body to its resting-place in the temporary tomb on Riverside Drive, the South as well as the North was represented. The outpouring of feeling gave people everywhere a renewed consciousness of nationality which soon took form in a project to erect a memorial worthy of the great man whose remains it was to enshrine. Under the impulse of the occasion a Grant Monument Association was formed and a sum of money amounting to $114,000 was subscribed. It was the ambition of the men responsible for the plan to build a mausoleum similar to those erected in Europe for the illustrious dead. No such monument existed anywhere in America—as a general rule, the remains of her great men lay in cemeteries—and the proposed memorial was altogether out of the range of experience of the average business man or ex-soldier whose contribution was to supply the money needed. Perhaps not fully realizing how serious an undertaking it was to raise a large sum for such an object by popular subscription, the officers of the Association announced a competition for plans and in due season gave the award to John H. Duncan of New York. The estimated cost of erecting the structure designed was over $500,000.

When ground was broken on Grant's birthday, April 27, 1891, nearly six years had elapsed since his death. In spite of repeated efforts to raise money, only $155,000 was then in hand, and there was little prospect of obtaining more. The work had begun, it is true, but it was impossible to see how it could be finished. Other parts of the country were ready to point the finger of scorn at New York, and when Congress assembled, a proposal was made that Grant's body be brought to the National Cemetery at Arlington, Virginia, there to rest among his comrades of the Army. To this plan, however, Grant's family were opposed; indeed, one of the reasons why Grant had expressed a wish to be buried in New York was that the remains of his wife might lie beside his.

One of the most vivid of my early memories is going Sunday after Sunday to Riverside Drive with my father, laying my flowers before the ugly brick vault, thrilling to the salute of the sentry, and listening to Father's laments on the nation's ingratitude to one of the greatest of its preservers. "Think what they do in Europe to honor their great men!" he used to say. "The splendid tomb of the Invalides—Trafalgar Square—Westminster Abbey—the Panthéon!" He would sum up the different monuments, describing them to me and adding, "Here we are, a great, united country, rich and prosperous. And the man who saved the Union, brought us peace, and paved the way for our prosperity lies in a little brick hovel. A fine monument to our ingratitude! Some day we sha'n't even remember where he is buried."

He felt the disgrace so keenly, he was so confident that the money could be raised if the right measures were taken that he agreed to become president of the Grant Memorial Association and extricate it from its difficulties. An appropriation by the State of New York had been suggested as the most feasible means; Porter urged that the money needed, $350,000, be raised, as originally planned, through popular subscriptions, and the method he proposed was what to-day we should call a "drive." The scheme was daring in its novelty, but if he himself could picture it as possible and could envisage the ways and means of carrying it out, men of less faith and energy were willing that he should take the load upon his shoulders.

It was now February of 1892. The construction of the lower course of granite was under way, and it was proposed to lay the corner-stone on April 27th. Unless the event were to be an empty ceremony, the money must be well in hand by that date. In order to reach all classes and conditions of people, Porter adopted the plan of forming committees, one for each line of business or profession in New York, each committee to make a thorough canvass in its own field. He soon had 215 groups, numbering 2,487 men, at work. These met at stated intervals to report progress, and he was invariably present himself to spur them on. The devices of "publicity" were, of course, put into operation to attract the attention of the entire city. The novelty of the enterprise was in its favor; but the strongest asset was Horace Porter himself, with his sincerity, his good management, and his winning personality.

The laying of the cornerstone of the monument, which came at the height of the drive, was made a ceremony to quicken the city's pride in its hero. The President of the United States took part in it; Chauncey Depew gave an oration praiseworthy both for its sincerity and for its appropriateness to the occasion; the representation of Civil War veterans,—men who had followed Grant to victory,—was unusually large; the seats provided for 9,000 people were filled, and a multitude stood in a solid mass far down Riverside Drive. As for the presiding officer, Porter himself, whose modest bearing deceived no one, he was able to report that at the halfway point in the number of days allotted to the drive the sum of $202,000 had been subscribed. If the workers did not relax their exertions, he urged, if the public responded as it should, the remainder of the amount would surely be obtained. He stood and looked at the vast throng below him: this was the greatest opportunity he had ever had to convince and fire an audience.

"While some generous subscriptions," he said, "will be received from other cities, the people of the Nation have seemed to say to New York: 'You have secured the honor of entombing within your borders the ashes of America's great captain; the memorial to be reared will be the chief ornament of your city, pilgrimages will be made from all quarters of the globe to visit that Mecca. You are the metropolis and the moneyed center; you must unaided build the structure.' New York has accepted the challenge and will make good her word.

"While the monumental tomb will be thoroughly national in its character and purpose, it will stand in history as a tribute of the greatest of American cities to the greatest of American soldiers. . . .

"You who are gathered here, should go forth from this impressive scene as missionaries in this patriotic undertaking. You should preach a crusade on this subject throughout the length and breadth of our city. By your presence at this ceremony you have identified yourselves with the work, and consecrated your services to the cause. If the effort fails, you will be parties to the shame. If it succeeds, you will be participants in the glory of the triumph."

A "drive" lasting sixty days is no slight strain on human nature, and after the climax of the laying of the cornerstone there was sure to be a sag of effort, and new means of appeal must be devised. Prizes of twenty and ten dollars in gold were accordingly offered to the pupils of the higher grades in the public schools of New York and Brooklyn for essays on the life of General Grant. Contribution boxes were placed in stations of the Elevated Road, in shops on the principal thoroughfares, and elsewhere, in order to reach people who could give only small sums. The quantity of five- and ten-cent pieces collected was astonishing; the number of separate coins, bills, and checks was 47,670. At the other end of the scale of giving were fourteen men from whom Porter had obtained contributions of $5000 each. When Memorial Day came and the exercises were held as usual at the little brick tomb on Riverside Drive, he was able to announce that the goal of $350,000 had been reached.[1]

It is instructive to compare this undertaking with "drives" as we know them to-day. In the first place, all service was given. A by-law of the Association provided that all officers should serve without compensation. The secretary, James C. Read, and the treasurer, Frederick D. Tappan, president of the Gallatin National Bank, performed their heavy duties as a labor of love; the offices were provided free of charge by D. O. Mills; nobody did any of the work as a means of earning his living. Of the directors of the Association, Porter's chief helpers were Elihu Root and General Grenville M. Dodge. The absence of professional publicity workers and canvassers meant not only a tremendous economy, but also a minimum loss,—less than $400,—from unpaid subscriptions. The spirit in which the 2,500 collectors went at their task made them unwilling to let go until they obtained the money which they had been promised.

As for Porter, he had thrown himself into this task because its fulfillment stood for one of the dearest wishes of his heart. All his capacity for hero-worship, all his sense of patriotism, were expressed in the planning, conferring, and speech-making which he crowded into the working hours of these sixty days. But his action had many unexpected consequences. A greater range of power was his, he discovered, than he dreamed of possessing. He found that he was able to inspire men with a vision and to get them to work for a great cause. He could stir impulses in the ordinary New Yorker, indifferent to matters of civic or national honor, and make him turn aside from his own affairs of the present to think of—and to care for—the past and the future of his city and of his country. When on Memorial Day he brought his flowers to the "brick hovel" and gazed at the spot where the great monument was taking shape, he knew it to be one more expression of his feeling for his old commander. A memorial was being built for the Chief which would rival those in Europe, and he, Horace Porter, through one more act of devotion, had made this thing possible.

As the walls of Grant's Tomb rose year by year, my father followed its progress with constant concern. With the architect he had traveled from one quarry to another to select exactly the right kind of stone; every detail in the construction was a matter of interest to him. Our Sunday walks now had a new goal, and many a time have he and I climbed up on the uncompleted structure and looked up and down the stately Hudson.

But still he was not satisfied. To him the monument did not express all that he wished posterity to know about his hero, and so he set himself to put in order his own experiences in a book to which he gave the title of *Campaigning with Grant*. He planned that it should be not a military history but a character study made at close range. Grant, during his career as soldier and as President, had been the subject of violent detraction. Even after his death disparagement, thinly disguised as judicial criticism, was persistently finding its way to the public.[2] Porter's object was to meet these attacks by explaining Grant: by making clear the workings of his mind, the secret of his power and his greatness, and by showing the simplicity and lack of ostentation which made his character one of such extraordinary contrasts. In short, Porter hoped to make Grant as real a human being to others as he had always been to himself.

As I have already indicated, my father's records made during the campaigns were full; his memory was clear and accurate; also the reader knows from my frequent quotations the qualities of his style in description and narration. The manuscript was prepared carefully during the period while the tomb was under construction and was finished fully a year before its dedication, the date of which was set for April 27, 1897. By arrangement with the Century Company the book was to appear serially in the *Century Magazine*, the publication to begin a few months before the exercises at the tomb.

How he found time to write the book has always been a mystery to me. He was constantly dining out: there had come to be a great demand for him as an after-dinner speaker; he was at his office all day; and yet he wrote and corrected in every spare moment. Much of the work was done in his own room, the second-story back, overlooking Fortieth Street and the roofs of the low houses behind ours. He used freely his own letters, which had been so long tied up in the linen bag. He carefully consulted the little leather-bound note-books in which he had written down so many tragic and humorous incidents of the war, Lincoln's stories, and finally the account of the surrender at Appomattox. In reading over those worn, closely written pages, in which every detail of that scene is noted, I do not wonder that he watched with anxiety Lee's manipulations of his one and only pencil. A great part of the manuscript of the book he wrote out with his own hand, not to mention innumerable letters to get what seemed to me unimportant information; he took time to verify the smallest detail. When I remarked upon this, he answered, "I want this book to be right in every particular." My own duty was to correct the first proofs and to see, as Father said, "if the spelling's all right," and I devoted to this spelling-match a good part of my holidays.

The *Century* articles proved so popular that they greatly increased the sale of the magazine. The book went through three editions and has taken the place that my father hoped for as an interpretation of his Chief's character. Through it, and through the monument, he has done what he could to fix in the minds of the American people a truthful and lasting image of his commander as a great and good man.

CHAPTER XII

CITIZEN OF NEW YORK

BY the year 1892, Porter being then fifty-five years old, his business affairs were well in hand and such fortune as he cared to accumulate was well assured; he was now in a position to spend his energies on things which interested him much more than money-making—writing, speaking, and public affairs. His work in raising the money for Grant's tomb, which had given him unquestioned leadership in public-spirited effort, was only one of these activities. 1892 was a presidential year, and the meeting of the Republican convention was set for Minneapolis in the early days of June. As one of the delegates at large from New York, he was an advocate of the renomination of Harrison, and to him was assigned the duty of seconding the nomination of his friend Whitelaw Reid as Vice-President—a task which he performed so well that upon his conclusion there followed "a prolonged burst of cheering that took the convention off its feet, and gave the most cold-blooded veteran among the delegates a thrill of contagious enthusiasm." [1]

In the campaign ensuing he bore his part in speech-making and regular party work. During the next few years, when New York was going through a period of civic house-cleaning, he served on one committee after another, and had his share in the labor that such responsibility involves. Inevitably the party managers were very anxious that he should take office, and repeatedly urged him to run for mayor and then again for governor. But if he had inherited his father's interest in politics and his facility as a speaker, he had equally inherited his independence of character, and this independence was one of the chief reasons for his continued refusal to accept any political nomination whatsoever.

In discussing with me these offers he clearly stated his reasons for refusal. "I want to be my own master. I won't be at the beck and call of any party, nor will I cringe to any politician. In your grandfather's time governors had things pretty much their own way; to-day they are the servants of the party who nominate them. They are almost as badly off as the President himself. No, it's better to be just Horace Porter."

New York was then not so large but that the men of distinction in different fields of effort could meet together and wanted to do so. In fact, it was the day of men's dinners. Any excuse was sufficient to bring men together for this purpose—the arrival of a distinguished foreigner, as Sir Edwin Arnold, Thomas Hughes, Paderewski, Henry Irving, or Li Hung Chang, the departure for Europe of one of their own number, or the achievement of something noteworthy in a fellow-citizen's career. There were, of course, large public dinners at Delmonico's and the Waldorf, when it was hard to say which was more appalling, the gastronomic or the oratorical orgy; but the choice occasions were at the Union League Club, the Lotos Club, or the Lambs' Club, where all were at their ease, and the guest of honor enjoyed the release from formality. It was mainly at these gatherings that my father formed the acquaintanceships of which he told me so many tales, and of which I found the mementoes among his papers.*

In 1893, when many distinguished visitors came from abroad as representatives sent by their governments to the

---

* "Not finding him [Li Hung Chang] at the Lotos Club, I went to see him at his hotel. I asked him for a photograph for my little girl, and he got the photograph out and got his paint-pot and his pencil, holding it as a drummer holds a drumstick, and he worked along from right to left, up and down, until he covered it all over with hieroglyphics. He said—I took his word for it—that on the left side was a list of his titles, and on the other side a list of the public positions he had held. I took it home, looking as if I had torn something off the end of a tea chest. My little girl looked it over curiously. I said to her: 'Here, there's what you wanted. If you can't read it, probably you can play it on the piano.'"—*Speeches at the Lotos Club,* p. 202.

World's Fair, my father found himself much occupied in this way. His outlook on international matters was broadening. He was becoming a citizen of the world as well as of New York, and his knowledge of French was of great assistance in making the stranger welcome. Thus he met Admiral Kasnakoff, whom he was to see later in Russia, and also the Infanta Eulalia, sister of the King of Spain. The princess, in appreciation of his courtesy to her during her stay in America, presented him with a sword of Toledo workmanship, worked with her arms and initials.

Under these circumstances Porter developed his talent for speaking. Though in conversation his voice was low in pitch and his enunciation not always clear, no one would have suspected it when he was on his feet. His bearing was alert, he had a knack of putting himself in touch with his audience, and at the end, if he so desired, he could lift them to a plane of feeling the mood of which did not die with the ceasing of his voice.

His systematic pains in supplying himself with material may have been influenced by the rivalry of Chauncey M. Depew, who was in equal favor as an after-dinner speaker; be that as it may, the little leather commonplace books which he kept show that he made a practice of noting down apt stories, bits of wit and wisdom, and original turns of thought characteristically American in their humor. The following paragraph, taken from a speech which he delivered at a dinner of New Englanders, is an example of the sort of thing he could turn on and off at will.

"The New England sire was a stern man on duty and determined to administer discipline totally regardless of previous acquaintance. He detested all revolutions in which he had no part. He was always ambitious to acquire a reputation that would extend into the next world. While always seeking out new virtues, he never lost his grip on his vices. As far as his own particular case was concerned, he manifested a preference for the doctrine of damnation without representation.

"When he landed at Plymouth he boldly set about the appalling task of cultivating the alleged soil. By a fiction of speech which could not have been conceived by a less ingenious mind, he founded a government based upon a common poverty and called it a commonwealth. In the rigors of a New England winter when he found a witch suffering he brought her in to the fire; when he found an Indian suffering he went out and covered him with a shot-gun."

These speeches, many of which found their way into print, were, as a general thing, put together hurriedly, often while he was dressing for the dinner in question; sometimes, indeed, he did not do even this, but trusted to his ability to "box the compass" on any given subject as the inspiration of the moment prompted him.

In another class are the many commemorative addresses which he made on important public occasions, such as the dedication of the Washington Arch in New York, in May, 1894, and of Grant's tomb, on April 27, 1897. To the preparation of these addresses he gave much care, but he was never dependent upon his manuscript. His voice was strong and had a carrying quality that made it unusually easy to hear out of doors. He breathed deeply, almost exaggerated the use of his lips for the sake of distinct enunciation, and set his voice at a pitch on which it rang clear, melodious, and vibrant. In motive these public addresses were patriotic; for the most part they dealt with men and events of the Civil War. The pitfall besetting speakers on such topics is insincerity and unreality; Porter usually spoke from first-hand knowledge, and however elaborate his phraseology may sound to-day his words rang true.

His addresses at West Point deserve mention by themselves. Every call upon him from his old school met with a ready response; I was struck to find, in the well-worn leather-bound books, that the first and the last entries, June,

1873, and June, 1909, were for speeches there at the time of the graduation festivities. West Point meant to him not only his training for those great years with Grant but the joy and romance of his youth, and when he spoke to the cadets he was stirred in some of his tenderest memories and deepest feelings. It was entirely fitting that at the celebration in 1902 of the centennial of the founding of the Academy he should be the orator of the day.*

One of the duties to which Porter gave much attention in the years between 1892 and 1897 was his service as President-General of the Sons of the American Revolution. The position called upon him to take the lead in many kinds of effort along historical and patriotic lines. The placing of memorial tablets, the erection of monuments, awarding of prizes and medals, organizing state societies North, South, and West, attending banquets, and arranging for the annual congresses—these and kindred matters occupied more of his time than when he accepted the office he would have believed possible. Most important of all, he was untiring in his efforts to bring about a union with the rival society, the Sons of the Revolution. The stumbling-block was the fact that the Sons of the Revolution accepted as members descendants through collateral branches—thereby, as Porter was fond of pointing out, making possible the election of descendants of Revolutionary Tories—and in spite of all his tact he found it impossible to bring the union to pass.

My father was President of the Union League Club from 1893 to 1897. No position within the gift of New Yorkers carries with it more honor. His immediate predecessors had been Hamilton Fish, William M. Evarts and Chauncey M. Depew. His inaugural address as president combines the spirit of good fellowship which made Porter such an admirable clubman himself, an appreciation of the historic importance of the Club, founded in the dark days of the Civil War, "when the fate of the Republic was

* His oration is given in full in the Appendix.

PORTRAIT OF HORACE PORTER BY DANNAT
In the Library at West Point

trembling in the balance," and a sense of its present duty to be "progressive, aggressive, and courageous" on all questions of civic or national importance. In all these respects he was well qualified to be its representative before the city of New York, and also to the many distinguished people whom it constantly entertained.

To turn for a moment from my father's public life to his personal affairs: His son Horace, who had been voted the handsomest and most popular man in his class at Princeton, was graduated in 1888. A year and a half later he married a pretty Philadelphia girl, Adelaide Watson. His happiness was short-lived: stricken by typhoid within a year of his marriage, this splendid handsome brother of mine was laid to rest in the little cemetery at West Long Branch beside his baby brother, William. It was after Horace's funeral that I noticed gray hairs over my father's temples and lines in his forehead that I had never seen before. Horace was his idol; he represented everything that a proud father could wish to find in his son. He had been taken in the bloom of his young manhood, at the age of twenty-five, leaving no child to bear his name. The day of his death marked the end of a chapter in my father's life. He seemed to age ten years.

As for myself, in looking back over those early years it always surprises me that Father found time to busy himself as he did with my little life. Deep as he was in business and politics, a severely hard worker, my many questions, for example, were seldom turned aside with an impatient answer. He took the greatest interest in helping me select names for all our different animals; we would discuss at length what was suitable for horse, calf, kitten, or puppy, and then generally decide on our favorite character in some story-book.

As regards my formal education, my father's chief hobby was modern languages. "Think," he would say, "think what it is to be able to go to the theater in the principal cities of Europe and understand what is going on! How are we to comprehend other nations if we can't speak their languages or read their literatures? To know another fellow's language should make you understand how he feels." Nearly every day during these years he managed to maintain his habit of reading aloud to himself in French, and from time to time he took lessons in French conversation or wrote speeches in French. He read and spoke French to me when I was still trying to master English. After my French nurse had been dismissed, Father engaged a German governess, a very superior woman who remained with us twenty-two years.

As a part of their purpose for me, he agreed to mother's proposal that she and I should spend a year abroad. All through the trip father and I kept up a lively correspondence: the following extract is from a letter written in reply to one from me describing Paris as I saw it.

> My dear darling little girlie-pearlie Elsie,
> I have your letter of the 26th, and also one from your Mama written on her arrival at the most beautiful city in the world—Paris. I am very glad you are seeing so many curiosities of the old world, and hope you will remember everything so that you can entertain me when you get home by telling me all about them when we sit in the big rocking-chair of an evening. You must recollect the names of all the great painters, so that when you see beautiful pictures hereafter you will know all about the artists who painted them. Now that you know so much German you must practise your French which I know you will do when in *La Belle France*.

On our return to New York our apartment at 10 West Thirtieth Street was given up. Father rented a furnished house at 202 Madison Avenue, and then bought and rebuilt a house farther up on Madison Avenue—Number 277, at the corner of Fortieth Street. This remained our home until we exchanged it for the Embassy at Paris. My father always said that one of his chief reasons for buying this property was that it was within comfortable walking distance of the Metropolitan Opera House and the principal theaters.

His mode of life was not changed for the new home; indeed, it never did change. He was a light eater and still lighter drinker, and he never smoked. His toilet articles were of the simplest, and though he was fastidious about his linen and believed in going to the best tailor and in buying the best material for his clothes, those clothes had to last a long time. I can still see him, standing well away from the window, looking at his overcoat and trying to persuade my mother that it would certainly last out another winter. "Anyhow, it's December now, and I'm sure we shall have an early spring, and then I can wear my light overcoat." In fact, it was difficult to get him to spend any money on himself, but where others were concerned it was a different matter altogether. He was forever helping widows and children of his former comrades, and it was hard for him to turn a deaf ear to the pleadings of an old soldier. To any expostulation from the family his answer was always: "That man has been through the war, and war is Hell. You don't know what you'd be like if you had been through Hell."

As childhood draws to an end and the years of equality between parent and child come gradually on, their relation takes on a new kind of happiness. This was recognized by my father and me, but tacitly, like so much else between us. Much as he depended on telling his experiences and expressing his ideas in talk, he was too reticent to express his feelings, except by action. "Preaching," moreover, was so distasteful to him that he never gave me anything that could be called religious or moral instruction—or, if he did, I never recognized it as such. He relied on indirect methods. He believed that deeds count more than words. The creeds and church-going in which his mother had brought him up had lost meaning for him, yet he knew that he owed to her certain spiritual values which remained with him always unaltered. Duty never ceased to appear to him a supreme reality; on the other hand, the applause that is usually rated high in men's desires he took, as she had done, for what it was worth. So, by his kindness, his moderation, his moral courage, he showed me how to live. My mother, who remained a consistent Presbyterian, had me go to Sunday School and took me to church with her, and it may well be that my father was satisfied that I should have this experience, as he had had it, since I also could receive it at the hands of a sincere believer. But by the time my childhood was over his way had won me, and my point of view was his. And this, too, was silently understood between us.

Thus these years in New York ran their course. My father was happy in his home, and he enjoyed being in public life. It is true that he did not find in that life anything that unified it for him by commanding his complete devotion. The careers that lay open to him—money-making, creative business, public office—could not command it. So it is easy to see why, in his estimation, no experience of his life ever equaled his experience during the war. But he did attain, to an unusual degree, the freedom which he prized, and he had great enjoyment out of the uses to which he put it. He liked to meet people; he liked to make speeches; he liked to see pictures, to hear music, and to go to the theater; he liked the hard work that he put into the various enterprises which he freely undertook. And, as time went on, he had the happiness of knowing that his fellow-citizens counted on him more and more, and that they did not count in vain.

CHAPTER XIII

THE CAMPAIGN OF 1896

AS the time drew near for the Republican convention of 1896, the strength of William McKinley's candidacy for the presidential nomination became more and more apparent. Porter's acquaintance with him dated back to the days of the Civil War; he had followed his career closely and believed heartily in him as a man worthy to lead his party and to become the nation's chief. The nomination of Bryan by the Democrats followed that of McKinley by the Republicans, and the question of "free silver" versus the "gold standard" was put before the people as the main issue of the campaign.

Under these conditions Porter could no more remain inactive than in the great struggle of his young manhood. All his experience in business, all his conceptions of straightforward dealing, compelled him to offer his services in the cause of "sound money." He regarded the issue not as a party question, but as one involving the honor of the nation.

The story of the fight made by the Republican party in this year is well known. Under the guidance of Mark Hanna, chairman of the Republican National Committee, an organization was created, businesslike and thoroughly efficient, to educate the people in the principles of a subject on which they were necessarily little informed. Printed matter must be prepared in many forms and generally distributed; speakers must be sent far and wide. As the emergency required that all these undertakings be carried out on a scale more extensive than ever before attempted, the work of raising funds had to be organized to correspond. For this purpose an Auxiliary or Finance Committee was created in New York, and Porter was made its chairman. His experience in obtaining money for the Grant monument undoubtedly suggested his name, and when, about the middle of August, he called his committee together, a plan similar to the one he had followed then was what he proposed to them. As before, it was to be a large committee composed of men representing all possible occupations and interests. Subscription-book in hand, each member was to canvass the men in his own "line," urging contributions on the ground that this cause, like the other, transcended party divisions.

The undertaking to which Porter had set his hand and which was to absorb him night and day for ten weeks was by no means an easy one. This method of soliciting from the rank and file in a presidential campaign was novel, especially in its thoroughness; moreover, newspaper publicity was obviously undesirable. On the other hand, it was of great moment that the business community should have pressed home to it the reality of the emergency; if it pledged support in cash, it would be likely to give aid in other ways also.

Porter realized that to make the effort successful the committee-men must have enthusiasm as well as faith and that it was his business to inspire these unpaid[1] workers with that enthusiasm. This he could do because he was an ardent as well as an indefatigable worker himself. In the speeches that he was constantly making his praise of the standard-bearer was full of the sincerity of his own conviction, and, it may be remarked, stands the test of time better than most encomiums.

As for Bryan's principles, they were, he was fond of saying, "like ghosts: everybody fears them, but nobody believes in them." The influence of an ignorant leader over an ignorant mass of voters was, he knew, a danger to be vigorously combated; but he felt that against such an evil the weapon of ridicule was fully as effective as that of denunciation.

Enlightenment, however, was the best weapon of all, and

as Hanna extended his network of speakers more widely and planned for a more comprehensive distribution of pamphlets, his need for the sinews of war became more insistent. Then Porter and his fellow-workers must form new committees and incite the old ones to fresh vigor: not infrequently men who had already given had to be approached again and informed that the amount they had subscribed was not enough. No figures are available to indicate what sum was raised by Porter's efforts, but whatever it was, it was more than adequate.[2]

As the campaign drew to a close, Porter's time was largely occupied with the arrangements for a "business men's parade" which was to be held on the Saturday preceding the election.[3] The tide was beginning to run strongly in McKinley's favor, and Hanna, in planning that this day should everywhere be observed as "flag day," was trying to emphasize in the last hours before the election not partisanship but patriotism. Just as for the raising of funds New Yorkers had been appealed to through their business connections, so for the parade they were to be grouped in the same way. No political organizations as such were to appear in line; the men were to march under such inclusive temporary titles as the Coal Trade Sound Money Club, and the Coffee Exchange and Lower Wall Street Business Men's McKinley and Hobart Sound Money Club. From the beginning it was assumed that the number of participants would be well over 100,000, a total much larger than had ever been known before in any procession. The arrangements for assembling, marshaling, and disbanding it needed to be made with the greatest care, and Porter's hours were crowded with attention to innumerable details. Meanwhile New York was decorating itself in such a fashion as to astonish even its own inhabitants; flags and bunting appeared everywhere, even on the churches; the city became as a small community, strong in civic sense and striving to outdo itself on a great occasion.

The weather on October 31 was perfect. Long before

ten o'clock the streets leading into lower Broadway were swarming with the men composing the first divisions of the parade; on the stroke of the hour General Porter, the Grand Marshal, was at the starting-point, the corner of Worth Street and Broadway. Preceded by a platoon of mounted police, he led the procession, sitting his horse as erect as if he were twenty. In spite of his civilian clothes no one could mistake his military bearing. After his escort of one hundred citizens, mounted, came the van, the Wholesale Dry Goods Republican Club, 18,000 strong, with twenty bands. They marched in a sixteen-file front, their ranks only four paces apart. In contrast to the red, white, and blue of the street decorations, the prevailing color in the procession was yellow. Sound money gave its hue to the banners and mottoes which were borne aloft and was reflected in the yellow chrysanthemums worn as boutonnières.

At Madison Square, opposite the Fifth Avenue Hotel, stood the reviewing stand. Receiving the salutes of the notables massed upon it, Porter proceeded up Fifth Avenue to Fortieth Street, where the parade was to disband. He had foreseen the many difficulties that might occur in crowded streets, when men break ranks at the rate of fifteen thousand an hour, and he felt that the end of the route was for him the post of duty. From this point he was in telephonic and telegraphic communication with every street-corner along the line of march, and he had at his command a multitude of active young aides. Here he sat his horse, hour after hour, as the steady ranks swept up toward him, all on schedule time, watching the divisions turn into Fortieth Street, alternately to the east and the west. The early darkness of a late October day descended, and on the Avenue, on Broadway, buildings grew bright with illuminations. Shortly after eight o'clock the groups of college students who brought up the rear, marching to the music of the one hundred and fifty-third band in the procession, had cheered the Grand Marshal, and the parade was over.

Following the election of McKinley and Hobart there were numerous feasts of rejoicing. The banquet of the New York Chamber of Commerce was arranged for by Porter himself, and he was especially proud of obtaining as one of the speakers Secretary Wilson, of Cleveland's Cabinet. Besides the mutual congratulations of men who had done good team-work in striving for victory, the awakened interest of business men in politics was noted at these gatherings as significant. This was the theme of Porter's remarks at the "Parade Dinner" on February 27, 1897. Mindful of the need of better government in New York, he called upon his listeners to pay more attention to what was going on in their districts. As the event proved, the return of the Republican party to power at this time meant that the influence of business upon government was indeed to be felt more strongly than ever before; unfortunately it manifested itself in less desirable ways than those which he indicated.

With the election over, the thoughts of those who had been directing the campaign were naturally turned to the inauguration and the personnel of the new administration. Porter's position was such that he was consulted in both matters. At an early date he received an invitation from Governor McKinley to come to Canton. The president-elect's first request of him was that he take charge of the inauguration parade. Next came the offer of an appointment. On this subject Porter evidently had views of his own.

Horace Porter to A. A. Woodhull

December 30, 1896.

. . . The Governor has had very full and frank talks with me about all his preparations for the future, Cabinet, etc. I told him at the outset that nothing could induce me to camp in Washington and undertake the African slavery of running a Department of the Government; that I was trying to get rest in these days rather than confining work. He is all adrift as to a Secretary of War, but he will no doubt be able to get a good man before the 4th of March. As you say, it is more important than ever that there should be a proper head to the Military Department of the Government, particularly if we should have more domestic insurrections or a foreign war.

It seems probable that at this time or not long afterward McKinley made an offer to Porter which he was quite ready to accept—the post of Ambassador to France. Whenever the arrangement was made, no inkling of it was given by Porter to any one, and he was continually parrying suggestions to the effect that he was destined to fill the position of Secretary of War. His firmness occasioned McKinley temporary embarrassment, for not only was there no suitable alternative for the War Department, but when his refusal to enter the Cabinet became known, the machine element among the New York Republicans,—"a few disturbing spirits," Porter discreetly called them,—became clamorous for recognition.

> The President was hard pushed in regard to a Cabinet officer from New York [wrote Porter when the affair was happily settled] but his judgment was sound, and he was in no real danger of making a serious mistake. When it was known that neither [Cornelius N.] Bliss nor I would enter the Cabinet except by force, a great many people were pressed upon the President, but he gave scarcely any consideration to their names. I felt an abiding faith that when the crisis came Bliss would be patriotic enough to go to Washington, and that brought about a splendid solution of the whole question, and left me to exercise my first choice, if I can say that I had any particular choice.[4]

The solution found for the other embarrassment was unfortunately anything but "splendid." The appointment of

General Russell A. Alger as Secretary of War proved most unlucky. The foreign war which Porter feared came, and Alger's unsatisfactory administration of affairs in the War Department compelled his retirement.

The new adjustments involved Porter in another negotiation much more delicate and far-reaching in its consequences than his own affair. Mark Hanna was desirous of obtaining at once a seat in the United States Senate. A vacancy in the Ohio representation could be created by appointing John Sherman, who was seventy-three years of age, to the first place in the Cabinet. Then, if the Governor of Ohio were so disposed, Hanna could be chosen to serve in Sherman's place. This official, however, as it happened, was of the opposite faction from McKinley and Hanna. In a letter to the latter Porter describes with keen relish the gubernatorial embarrassments and his own efforts to make the gentleman's path plain before him.

Horace Porter to Mark Hanna

January 18, 1897.

On getting the intimation as to the desirability of Governor Bushnell appearing conspicuously in the Inaugural Parade, I addressed him a very polite letter, offering him the command of any Division in the Parade he chose to accept. He was profuse in his acknowledgments, and on his arrival here on Saturday he sent a staff officer to me saying that he wanted to call with his staff in uniform to pay his respects to me at the Union League Club that afternoon. I fixed an hour and had a captivating lunch prepared. A few mutual admiration speeches were made and he went on his way rejoicing. He and I both spoke at the Ohio Society's dinner Saturday night, and I had some quiet talk with him afterwards and tried to draw him out a little on the Ohio situation without lugging the subject in by the ears. He was rather non-committal, intimated that he had not been advised officially whether Sherman was really

going to leave the Senate, did not know for a certainty
whether you were to be a candidate for the place, that he
was debating whether to call the Legislature together to
elect a Senator, and then went on to make some flattering
allusions to you and Governor McKinley. I judge from all
that he is in quite a state of mind over the subject, and
really does not know himself what he is going to do. . . .

Meanwhile most of Porter's energies were devoted to
the inaugural parade, which was to be such an important
incident in the day that would crown Hanna's campaign.
In one respect Porter's plans were blocked. He had wished
to have the cadets from West Point and the naval cadets
from Annapolis ordered on; but the "Populists, the Free-
Silverites, and I am sorry to say some of our Republican
friends, opposed this and beat it by eight votes." Apart
from this annoyance, the detail to which he gave most
thought was the selection of the men who were to ride beside McKinley's carriage. Four of them were sons, one
was a grandson, of former presidents. It was like him to
be guided in his choice by sentiment and to leave no stone
unturned to secure the men he wanted. Thus as the new
chief magistrate rode from the Capitol to the White House,
past cheering multitudes, he was to be escorted by riders
bearing the names of Hayes, Garfield, Arthur, Harrison,
and Grant.

The Fourth of March, 1897, was cold and blustery, as
usual. My mother and I decided that we preferred to see
Father in all his glory rather than witness the inauguration
ceremony at the Capitol; accordingly we were escorted by
one of the aides to seats on the reviewing-stand in front of
the White House, whence we heard McKinley acclaimed
when he arrived at the Executive Mansion from the Capitol.
Later he took his place on the reviewing-stand—just in
time to meet the head of the procession. A line of police
cleared the way; then, after an instant of silence, I heard
shouting and cheering, and there, coming from the right,

was Father, erect and military on a splendid horse. He was wearing the full General's uniform of that period: gold belt, broad sash, medals, enormous gold epaulettes, a plumed black hat, and, at his side, the sword presented him that morning by his staff. It was the first time I had seen him in full regalia. To my prejudiced eyes he made a very fine appearance, and to judge from the enthusiasm of the crowd they were entirely of my opinion.

A brilliant spectacle of another sort—the inaugural ball —succeeded the procession. In spite of his seven hours on horseback Father was on hand to dance the opening quadrille and was not ready to walk home until the small hours. During the evening the public buildings were illuminated, a sight that Washington had not witnessed since the fall of Richmond.

Thus with ceremonies which, in the words of the New York *Tribune's* correspondent, were "for magnitude, color, intensity of interest, and dramatic effectiveness the most imposing and successful that ever ushered a new administration into place and power," William McKinley assumed his duties as head of the government. Hanna's campaign was concluded, and a new era in our history was begun.

President McKinley's nomination of General Porter as Ambassador to France was announced on March 16, being coupled with that of John Hay for the corresponding post in England. The appropriateness of both appointments was immediately recognized; the Administration received high praise, and the men thus honored were overwhelmed with congratulations. It was a turning-point in our diplomatic history. The bill creating the rank of ambassador had been passed only in 1893, and McKinley was the first President to have the opportunity of choosing men to fill a position of this rank.

Father brought back from Washington a vivid account of the President's talk with him about the new appointments. The whole diplomatic service, McKinley felt, was bound to change with the creation of the rank of ambassador to the larger European countries, and it was absolutely essential that the men sent to London and Paris especially should have not only knowledge of the world but tact, distinction, and force of character. I could see that my father was stirred, and eager to take up his new work.

There was one duty, however, which he could not possibly omit to perform before leaving the country. The dedicatory exercises at Grant's tomb had already been set for April 27, Grant's birthday. That day would see the completion of Porter's long labor of love [5] and the transfer of the great monument from the Association to the City. Although the event was in charge of the city authorities and Porter's sole direct responsibilities for it were to deliver the oration and go through with the formalities of the transfer, there were still a quantity of preliminary details for him to attend to.

In addition to the exercises at the monument the plans for the day included two parades: one of civic and military bodies in which over 50,000 men were expected to march; the other, on the Hudson, of a multitude of vessels, among them the warships of five nations. The city was decorated with flags and swarmed with visitors. The entire program had been planned on a scale of dignity and impressiveness which should show that the great community knew how to value the charge about to be entrusted to her. On the speakers' stand, on the morning of the dedication, was gathered the sort of assemblage rare in any of our cities except Washington—President McKinley, Vice-President Hobart, ex-President Cleveland, members of the diplomatic corps, officers from the foreign warships, Senators and Representatives, besides many unofficial persons of national distinction. No figure, however, attracted more attention or put the audience more in tune with the spirit of the day, than that of the hero's widow.

After President McKinley's remarks, Porter came forward to pay the tribute that was to be the crowning justification of his faith and works. He stood an instant, rapt entirely out of himself, and began: "It is all like a dream." Then, in an address wonderfully compact, he set forth the qualities of Grant's greatness as a man and the significance of his deeds in arms and in statesmanship. Here, as always, he recognized the attacks to which his Chief had been subject and met them as always, with the ardor of a champion. In style the oration is particularly effective. For a dozen years his mind had been full of the subject, and through much practice in presenting Grant to readers and to audiences, he had a treasury of illuminating phrases and a sense of proportion as to the parts that gave the address a high literary quality. These merits, which make it admirable reading, must have been lost on the occasion, along with the very words themselves, for a blustering cold wind scattered all sounds and, indeed, cut short the exercises.

At this time, one might say, my father had reached the pinnacle of his career: in New York he held a unique position. More than this, he was known and respected throughout the country. Honors had been heaped upon him, and new honors awaited him as Ambassador to France. He was happy, and I remember his saying to me once, "I wish your grandmother were alive and I could tell her." Yet, though the years following contained, to the eye of the world, more brilliant episodes, in which he played a prominent part, I do not believe he had a happier or prouder day in his life than that on which he stood beside Grant's successor in the shadow of the monument and spoke to the thousands that had come from all parts of the Union to see and acclaim. His Chief was justified and could sleep in peace.

BOOK III
THE DIPLOMAT
1897-1905

CHAPTER XIV

GETTING ESTABLISHED

WE sailed on the old *St. Paul* May 5, 1897. During the last two weeks in New York, clubs and societies vied with each other in giving dinners in my father's honor. In the daytime he tried to round up his business affairs; the evenings were taken up with banquets and speeches. The climax was reached at the large dinner given by the Union League Club on May 3, when he was presented with a silver-bound book, heavily embossed with the arms of France and America, the parchment leaves of which bore the signatures of President McKinley, John Sherman, Elihu Root, and scores of other men prominent in the worlds of politics, finance, art, and literature.

It was only the last evening before sailing that Father found time to sort his papers and superintend his packing. In the confusion I slipped into my own trunk the linen bag of his war-letters; I was no more willing to be parted from them than he was to be parted from the portraits of his father and mother or his mother's old chair. Meanwhile our elderly German housekeeper, Emily, hovered over his trunk. A supply of mufflers was her chief care: his throat was delicate, and he must reach France in good shape to begin his speech-making to "dem Frenchmen."

At the wharf next morning we were met by a crowd of friends, who literally carried us on board the boat. I had a vision of a deck suite piled with flowers, heard continual calls for "General Porter" or "the Ambassador," saw Father standing in the midst of a talking, gesticulating crowd, shaking innumerable hands and vainly trying to appease the frantic efforts of the reporters clamoring for a last interview. Finally, with a great deal of shouting and waving of flags, we steamed out of New York Harbor.

During the voyage the main subject in my father's mind was what he must accomplish on reaching his post. He fully realized the old-world prejudice against the upstart republic across the Atlantic which he represented; he recognized, too, the reasons for these prejudices. However, the Americans themselves had not always been to blame, for they had been subject to more than one handicap. First and foremost, "our official representatives to foreign countries had suffered from the inferiority of their rank as Minister. When the United States had ministers only, and one of them wished to present to the minister of foreign affairs a matter even of the utmost importance, he had to wait and follow ministers, often those from the most insignificant states, who had arrived before him, and after having danced attendance for hours, just when he believed that his patience was about to be rewarded, perhaps an ambassador would arrive. As there were usually eight ambassadors to take precedence of him, his sense of dignity had to be thrown to the winds." [1]

General Porter, as Ambassador, was in a position of dignity and influence, and was animated by an earnest purpose to lay the foundations of a better understanding between France and the United States than had existed for many years. He must if possible make even the greatest nations of Europe feel that the American Republic had come to stay, that she must have her say, that she was not to be accepted on sufferance only on account of her wealth, but because she too had brains, culture, and tradition, and counted among her people men who represented higher things than the almighty dollar. In this new position, to make his personality felt, he must follow out the old tradition of pomp and circumstance surrounding the ambassador of a great country to the most brilliant capital in Europe. Although the United States Government provided the rent for the offices, or Chancery, it supplied him with neither an official residence nor the means for hiring one.[2] But a large house he must have, furnished to meet the approval of a people famed for its taste in art. It must be equipped with an excellent staff of servants, although he did not choose to have the usual number of footmen required by the other embassies: a certain simplicity he considered should mark the difference between an imperial embassy and the embassy of a republic.

When the new Ambassador arrived in Paris on May 13, he was met at the station by his predecessor, Mr. Eustis, the two Embassy secretaries, Vignaud and Scott, the military attaché, Kellogg, and the naval attaché, Sims, and some of the resident Americans, among them his friend, General Edward Winslow. His informal introduction to Hanotaux, Minister for Foreign Affairs, took place on May 18. I can answer for his inward thrill when, after long years of faithful devotion to the French language, he found himself able to do it justice in conversation with that most polished of Frenchmen. For his formal presentation to President Faure on the twenty-sixth, he took a characteristic resolve, in the face of the stereotyped instructions of the State Department to diplomatic officers that their ceremonial address be delivered in English.[3] In his account of the occasion written next day to the Secretary of State, he alludes with a discreetly light touch to what might be described as the first hit of his ambassadorial career.

Horace Porter to John Sherman

Embassy of the United States,
Paris, May 27th, 1897.

Sir:

My predecessor, Mr. Eustis, handed his letter of Recall to the President of the French Republic on the 24th instant, and my official reception took place yesterday, upon which occasion I presented my Credentials as Ambassador. This function, as you are aware, is attended, in France, with elaborate ceremonies. The newly accredited representative is driven from his residence in the Presidential carriage, is accompanied by all the members of his Embassy, and escorted by the official Introducer and a squadron of cavalry.[4] Upon his arrival at the Palace of the Elysée, a regiment of Infantry is drawn up which salutes while the band plays "Hail Columbia." Upon departing from the Palace the same honors are accorded.

I found that the speeches addressed by the various ambassadors, and the Ministers to the President upon presenting their credentials have been delivered invariably in French, and in view of this practice and from the fact that I had received a polite intimation from the Foreign Office that it would be particularly agreeable to the President to have me follow this custom, I decided to make my remarks in the French language. I submitted at the same time, in writing, an exact translation in English. In view of the hearty welcome I had everywhere met with, and the friendship really felt by our country for France, I made especially prominent in my remarks an expression of our amicable relations and traditional sympathies, and the President's reply was marked by extreme cordiality.

I enclose copies of both speeches.

In the conversation which followed and which was also conducted in French, the President extended to me a most hearty welcome to France, said many pleasant things in regard to our country, and asked numerous questions about the President of the United States; as to his method of distributing his official business; his personal characteristics etc.; and seemed to be particularly interested in his career as an American statesman.

I have now assumed official charge of the Embassy.

I take great pleasure in availing myself of this occasion to express my deep sense of appreciation of the extreme courtesy extended to me by my distinguished predecessor in office and the many useful suggestions made by him with a view to my assistance.

I wish also to make my acknowledgments to Mr. Vignaud for the important aid he has rendered me in familiarizing myself with the affairs of the Embassy. His varied and useful experience and his thorough familiarity with the manifold details of the work acquired during his long and honorable term of duty here render his services of peculiar value.[5]

Immediately after his interview with the President, the new Ambassador, according to custom, called on all ministers of the French Government (corresponding to the members of the American Cabinet), and on the eight ambassadors of foreign countries, that is, the Papal Nuncio, the Ambassadors of Russia, Germany, Austria, Italy, Spain, Great Britain, and Turkey. On the ministers of countries represented only by legations, the Ambassador was not supposed to make the first call.

The presentations and official visits finished, General Porter pursued the difficult mission of house-hunting. "The embarrassments of an American representative," he writes, "begin the moment of his arrival at his post. Instead of devoting himself to arranging for his formal reception by the Chief of State, and the preparation of his address to be delivered on that occasion, and familiarizing himself with the etiquette of the country and the work of his embassy or legation regarding official matters which may require immediate attention, he is compelled to spend his time with house brokers, real estate agents, and speculators, in finding a suitable residence. These people are clever enough to know how few suitable houses are obtainable and, when they find an American representative in the market, prices are advanced and many obstacles placed in the way of the lessee. He can generally get better terms by making a lease for a long period, but his tenure of office is so doubtful that in doing so he takes a grave pecuniary risk. Even if our representatives are able to install themselves properly, each one selects a different domicile, and while other embassies are permanent and their location often historic, our own are as itinerant as a houseboat. When a city cabman is asked by a stranger where the American embassy is, the reply often given is, 'On wheels. Year before last it was on such a street, last year on another street, this year I don't know where.'" [6]

After a long search my father found a house that was hardly second to any of the favored nations' embassies in Paris; incidentally its rent was the same as his salary. It was situated on a small street running from the Avenue Victor Hugo to the Avenue Bois de Boulogne, number 33 Rue de Villejust. The house had been bought and re-modeled by the celebrated antiquaire, Spitzer, for his collection, the finest private one in France. At his death some of the works of art had been sold, but many still remained in the house.

As to its exterior the building was not distinguished, but it had a garden which opened upon the Avenue Victor Hugo through which carriages left the premises instead of having to turn in the courtyard. From the large hall of the *rez de chaussée,* a broad staircase (covered with the invariable red carpet) with a wrought-iron balustrade led to the second floor, the *premier étage.* The square space over the stair-case, which was lighted from the roof, was hung with an early Louis XIV Beauvais tapestry, to me the gem of the whole collection. Two early gothic tapestries, remarkably fine, hung opposite the entrance of the salle d'armes, at the great doors of which the stairway stopped. This salle d'armes was a huge room running the width of the house, its two windows filled with fourteenth century stained glass. Opening out from the salle d'armes were the two Louis XV salons. The white and gold wood work had been taken bodily from a French château, part of the paneling was filled in with old Sèvres blue brocade, the curtains were of red soft taffeta. The wonder of this room was the chan-delier, with its hand-cut crystals tinted pink and holding once a hundred candles, but now, alas, electric lights. The dining-room had been treated in the same manner; the

SALON AND SALLE D'ARMES AT THE EMBASSY

woodwork, of carved oak with a small gold filet, was even finer than that in the salons. The rest of the suite consisted of a large comfortable sitting-room, two other rooms, and a so-called "bibliothèque." Valuable pictures adorned the walls; old carved chests, fine bronzes, one or two marbles, some rare majolica, and a priceless collection of old armor were arranged according to the period and style of the different rooms.

In contrast with all this magnificence, the bedrooms, situated on the rez-de-chaussée, were inadequate, badly and cheaply furnished, and without the slightest attempt at comfort. The proprietor of the house, Mr. Spitzer's son-in-law, had told us as a great piece of news that there was a bath room, "une salle de bain magnifique!" I discovered that this salle de bain had been partitioned off as a *cabinet de toilette;* it was large and its walls were done in priceless old delft tiles. Standing solitary in its grandeur was a much battered high tin tub, from which the water could not run out until the stopper had been secured on high with a string.

We moved into our "hôtel" as quickly as possible, and on the evening of July third the new Ambassador held his first official reception, his "recivimento." "This is a very formal function, and involves no little expense. A minister, if he chooses, may hire accommodations in a hotel for this purpose, but an ambassador is compelled by usage to receive in his own domicile, that is, his Embassy." [7] Usage, indeed, exercised a firm control over the Ambassador's every social act of an official nature. The department of the French Government which thus dominated his movements was called the Protocol, and when he had occasion to consult it about matters of etiquette the answer was always brought by the hand of a resplendent cavalryman from the Garde Républicaine. From that answer there was no appeal: it was as final as the laws of the Medes and Persians. In the case of the invitations to the recivimento, the Ambassador was furnished by the Protocol with a list of all the high officials of the French Government and of all the members of the resident Diplomatic Corps, together with their families. Although General Porter was not expected to go beyond this list, his American spirit of hospitality and his independent nature would not permit him to accept such a strict rule. "In my case," he writes, "I announced my intention of inviting about two hundred Americans then in Paris, consisting of persons of some distinction and all of them personal friends. My suggestion was adopted by the Government, though it was quite an innovation. The total of invitations issued amounted to about fifteen hundred." [8]

Not only was this reception characteristic of the atmosphere in which Porter was to spend eight long years, but also the world it characterized is a thing of the past— "ça n'existe plus." The big entrance hall of the Embassy was decorated with flowers and plants amongst which were cunningly concealed tiny electric lights. In the salle d'armes the beautiful stained glass windows were lighted from behind to show their delicate traceries. Flowers were everywhere in profusion. From the Protocol had come the official introducer, a tall, pompous man in black, with knee-breeches, a silver chain around his neck, a rod in his hand, and a voice like a megaphone. It was his business to know every official person of importance in Paris, to inquire the names of the other guests, and to bellow all names as loud as possible: the more important the guest the more he yelled. The following introduction is typical of the manners of this august person, as he stood at the head of the stairs, beside the entrance to the salle d'armes:

"Son Excellence, M. le Comte Tornielli, Ambassadeur de Sa Majesté le Roi d'Italie auprès de la République Française et Mme. la Comtesse"; but at the height of the crowd there were times when he had to omit the King and the Republic.

Within the broad entrance to the salle d'armes, at the top of the staircase, stood the American Ambassador, immacu-

late in his black dress suit, tall, slender, erect, his eyes very
blue and bright, his face a little flushed. Paris might well
believe him under fifty: his iron gray mustache and the
touch of gray in his thick black hair were the only signs
that could have suggested sixty. Beside him stood his pretty
wife. Her curly hair was now quite gray; her neck and
shoulders retained their graceful outlines, and her com-
plexion was the same pink and white; her dark laughing eyes
had not changed since the far-off days when Horace Porter
had first seen and loved her. That evening she stood beside him dressed in soft white satin embroidered in silver,
with diamonds around her neck and in her hair. No wonder
her guests called her "une belle femme" and "une femme
délicieuse."

To my great disappointment, I was considered too young
to assist at such an event. So I stationed myself behind the
palms in the hall, watched the staircase, and listened to the
megaphone voice shouting the names. With the help of
Bailly-Blanchard, my father's private secretary, I began to
understand who the people were. The guests were invited
at nine, and of course the whole Embassy staff, Sims and
Kellogg in full uniform, were the first arrivals, for in those
days no one ever dared to be over a quarter of an hour late.
The ambassadors and ministers representing "sovereigns
by the Grace of God," were generally, like Royalty, on the
minute. At the moment when the street and courtyard were
filled with carriages and the first guests were mounting the
stairs, every light in the house went out! The electrician
had disappeared, there was no telephone, we were left in
darkness for half an hour. Many of the guests waited in the
hall and on the staircase, and when at last the lights suddenly flashed on there stood revealed a truly brilliant
throng.

Each Ambassador arrived with his wife, the gentlemen
of his suite and their wives ranged behind him according to
rank. The Russian Ambassador was little old Baron

Mohrenheim (he was soon replaced by Prince Ouroussof).
The Austrian Ambassador, Count Wolkenstein-Trostburg,
was in a gorgeous uniform. His wife was a very pretty
woman, with small, regular features, a perfect skin, blue
eyes, and a mass of wavy white hair. She had been brought
up in two of the stiffest courts of Europe, first as lady in
waiting to the old Empress Augusta (wife of Emperor
William I), and later, when she married Wolkenstein, at
the court of the Habsburgs.

Close beside the palm behind which I was hidden stood
for some moments a long, thin, distinguished-looking person of erect military bearing, with neatly trimmed white
beard and a face expressing character and determination.
This was Count Münster, the German Ambassador, a man
of seventy-five and for the last dozen years a well-known
figure in the Paris diplomatic and social world. Münster
was shortly afterwards created Prince, and it was under
this title that we knew him. Beside him was his unmarried
daughter, known in Paris as the Countess Marie. On her
thin, tightly drawn gray hair was a small coronet in pearls
and diamonds; it was on perfectly straight when she went
upstairs, but when she came down it had slid almost over
her ear. I discovered later that that coronet never managed to stay straight for more than a few minutes at a
time. Following the Ambassador were the different members of his staff, and bringing up the rear were two immensely tall, fine-looking officers in the white and gold uniform of the Potsdam Guards.

Another diplomat, who strongly resembled the portraits
of Michael Angelo, was Count Tornielli, the Italian Ambassador, later, in 1907, co-worker with my father at the
Hague Peace Conference. With the Count was his wife, a
great-granddaughter of that Rostoptschin who had defended Moscow against Napoleon. Then appeared the
Papal nuncio, Monseigneur Clari, resplendent in his purple
robes, purple gloves, great emerald ring, and little cap;

following him were Monseigneur Peri-Morosini and the handsome, clever Monseigneur Belmonte, quite a young man, who looked like a Titian portrait. Her Britannic Majesty's Ambassador, Sir Edmond Monson, was conspicuous on account of his brilliant uniform, covered with heavy gold embroidery, orders, and ribbons. He himself, though tall, stooped, and had little personality.

There were innumerable members of the French Government, each department being represented by its head and so many secretaries and undersecretaries. These men were all in dress suits, but generally with a broad colored ribbon and several orders. The officers of the military household of General Billot, who for the moment was Minister of War, came in the uniforms of their various regiments, among them old General de Freycinet, the Marquis de Gallifet, and Captain Sadi Carnot, son of the murdered President. Mingled with this brilliant official assemblage were the two hundred members of the American colony whom, with the consent of the Protocol, General Porter had invited. The women of the group made a wonderful showing of chic dresses and splendid jewels; the men were conspicuous as the only people there in plain black evening clothes except their host himself.

To-day, as I read over the list of the fifteen hundred invited guests which I found among my father's papers, so many faces, so many other scenes, come before me! Those gay, pleasure-loving Americans, their clothes, their jewels, their scandals, and their dinner-parties! The cultivated, aristocratic Frenchwoman, unmatchable in her calm superiority, wearing just the right amount of jewels, and her clothes never too chic. Beside her, her sisters of the Haute Bourgeoisie, affable and smiling. That glittering throng passes before me, as it did in reality thirty years ago. The recivimento is drawing to a close: down the great staircase they come, alone, in groups, and in couples. The women gather the folds of their evening wraps around them, the men their broadcloth coats with capes. Each settles his feathered, gold-braided hat upon his head (it never fits, because it is made to carry under the arm), swords are held to permit their wearers to move more easily. One by one the carriages enter the courtyard; there is an impatient stamping of horses' feet, the slamming of a door, a roll of wheels, and another group of figures has disappeared. At last all are gone. I hear my father giving a few final orders, I see the figure of my mother, silver-white, wearily descending the dimly lighted stairs. Sinking into a chair in her dressing-room, she cries, "Thank goodness, that's all over. Now I'm going to bed!"

Two days later a still larger company poured through the house in honor of the Fourth of July. After that the Ambassador found time to write to President McKinley.

Horace Porter to William McKinley

July 13th, 1897.

My dear Mr. President:

Knowing the vast number of letters you receive, I have not written you heretofore; but now that I have become fully installed and have got the "hang of the schoolhouse" in France, I venture to send you a few lines to give you a little news regarding your representative here which does not find its way into official despatches. My first five weeks were spent largely in getting through with my official receptions, exchanging official visits and house hunting. Apartments are plentiful, but as to separate houses appropriate for large entertainments one can say of them what Curran said of the books in his library: "Not numerous but select." I finally succeeded in leasing for a residence a house in the best quarter of Paris and the center of the American Colony which fulfils every requirement. The reception floor has a space more than half as large as the first floor of the White House, and its appointments are in keeping with its size. I managed to get into it in time to hold my official reception on the evening of the 3rd of July, which was attended by the Ministers of the Government and my Colleagues of the diplomatic corps with their families and by many prominent Americans. On July 5th to celebrate Independence Day I held a public reception in the afternoon to which all Americans in Paris were invited by notice in the newspapers and which was attended by about two thousand of our countrymen. I fortunately had a large picture of you and this, draped with the American flag, presented a patriotic feature of the occasion greatly enjoyed by people three thousand miles away from home.

President Faure creates a most favorable impression upon all who are interested in Republican institutions. He is a man of distinguished presence, extremely courteous in manner, possessed of great tact, unpretentious but not lacking in dignity, and understands the French people thoroughly. He has been excessively civil to me from the start, inviting my wife and me to his box at the Opéra, and at the races, to little theatrical entertainments and garden parties at the Palace, and always has much to say about our country and a great many interesting questions to ask about you personally, as to your hours of work, manner of receiving the public, method of dispatching business, etc. He speaks English a little but always prefers one to speak with him in French. . . .

Yours very sincerely,

HORACE PORTER.[9]

From the moment of my father's decision to go to France, I had been looking forward to the help that I should be able to give him. The French I had learned at school at Dobbs Ferry, I thought, equipped me for all emergencies in the life of an ambassador's daughter. (One knows so much at seventeen!) Such simple work as marking visiting cards or preparing lists I was able to do; but although I understood French perfectly, when it came to answering the most ordinary letter of social courtesy I was beyond my depth. I was therefore not long in making up my mind to go to a convent school where I should speak nothing but French and hear only the best. When I broached this idea to my mother, her Scotch Presbyterian blood rose in indignation; but my father approved, and in the end entered me at the Convent of the Assumption, Rue de Lubeck, where I was the only American scholar. I shall always be thankful for my experience there; it gave me an understanding of French ways, ideas, and character that I could not have got otherwise.

When Mother installed me, she had to choose between an unaired dormitory accommodating forty-five girls, and a room to myself in a new building across the garden. This house, as I found when I took up my abode in it, was occupied chiefly by the boarders,—elderly ladies who preferred a convent to an ordinary pension.

A great variety of prejudices and erroneous notions concerning my native land were represented in the convent. I am afraid I could not always resist the temptation to encourage some of these imaginings: one old lady pensionnaire, who was always harping to me on the wealth of Americans and the good uses we might put it to in French-African missions, used to get in reply shameless descriptions of the thousand-dollar bank notes that we pick up any day on Wall Street. Years before, when Father saw in Paris a performance of *Round the World in Eighty Days,* the population of New York was represented as consisting wholly of Indians and negroes; at the convent the idea was not dead yet. Another old lady cherished a peculiar dislike for Americans and did not hesitate to express for my benefit her conviction that our "mixed blood" could not but make us vulgar. I was sorry for her and one day took her some violets. I shall never forget how her look of suspicion faded. From that time on I went to see her almost every day, and spent many hours listening to her stories of the Paris of the Second Empire.

It was not only America that was misunderstood there. The attitude of the nuns, the pensionnaires, and almost all the pupils toward the entire world outside France was soon made clear by a hundred chance remarks. "Why should we travel?" they said. "Every one who can comes to Paris. If your country has beauty in it, too, why do you Americans risk your lives to cross the ocean every year?" Although Mother Marie Emelda had been ten years in the convent in England, she had never learned English. In our studies, whatever was connected with France in history, art, literature we learned in the most minute and interesting detail. Of the history, art, and literature of other countries we were given the merest smattering.

All the teaching was done by the nuns, from books revised by dignitaries of the Catholic Church, and it may be imagined that their presentation of history was not calculated to make their pupils firm believers in the government of the République Française. We heard a great deal about the glories of Le Roi Soleil and the virtues of Madame de Maintenon, but never a word about the untold miseries of the French peasant; of the crimes and horrors of the Revolution we were given detailed accounts, but little mention was made of the excesses and crimes of the old Régime which brought about that revolution. Lafayette was a traitor; Napoleon was a great man, though he had made the mistake of not putting back the Bourbons on their throne. We were never to forget that it was under the monarchy that France experienced the most glorious epochs in her history.

All these things and much more I poured out to Father as I came back to him week after week. My new leanings toward the monarchy, in particular, led us into many a Saturday evening discussion. Some of his trenchant sentences proved unforgettable. "Let the French be proud of their history, their literature, their art; no one disputes these. But no one can afford to refuse to see the good in others. A nation that will not try to understand other nations puts itself at a terrible disadvantage." And again: "Fine feathers don't always make fine birds. M. Faure

would look just as well in a periwig and cocked hat as most
of the courtiers of Louis XIV. . . . The young man who
is trying to become King of France is not fitted to be King
of Anything. . . . The world is marching toward democ-
racy. Some countries may keep their royal families, but the
government will be in the hands of men of the people."

So the winter passed. Then suddenly, one April morning, my peaceful life was brought to an end by the arrival
of my father. Circumstances launched me, as yet against
my will, into the fashionable life of the great capital. But
before I embark upon that story, which was a small incident
in one of the most important episodes of my father's career
as Ambassador, I must stop to tell something about the
Chancery and his labors there.

CHAPTER XV

AT THE CHANCERY

THE Embassy staff, as General Porter found it, consisted of two secretaries and a clerk. The first secretary, Henry Vignaud, was a Southerner who had come to Paris in the suite of John Slidell, the Commissioner appointed to represent the Confederacy at the court of Louis Napoleon. Stranded in Paris at the close of the Civil War, Vignaud eked out a living as a correspondent, and in time obtained a position in the United States Legation, where his devotion and ability had presently brought him to the top.

The most important of the successive occupants of the post of second secretary was Colonel A. Bailly-Blanchard, who, coming from New Orleans after the Civil War, had finished his education in Paris, becoming in the course of time, through his family connections, thoroughly versed in the intricacies of French society and politics. The value of his services at the Embassy and his devotion to General Porter can hardly be overestimated.[1] Later, when a third secretary was added, the office was filled successively by R. S. Reynolds Hitt, Peter Augustus Jay, recently Ambassador to Argentina, and Lewis Einstein, now Minister to Czecho-Slovakia. Other men connected with the Embassy for short periods during Porter's ambassadorship were T. Edgar Scott and Spencer Eddy. The military attaché at the Embassy was at first Major Sanford C. Kellogg; Captain (now Colonel) T. B. Mott, who came later, is still there. The naval attaché was Lieutenant (now Admiral) William S. Sims, whose keen mind and alertness were much valued by my father.

A passage from a letter recently written by one of the younger members of the staff throws light on the traditions of the Chancery as they were maintained by the first secretary.

"Vignaud would not allow a telephone to be installed . . . because we would be too much bothered. Also, incredible as it seems, all dispatches to Washington and notes to the Foreign office were sent in long hand, being copied by Biesel [the clerk], who had a beautiful copperplate handwriting.[2]

"Vignaud was a tremendous worker and liked to do everything himself and in his own way. He kept things so much to himself that I never knew what was going on, nor did I venture to see the Ambassador for the purpose of asking him. Things were different in these days and young men were less fresh. Once I screwed up my courage to ask General Porter for a short leave. He was, as always in his personal relations with me, most kind; but explained to me that all applications must be first approved by the First Secretary, who would then submit them with endorsement. I have often thought of this little incident, when I see the free and easy way our young secretaries nowadays carry on. A few months under General Porter and Mr. Vignaud would do them good."[3]

It thus appears that the new Ambassador did not disturb these old-fashioned ways if he could help it. Nevertheless, his military habit made it impossible for him not to take command, and his decisions were as clear-cut and positive as his attitude was considerate. Bailly-Blanchard in speaking of those days in Paris said: "For a time the General was the only Yankee in the camp; the rest of us were 'Rebs,' but there was nothing we wouldn't have done for him."

The Embassy was wretchedly understaffed, and from the time of his arrival Porter made appeals to the State Department for relief. In comparison with the five men allowed to the United States, Italy had eight, Turkey seven, England and Russia each thirteen, and Spain fifteen.[4]   When the State Department suggested a third secretary Porter replied that what was needed was a stenographer and typewriter,—a man who could speak and read French fluently. Nevertheless, the assistance when it came was in the form of a third secretary.

The following extract from a letter to the Secretary of State gives some idea of the variety of work that it fell to the officials of the Chancery to perform.

Horace Porter to John Hay

March 2nd, 1899.

. . . .

Besides the strictly official business, the work thrown upon this Embassy is exceedingly burdensome from the fact that there is every day a flood of demands personal and by mail from U. S. citizens regarding the coming Exposition, for information as to getting public documents, entering the French schools, opening new branches of trade, searches after imaginary estates left them, inquiries about decayed ancestors, admission on the part of visitors to see all the sights of Paris, etc., and before long there will be requests, no doubt, to sit down in the laps of public men and caress them for a reasonable length of time.   For the reputation of all concerned, these communications all received careful attention and answers.   It was for these reasons that I suggested a stenographer and typewriter familiar with both languages, if it should be found convenient some day in the course of things to squeeze out a small stipend for such purpose.

I agree fully with you that our system, established by Congress, of providing for the Diplomatic Corps will not be materially changed in our time, and in the present days of exceptionally large government expenditures it would not be prudent to attempt to make our Embassies size up in general equipment with those of other powers.   We are getting along pretty well just as we are. . . .

I am expecting a visit from Harris soon on his way to
Vienna. I have to play the rôle here of the St. Bernard
dogs of the Alps in looking out for passing travellers and
trying to warm them into life at my monastery, 33 rue de
Villejust. This recalls the remark of the ancient maiden
lady here: "I do so love those big Sarah Bernhardt dogs that
dig down in the snow and eat up those dear old monks." [5]

.   .   .   .

The Ambassador's initiation into the French method of
transacting affairs, with its formalities and red tape and its
long interruption in the middle of each day for lunch, came
in connection with the arrival in Paris, close upon his heels,
of the Commission appointed by President McKinley to
discuss with the governments of Europe the possibility of
adopting a bimetallic standard of currency. In personnel
the Commission was distinguished; it represented a sincere
effort on the part of the new Administration to study im-
partially and without delay the subject which had been the
cause of such prolonged and bitter controversy. Porter's
business was to arrange for the meetings, formal and informal, with the French government, and to temper as well
as he could his own impatience and that of his fellow-
countrymen at the unfamiliar procedure in which they found
themselves enmeshed. His comments on this point are
those of a newcomer: his philosophy soon taught him to
endure the inevitable with humor.

Horace Porter to William McKinley

July 13, 1897.

You have been advised as to the progress made here on
the subject of bimetallism. Senator Wolcott presented the
matter with signal ability to the officers of the Government. With him it is an all-absorbing question, and his
intense anxiety to press it and secure for it the "right of
way" at all times is quite natural and is evidence of his

ardent advocacy of the cause. Every possible assistance was given by the Embassy to further the object of this important mission. The methods of transacting official business here are distressingly slow, and it is impossible to hurry matters very much, however great the effort. I took a deep [interest] in the progress of the negotiations, not only on account of your instruction to that effect, but because I have been an avowed advocate of seeing a serious and geniune effort made to thoroughly test the question as to whether the principal European powers can be induced to unite with us and thus bring about the only possible means of securing bimetallism in a practical form. The French Ministry gave what I think is a genuine expression of its views in the paper shown to our Envoys and also to our Secretary of State through the French Ambassador at Washington. But here as with us there are too many who would have us believe that the short cut to bimetallism is free coinage of silver. The Ministry did not take public official action at this time for various reasons. We have to keep in mind always when judging the acts of a Ministry here that a vote of want of confidence in the Chamber of Deputies can end the term of the Ministers, and this fact naturally makes them hesitate to propose measures upon which the Deputies are divided and which might give rise to heated discussion and the result of which might be doubtful. Since the establishment of the Republic the duration of the Ministries has not averaged eight months. The present one has had the longest existence, over a year and a half, and it moves very cautiously in matters of grave importance. The more one sees of the want of stability in the Ministries here the more one appreciates the advantages of our own system of Government in this respect.[6]

One of his ambassadorial duties, as Porter soon found out, was to keep the State Department informed as to possible legislation concerning American exports. For a number of years French agricultural interests had been agitating against the entrance into the country of American meat products, and the laws which had been passed in consequence had proved very embarrassing to the Chicago packers. On this topic Porter had numerous conversations with the Minister of Foreign Affairs and sent home many dispatches; but since the subject is one which has little general interest at the present time, it is not worth going into here. There was only one aspect of the situation that had any fundamental concern for Porter: he cherished the idea, then and always, that America's need of getting hogs into France might some time induce her to admit light French wines practically free of duty. He believed that one of the best things that could happen to his fellow countrymen would be to substitute light wines and beer for the cocktail, which he looked upon as nothing short of poison. A reciprocal commercial agreement which was made at this period did much to establish better relations between the two countries; but as the negotiations were conducted in Washington, the work of Porter and his staff was confined to the supplying of information.

CHAPTER XVI

FRANCO-AMERICAN CRISIS

WHEN my father appeared at the convent that April morning in 1898, it was to tell me that he was to give a big official dinner in the evening, that Mother was ill,—she was subject to trouble with her heart,—and that I must come home and take her place. As we drove off he answered all my questions and settled all my objections with the utmost speed and firmness. No, considering the international situation, it was not possible to postpone the dinner; certainly, I should have to sit between the President of the Senate and the Minister of Foreign Affairs; yes, he would take me at once to see Paquin and would make him have my new evening dress ready in time even if the embroidery had to be pinned on. When I appeared at dinner as a full fledged young lady he told me to my great delight that I reminded him of Mother at West Point; in my innocence, my self-satisfaction was further increased by praises of my French from M. Hanotaux, the Minister of Foreign Affairs. He was slender, of medium height, with all the subtleness and keen understanding of his nation. By his charming manner and witty conversation he put me immediately at my ease. M. Loubet, however, had no small-talk, and with both gentlemen I naturally felt my youth more and more as the dinner went on. In my nervousness I parted with one of my slippers, and my efforts to get it back and to walk into the drawing-room with it only half on would have been a tragedy if it had not been for M. Hanotaux. He saw my predicament and, gravely standing for a moment between me and the others, let me balance myself on his arm while I got the slipper into place.

The serious international situation which called a young girl from a convent to preside at a State dinner was brought about by the excitement in France on the outbreak of the Spanish-American War. The words of President McKinley which my father had so deeply pondered as he crossed the Atlantic proved true to the letter. When he began his service, the United States, hitherto an outsider in world affairs, already stood upon the threshold. Cleveland's action at the time of the Venezuela difficulty in 1895-96 had given notice of the arrival of the stranger, but the announcement had been little heeded. Busy with their own concerns in Africa and Asia,[1] acquiring "spheres of influence," strengthening themselves by alliances against enemies real or potential, and guided by statesmen who were either controlled by militaristic aims or dependent upon the support of an uncertain majority in a representative body, the European powers ignored the existence of an external force which might disturb their plots and counterplots. The arts of diplomacy and the long-tried devices of the Foreign Offices could, they believed, be trusted to control any crisis that might arise. Then the outsider knocked at the door.

A satisfactory adjustment of the Cuban question was one of the hopes of McKinley, and he chose General Stewart L. Woodford as Minister to Spain in the belief that his skill as a negotiator would accomplish everything that could be done to prevent war. General Woodford, on his way to Madrid, stopped in London and in Paris to get the benefit of whatever information and advice Hay and Porter might be able to give him. At Paris he met also Andrew D. White, our Ambassador to Germany, who had been directed by the State Department to come there to confer with him. General Porter, in writing to Secretary Sherman, leaves to General Woodford the duty of reporting on the main subject of discussion, but he has something to say about the state of things in France.

Horace Porter to John Sherman

August 19, 1897.

.   .   .   .

There have been some persons at work for some time trying to create a sentimental sympathy for Spain, looking to some sort of an understanding between the countries which would strengthen both, but the effort has made no progress, and will not be revived. When Spain made an attempt last year to have the European powers unite in a protest against the contemplated action of the United States in favor of the Cubans, members of the French Government did not favor such action and behaved in a very friendly manner to us. Frenchmen have a large ownership in Spanish railways and in Spain's national debt, the total of which is about $2,000,000,000 at this time. France bought nearly all the bonds which were taken outside of Spain, namely about $400,000,000. The people owning these securities watch with much anxiety Spanish affairs and will naturally exert all the influence they possess to so shape action on the part of France as to protect their interests; but I find shrewd men realize that if the Cuban war goes on very much longer the resources of Spain will be so crippled that the debt holders will suffer serious loss, while if Spain lets Cuba go, stops the enormous expenditure of men and money incurred in conducting the present struggle, and devotes her energies to developing her resources at home and her possessions in Africa, there will be a prospect for the creditors to get a better price for the securities they hold, which are much depressed in value. Canovas, whose dastardly assassination touched all our sympathies, was regarded by the most influential Frenchmen as the only real statesman Spain possessed, and there is never much disposition on the part of a nation to entangle itself with the affairs of a country which has neither statesmen nor money. I feel for these reasons and as the general result of most careful investigation of the whole subject that France would not only not commit any overt act in behalf of Spain, but that she has no disposition in her present

temper to enter any formal protest against such action as
the United States may be compelled to take to put a stop to
the disastrous Cuban war.[2]

These official utterances may be supplemented by Porter's
personal opinion as expressed to his friend, Cornelius N.
Bliss, then Secretary of the Interior.

If we ever get this infernal Cuban question settled we
shall have some peace and quiet. It is perfectly absurd that
Spain, with 200,000 regular troops, cannot handle 30,000
insurgents, and it is the best proof that Cuba will some day
be free in spite of everything. The Administration has
shown great patience, which is wise.[3]

Through the fall and winter General Porter's part was
no more than that which an Ambassador does as second
nature—that is, to keep himself in touch with sources of
information on which he may rely when the need comes.
With the outbreak of hostilities, however, he had, in addition to this duty, which he described as "keeping tabs, day
and night," the task of presenting to the French Government, through its Minister of Foreign Affairs, Gabriel
Hanotaux, the case of the United States and urging the
observance of strict neutrality on the part of France. Besides influencing the Government, he must do what he could
to get a favorable hearing for his country in the Paris press,
a considerable part of which was unfriendly, and, in the
right quarters, to stress the fact of Spain's financial weakness.

Hanotaux had been Minister of Foreign Affairs for an
unusually long period, having held office, except for a few
months, since May, 1894. He was guiding French diplomacy with the aim of improving the position of his country
among the European nations and of extending her colonial
empire. The strengthening of the Franco-Russian alliance
was the result of the first point of his policy; the clash with

GABRIEL HANOTAUX

Great Britain at Fashoda in 1898 put a check for the time being to French colonial expansion in Africa.

Whatever may have been Hanotaux's feeling before the war about the merits of the controversy between Spain and the United States, he has recently borne witness to the course of action pursued by the American Ambassador at this crisis: he displayed, says the Minister of Foreign Affairs, "sound judgment and friendly good sense." "Systematic work" was the American's own phrase in describing his method. The French minister was for many reasons in a difficult position. Spain was importunate, his own people were for a time in a high state of excitement, both over the war and over the Dreyfus affair, which latter, indeed, presently contributed to the downfall of the ministry of which Hanotaux was a part.[4] The wishes of some of the continental powers to take advantage of the situation in the Philippines and their inability to do so from fear either of each other or of the United States, appear in dispatches printed in *Die Grosse Politik der Europäischen Kabinette*.[5] One proposal, considered by the Kaiser, was the neutralizing of the islands. Another plan, proposed by Spain, was the joint occupation of Manila by the powers; this scheme, Hanotaux had to point out, would be a violation of neutrality.[6] Above all, as both Hanotaux and Porter soon found out, the delicacy of the situation lay in the irresponsible journalists who, controlled by motives with the results of which the world to-day is all too familiar, saw in the crisis nothing but an opportunity to stir up national antagonism and to increase the sale of their papers. Thanks to the courtesy of M. Hanotaux, it is possible to present here an authoritative statement of the course of action taken in the premises by the French Government. This communication, dated 27 July, 1925, he calls *Le Général Porter et l'Affaire de Cuba*.

I had had no reason to be anything but pleased, in every respect, with my relations with the General; and the relations existing between our two countries were equally satisfactory.

On the other hand, the proximity of France to Spain created a feeling of friendship and good will here toward the neighboring kingdom.

France had no special interest involved in the Cuban affair. Her position was therefore naturally one of neutrality, and that was the position which she at once adopted by official declaration.

We were having at the time rather serious difficulties with England in regard to colonial policy. If I remember right, Mr. Chamberlain, the elder, was close to Lord Salisbury in the government, and he was not averse to making some arrangements on a basis of understanding with Germany. It was a pretty strained period, though there was no definite crisis in general European affairs.

We were much astonished in France when suddenly, after hostilities had broken out between Spain and the United States, there began, in the English press first and immediately afterward in the American press, a campaign asserting that French opinion was favorable to Spain and hostile to the United States and that France was intervening to help Spain in the struggle. The German press played the part of chorus, and energetically fanned the spark.

The situation soon became inflamed, as if by poison; or rather, gossip inflamed it. Every day new stories [*canards*] made their appearance. People told, in all seriousness, both in Europe and America, how Americans were being molested in Paris, how there had been scenes of violence in shops on the Rue de la Paix. Finally it was said that France was furnishing arms to Spain, that she was helping her in every way, and that she was taking this stand in order to protect her own interests.

Things came to such a pass that, as Minister of Foreign Affairs, I had to devote ceaseless attention to this singular press campaign, which was made up out of whole cloth. I saw plainly that it was of European origin, without being able to decide just what was its actual source, and I could only regret to see the American press let itself be carried away by it without my being able to counteract it.[7]

Feeling that the state of the public mind, which in America was in an unnatural condition of excitement on account of the war, might let itself be swept into some dangerous act, I kept myself constantly on the lookout; and well it was that I did so. For, on one occasion during the war, which was, of course, very short, while I was going every evening to superintend myself the arrival and translation of dispatches, I received a telegram from one of our consuls warning me that someone had just informed him of the presence, on board a French vessel,—the *Jemappes,* I think, —of a consignment of arms and munitions destined for the Spanish army in Cuba and that orders had been given to the American naval authorities to seize this French boat. The affair of the *Maine* was very recent; serious consequences might follow, if such a complication as this, which had no foundation in fact, had any sort of sequel that touched the national honor. I knew positively that this supposed information was absolutely false and trumped-up,—which shows how one must be on one's guard against the famous "press rumors." And so, even before going to bed, and without waiting for the opening of the offices next morning (for it would have been too late) I sent immediately the telegrams necessary to prevent the occurrence of an incident of "search" or the like. The boat was turned from her route, explanations which could leave no doubt in people's minds were exchanged with the American authorities; and this sham incident, like that of the Americans molested in the shops on the Rue de la Paix, fell of its own accord.

I hardly need to add that during this critical period,— which was more important and more dangerous than one can imagine so long afterwards,—I kept myself in daily touch with General Porter. I answered with the greatest directness and sincerity the questions that he asked me;[8] and he, on the other hand, in dealing with his government and his friends, always supported me in my efforts to ascertain the exact truth. He knew perfectly that there was nothing *underneath,* in the policy of France toward the United States; or rather, if there was anything underneath, it was all sympathy and cordiality. At one moment it was possible to conceive the idea of arbitration by Pope Leo

XIII, to which I think the United States would have agreed, but which the Spanish government then in power had not the wisdom to accept. All along, through the confidence and sympathy which existed between the Minister of Foreign Affairs and the Ambassador, all difficulties were smoothed away: we were on the point of reaching a road toward mediation to put an end to the war, when the cabinet of which I was a member fell; but this same conciliatory policy, continuing between General Porter and my successor, furnished grounds for the negotiations which ended the war and in which the French Ambassador [to the United States], M. Jules Cambon, performed a friendly act acknowledged by both sides.

I have had in view especially, in this short account, the part played by General Porter during the serious Cuban incident; no one contributed more than he, if I may trust my memory, to maintaining and strengthening cordial relations between France and the United States. These relations then expressed themselves by other important acts: the United States was the first power that recognized the protectorate of France over Madagascar, and this recognition had great influence in the general settlement of the question which was then dividing France and England. Presently a commercial *modus-vivendi* was concluded between France and the United States, and the better economic relations did much for good political relations. . . .

From that time on the sky, so to speak, became clear. And so, when I think about that delicate episode,—which now belongs to history,—I always remember with real feeling the qualities of mind, sound judgment, and friendly good sense which were shown throughout by the admirable and loyal ambassador, General Porter.

Porter's dispatches to Washington throughout the spring and summer reflect the constant occupation of his mind, and they have the further value that they relate the Spanish-American War to the general European situation as he saw it. To the powers, it appears, the struggle became of vital moment when, with Dewey's arrival in Manila, it threat-

ened to interfere with their quiet plundering of China.   As
Hanotaux's memorandum indicates, indeed, they would have
been glad to help in bringing the war to an end, for the purpose of their own protection, if not for direct advantage.
Hence the wisdom of the State Department in insisting that
the preliminary negotiations be carried on at Washington.
All this makes the first page of a brilliant period in which
the high aims and bold leadership of the New World diplomacy stand out in striking contrast to the confusion of purpose, the jealousy and the greed that characterized the governments of the Old World in their international dealings.

Our Ambassador's dispatches follow.   They touch on
familiar ground and require only such comment as is necessary to clear up minor obscurities.

Horace Porter to John Sherman

April 8, 1898.

. . . There is a great dread expressed of a war [9] between
the United States and Spain and a very exaggerated view
taken of its magnitude and   consequences to general commerce, and vague fears are expressed that in some unanticipated way, war may become contagious and lead to other
nations appealing to the arbitrement of the sword in settling
the many delicate and grave questions which are arising
between European Powers in reference to proceedings in
Africa and Asia.

Notwithstanding the very ardent desire here to prevent
hostilities and the appeals made by the Press in that interest,
I cannot learn that any European country has been con-
templating any action at this time regarding the Cuban
question except the mild note of the foreign Ambassadors at
Washington which was presented to the President yesterday.[2]

The reference in the next letter to ill-feeling in Paris
against Americans recalls the fact that at the outbreak of
war the French Government promptly placed a guard at

the door of the American Embassy, which guard the Ambassador with equal promptness sent away.

Horace Porter to William R. Day [10]

Confidential

May 24, 1898.

I am in receipt of your letter of May 8th in reference to the tone of the French press regarding the present war and asking whether measures can be taken to change it.

There has been so much loose talk lately about the sentiment here that I have been on the eve of writing you the exact state of things, but have always been delayed because the conditions change rapidly even from day to day and it is difficult to write a circumstantial account which would be up to date when it reached Washington. I have given the subject constant attention and have taken some steps which have already resulted in good.

When the war was certain to be declared I had very full interviews with officers of the French Government and early received assurances that everything would be done to preserve in all respects a strict and impartial neutrality and there has been no departure from this attitude, the Minister of Foreign Affairs taking pains to treat me with entire frankness, answer communications promptly, give me all information in his possession and to deplore the attitude of the many journals which have been so pronounced in the expressions of their sympathy for Spain. I have in my conferences warned the government in very positive terms that the action of certain elements here adverse to the United States might result in endangering our commercial negotiations, changing the current of trade with France and diverting it elsewhere, putting in jeopardy our contemplated representation at the Exhibition of 1900 and fostering an alliance with their hereditary enemy, Great Britain. The government, which has always been apparently friendly, is now thoroughly alive to this state of things and is anxious to change the tone of what would seem to be public sentiment. They say with truth that the Paris press does not represent the government nor the mass of the people. The Royalists who have a strong voice in the higher society of Paris naturally side with the Spanish monarchy. They dislike the Republican Government of France and look with horror upon another Republic in Cuba. The society journals which cater to this element express a pronounced sympathy with the Spaniards. The bankers, who are interested in Spanish bonds and enterprises, and the papers influenced by them are generally inimical to the United States. The radical clericals make common cause to a large extent with Spain, the most prominent of Roman Catholic countries. These elements have a voice, while the great mass of the French people who are friendly or at least not unfriendly to the United States have no means of giving public expression to their feelings.

Some are influenced stupidly by a fear that the United States, after finishing with Cuba, will at once seize upon all French Colonies in the new world. They overlook the pledges of our government not to take an ownership in Cuba and our history as a non-annexation people.

The race question has not much to do with the matter. The French consider themselves a pure race and superior to a nation composed of Latins, Moors and Arabs.

The claim of England that an Anglo-Saxon Alliance is to be formed to menace and hold in control the acts of European powers has considerable weight with the more impressionable element in France and has greatly excited many of the people.

The natural retaliation on the part of our American journals has added to the crimination and recrimination in the press. After the totally unexpected result, to people in Europe, at Manila,[11] the general opinion began to change very perceptibly. Another victory will speak more eloquently than any newspaper articles.

The government has exerted a good influence in certain quarters. I got at least three articles on our side inserted in one of the most inimical of the Paris papers. The Temps, one of the most serious journals, now has some very excellent articles entirely fair to us. Many of the papers are somewhat neutral, and the six or eight radical Republican and Socialist papers are waging daily warfare against Spain.

Many of the leading merchants are now coming forward and protesting against the action of the press, which is having an adverse effect upon their trade, and because they are really friendly to America. I have urged the correspondents here of several American papers not to exaggerate the state of things and widen the breach, and they are now reporting that there is a change here for the better. As a sign of this change, I may mention that at a large theatre the other evening a very popular actrice introduced a sentence about those "ill-mannered Americans," thinking to catch applause, but there was a dead silence, and a look of disgust on the faces of the audience, and I am told the words have not been repeated.

The rumors of "boycotting" of Americans in France and offensive remarks made to them in French society are without foundation. The members of this Embassy have encountered no such experiences in any quarter and Americans, generally, notwithstanding the fact that the sympathies of so many are against them, do not find any difference in their treatment except in some cases where a heated discussion is brought about, when the language used becomes a little "peppery" on both sides. It is generally believed that Spain subsidizes some of the papers here. They certainly give great space to her cause. I have let it be known from the start that this Embassy has no funds for such a purpose. When persons are seeking that kind of aid and think such methods are practiced they are sure to make persistent attacks in order that funds may be employed to stop them. I would not recommend subsidizing any papers, but as facts are expensive to obtain and as papers here do not have a great amount of advertising, an important item of revenue, they cannot spend the money our papers use in getting full and important news from a distance. I think some skilful writers might be employed to advantage to obtain useful facts, prepare solid arguments, represent our side of the case, interview tradesmen and others, and arrange to get their articles published wherever opportunity occurs in a manner to reach the thinking public. If you approve of this and will place four or five thousand dollars at the disposal of the Embassy I will see that so much as may be necessary shall be used very cautiously and economically.

If the war ends soon all this forced and sentimental expression of sympathy for Spain will disappear and be looked back upon as a nine days' wonder.

I trust our people will not prevent our merchants and manufacturers and farmers from being represented at the Exposition of 1900, not on account of France, but in their own interest, for I am convinced that the effects of an important exhibit here will increase very largely the American export trade to all Europe, for all Europe will attend and have an opportunity to see and admire our superior productions.[12]

Horace Porter to William R. Day

June 7, 1898.

M. Hanotaux has, several times, as I have before intimated, expressed a desire to assist in maintaining and, since the outbreak of the war, restoring peace, provided that he could feel that the United States do not object to having him use his good offices in this direction, and would not misinterpret his motives, for he knows very well that any act which might seem officious on the part of a European statesman might defeat the end in view. He has had a long conversation with me again on this subject, which he distinctly stated was confidential, personal and not official, and which he desires should be so treated.

His relations are very close with the Spanish Ambassador here, who is a man of ability, has always been desirous of peace, and possesses the entire confidence of his Government. M. Hanotaux is, I feel certain, the person whom Spain would trust rather than any other statesman in Europe to bring about negotiations for peace. His relations with me are so intimate that he talks with the utmost frankness upon every phase of the question.

He is earnestly desirous of peace for several reasons. He

regrets the animosity which has been engendered between the Americans and the French, and sincerely wants the friendship of our country, and fears that it might be weakened by a continuance of the war, and as wars are contagious, that it might possibly start a conflict among the European nations. He sees that a continuance of hostilities will further depress the Spanish bonds held by Frenchmen, who have already lost enormously, and that each day's delay is making matters worse in this respect and also having an injurious effect upon French commerce. His information leads him to believe that the Spaniards are determined to fight to the bitter end unless some pressure be brought upon them by friendly parties outside of Spain, and he would gladly feel her upon the subject of peace if some feasible terms could be suggested which would in any measure help to break her fall, and make the present Government feel that it could make peace without being overthrown.

He started with an idea of this kind: a general election based on manhood suffrage to be held in Cuba, surrounded by all the safeguards practicable to ensure a safe count of the votes, to decide by a majority vote what form of Government should be adopted, and coupled with this, an assumption by the new Government of the Spanish obligations known as Cuban bonds, or such part of them as might be agreed upon, the United States possibly to guarantee these bonds, or bonds issued in lieu of them bearing a lower rate of interest, the United States to release the Philippine Islands.

He has in mind the loans or guarantees of loans which have been made at different times by the great powers of Europe to smaller states for the purpose of preserving the peace, in the belief that this is a method much cheaper and more humane than suffering wars to occur or continue.

I suggested that before any fair vote could be taken it would be necessary to remove all the Spanish troops and civil officers from Cuba, which would take several months with Spain's means of ocean transportation; that there would be many details to consider before a ballot could be framed which would express, when voted, the precise form of Government which was to be adopted, and that with the unfamiliarity of the people with the ballot and the lack of good communications on the island, there would have to be a very comprehensive organization perfected in order to insure a perfectly fair and satisfactory result, and that the carrying out of any such detail could not be made a condition precedent to a declaration of peace.

It could be taken for granted, however, that Cuba once being free, free suffrage would prevail there and that generally speaking, she would establish a government in which all powers would be derived from the consent of the governed.

The suggestion that the people, by a general vote, decide upon the form of Government comes, I think, from Spanish officials, thinking it would look like some concession however unsubstantiated with which the Ministry could go before their people in consenting to peace.

Regarding a guarantee of obligations, I said that, as we did not expect to take possession of Cuba or establish a Protectorate, we could not be expected to assume any debts, although looking at the subject in a pecuniary light it might be considerably cheaper than to continue the war. I said Spain knows very well that she can stop hostilities at once by abandoning entirely Cuba, and at the same time get rid of the enormous drain which that island has been upon her treasury, and save the ruinous expenses of war; but that if the United States have to make further sacrifices the terms of peace will naturally become more exacting. I explained clearly that I had had no communication with my Government on this branch of the subject and was not authorized to act in the matter, but that if he could ascertain from Spain by means of his relations any practicable terms upon which that country would conclude peace, I would inquire whether it would be possible for my country to entertain them. But it is evident that Spain is waiting to receive some intimation from us as to the terms which would in some measure sugar coat the pill she will be obliged to swallow—the relinquishing of Cuba—and could be used as a basis for opening negotiations looking to peace.

I have been particularly guarded, at all times, in avoiding everything that could lead to any meddling in this affair by persons in Europe. However, this suggestion of M. Hanotaux is not with a view to meddling, and I am sure that it is an earnest effort actuated very naturally by the motives herein above mentioned, and I therefore report it to show that there is a channel open in that direction, and one which could the most readily be availed of. If our Government is prepared to let any suggestion reach Spain by this indirect means and will communicate it to me, I shall use it discreetly with a view to having it urged upon the Spanish Ministry and calling forth some action on their part. I could make the suggestion as if on my own personal responsibility, if so desired. In view of the nature of this despatch, I ask that it be treated as confidential.[2]

Horace Porter to William R. Day

June 10, 1898.

There is an increased disposition every day on the part of the diplomatists of Europe to bring about an end of the war, but the impression prevails generally at this moment that these efforts should be directed to bringing a pressure upon Spain to make peace and not to attempt to dictate terms to either party. A prominent bishop here wrote to the Pope recently urging this view. I have many reasons to believe that a visit just made to Paris by the Austrian Ambassador in London was for the purpose of conferring with Spaniards here and assisting in this direction.

The dominant question with the European powers is still the occupation of territory in China. At first I found that this matter was so prominent in their minds that they were inclined to look upon our war as a matter of little importance relatively. Since our decision, however, to send troops to the Philippines and the impression that we may retain possession of those islands, the representative diplomatists are apprehensive that this may still further complicate the Eastern Question, and they are growing very anxious to see the war ended and a decision reached about the Philippines. Suggestions are made that it would avoid all possible complications if the United States would take possession of Cuba and possibly Porto Rico and release the Philippines. They do not seem to understand that we do not want Cuba.

I am still unable to see any disposition on the part of the European powers to take joint action of any kind, but it looks as if France and Austria would bring their influence to bear upon Spain to make peace at the earliest possible day. It has been suggested to the Spaniards that it would be a great advantage to make peace before the destruction of their fleet at Santiago,[13] but we are moving so rapidly in that direction that it is not at all likely that any steps will be taken early enough to save that fleet. I am watching movements here very closely and if anything of a definite nature occurs, I will, of course, cable you.[2]

Horace Porter to William R. Day

(Cipher Cable)

June 13, 1898.

In my confidential letter of the 7th instant, by English mail, I fully explain the wish of M. Hanotaux (Minister for Foreign Affairs) to bring about treaty of peace, and his willingness to lend himself unofficially, and in a friendly manner to any desired action which may lead to that result. He now says he can place the Ambassador here in contact with Madrid (?) if I am authorized to talk with him on the subject.

He supposes an armistice (?) will be suggested or asked as a means of opening negotiations,—but that of course cannot be conceded now. Spain, he believes, is ready for making peace now, when she may still save something.

After reading my letter, please telegraph me if I can consent to see the Spanish Ambassador, and how far (?) I can go in discussing the subject with him, without making any committal.[2]

William R. Day to Horace Porter

(Telegram received June 18, 1898.)

Your letter of the seventh, your cipher telegram of the thirteenth have been received. The President cannot directly or mediately make proposals for peace. Action on our part in the direction of indicating terms of settlement would be premature and liable to misinterpretation. We can under no circumstances permit ourselves to be put in the position to be obligated by any arrangement made abroad or to admit European intervention in any form. If the Spanish Ambassador seeks an interview and he has authority from Spanish Government to negotiate for peace the President has no objection to your receiving his proposals for transmission hither and consideration by the President. In the meantime conversation in a quarter as to possible contingencies and terms of peace should be avoided because any utterances by you may be misunderstood.[2]

Horace Porter to William R. Day

June 20, 1898.

I received your cable of the 17th, and in accordance with its instructions I shall telegraph you in case the Spanish Ambassador seeks an interview with me and presents by authority of his Government any proposition for peace.

I had anticipated the view you would very naturally take regarding any suggestions from our side looking to peace when in the personal talk M. Hanotaux had with me, I used the following language (I quote from my despatch to you reciting that conversation) : "I explained clearly that I had no communication with my Government on this branch of the subject and was not authorized to act in the matter but that if he could ascertain from Spain by means of his relations, any practicable terms upon which that country would conclude peace, I would ascertain whether it would be possible for my country to entertain them."

As I mentioned, the talk with M. Hanotaux was purely personal, merely that of two individuals not entrusted in any manner with matters relating to Spain.   He was very emphatic in repeating that he was not talking in an official capacity, and indeed, a ministerial crisis was then threatened which it was thought would soon lead to his retirement from office,—an event which has since taken place.   I reported the conversation in some detail, largely for the purpose of giving you the nature of certain ideas which are entertained here and to show the vague notions which still exist as to the true attitude of our country in this war and the practical conditions which might form the basis of a peace.

While I am keeping in close contact with my Colleagues here and others who are generally well advised as to the views of neutral Governments in order to learn, if possible, any contemplated action in any quarter which might be of interest to us, you can rest assured that no views will be put forth by me except in the strictest compliance with such instructions as you may send me.[2]

Horace Porter to E. A. Hitchcock *

Confidential

June 26, 1898.

. . . Spain has made the most urgent efforts to have the powers intervene in her behalf, but in this part of Europe there has been no such thing seriously contemplated, and she now seems to have abandoned all hope in that direction.   She has failed, up to this time, after an earnest effort, to raise money here by a sale of her tobacco monopoly, and her financial condition is very serious.   There was a disposition shown here for some weeks, by parties who do not represent the Government or the people, to sow dissensions and break up the traditional friendship between our country and France, but this has been successfully counteracted, and peace reigns here.[12]

* Ambassador to Russia.

Horace Porter to William R. Day

June 29, 1898.

During a visit to M. Hanotaux yesterday for the purpose of bidding him goodbye officially upon his retirement from his position as Minister of Foreign Affairs, I asked him to tell me frankly whether there had been any substantial foundation for the rumors several times circulated in Europe that some of the Powers had been in communication with France, with reference to combined measures looking to mediation or interference in the present war. He assured me emphatically and without reserve that there had been no such communication whatever, that no such suggestion had been received by France, and that France had never made any such suggestion to other powers, or entertained any such ideas, and that he felt that the policy of his country was definitely settled to observe a strict and impartial neutrality. He has every reason to believe that the same may be said as to Russia, and the relations of these two powers are so close that each generally knows what the other is doing.

This is only a more full and emphatic declaration of what he has said to me several times before.[2]

Horace Porter to William R. Day

July 1, 1898.

I have seen today a French gentleman, a private citizen, who has just returned from a visit to Madrid and who related to me some interviews he had had with Sagasta, Gamazo and Moret. I have confidence in his intelligence and think his truthfulness can be trusted. He says the view expressed by each was that he was decidedly in favor of an early peace, but that he feared it could not be brought about before a crisis was reached at Santiago and that there was great reluctance as to making peace overtures *directly* to the United States Government. My informant says that

the peace party was evidently making progress in Spain
until the news was received that a fleet was to attack her
coasts, but that now the war party is regaining some of its
lost ground, by calling on the people to defend their homes
and firesides, and making them believe that European
powers will intervene in their behalf if America attempts
to occupy any European territory or bombards a European
port.

Several rumors which have come from Spain in the last
few days corroborate this statement. There was no design
in my informant giving me this account of his visit to
Madrid. It was said in a casual conversation and brought
out by questions from me. I forward it for what it is
worth.[2]

On July 1-3 occurred the fighting about Santiago; on
July 3, Cervera's fleet, in attempting to escape from Santiago Harbor, was destroyed.

Horace Porter to William R. Day

(Telegram)

July 8, 1898.

I am indirectly informed confidentially that the Spanish
Ambassador again wishes conference with me to discuss
conditions of peace and negotiate therefor by authority of his
Government which is desirous of ending war but thinks it is
the place of the victor to name his terms. As I am satisfied he is not prepared to make a proposal for submission,
I am avoiding a meeting and all discussion.[2]

Horace Porter to William R. Day

July 13, 1898.

As Paris is the city in closest communication socially and
financially with Madrid, and as I have several good sources
of information, *one entirely trustworthy* as to the actions of

the Spanish Ministry, it may interest you to know the result of my present knowledge though I do not deem it of enough immediate importance to telegraph you. Last week, after the annihilation of Cervera's fleet, the Sagasta Ministry, and especially the Queen Regent were extremely anxious to open negotiations for peace, first, because of the expected fall of Santiago, and secondly, on account of the approach of a ministerial crisis which would bring into power, in all probability, a representation of the military element and make it more difficult for the Queen to conduct negotiations.

They evidently thought at one time last week of making a proposal simply to abandon Cuba, but probably deeming that futile, they reached the opinion that they could afford, in addition, to admit the principle of an indemnity, and having no money and no means of raising any, to offer to surrender to the United States either the Philippines or Porto Rico; but it was deemed more advantageous for them to let us keep the Philippines than to turn over Porto Rico, as it would be difficult to control the large population, in great part in insurrection, and especially as Spain has no adequate fleet left, while Porto Rico has a quiet and much smaller population, is easily governed, and would still leave Spain a foothold in the Antilles. They hoped to retain all the rest of their colonies.

This seems to have been the utmost limit to which any of the Cabinet would go, and it is not certain that a majority committed themselves to these terms. Just then it became evident that the ministerial crisis had been reached, and the decision to form a new Ministry, but with Sagasta still at the head, was made public yesterday. The question will now come up anew. Spain's great desire unquestionably has been to endeavor to get the United States to "speak first" in making a proposal as to terms of peace, though I doubt whether at heart she has any real hope that any such action would ever be taken by our Government.

Nearly all the newspapers in France are now urging her to try to make peace immediately on the ground that she is whipped and comparatively helpless. Some of the articles are strong and logical and have had an effect in Madrid.[2]

On July 17 Santiago surrendered, and within twenty-four hours Spain requested the French Ambassador at Washington to obtain a statement of the terms on which the United States Government would conclude peace. From this moment Porter had no further part to play. The preliminary negotiations were carried on at Washington, and there, on August 12, the protocol was signed. It provided for the immediate evacuation of Cuba by Spain, and for the meeting of Commissioners in Paris on October 1 to draw up the formal treaty. The reader who has followed the story of Porter's work at his own post of duty will appreciate the force of his praise of the men who had been leaders at Washington.

Horace Porter to Mark Hanna

August 2, 1898.

Now that this "cruel war is over," or nearly so, and you will have time to read letters, let me say how much we appreciate, on this side of the water, the work accomplished by our friends at home. Some of the measures before the Senate looked impossible of accomplishment at times, but you worked them all through. No war in history has accomplished so much in so short a time and with so little loss. If the President stands a head and shoulders above everybody at home, he has come to be looked upon by able men in Europe as the leading statesman of the day. Nothing is so successful as success, and people are everywhere lifting their hats a little higher than usual to Americans.

The anti-republican press in France criticized our Republic nearly as much as it criticizes this Republic, and for some weeks it was annoying; but the Government behaved well throughout, and by dint of systematic work we got the press turned round far enough to be fair in most of their articles. Many papers have been with us heartily from the start, but their articles are never quoted at home. I never heard of Americans in Paris being called hogs, insulted in theatres, threatened in the streets, and snubbed in society, and their custom refused in stores till I read the interview of Chauncey Depew, that great teacher of the American public. He learns this all in five days in Paris! . . .

I am very glad for the sake of our trade that you passed the French Exposition bill. We ought by a good exhibit here to increase our exports largely.

We have been keeping tabs day and night on movements in Spain, and the information sent from this Embassy regarding every act has been complete down to the smallest details. This work is now about to be ended. I hope you will get a good rest this fall and come back to Washington well braced up for the next session. . . .[12]

Horace Porter to William McKinley

September 6, 1898.

Now that you are able to take some well-earned rest and may have a spare moment to read personal letters, I wish to express to you my cordial congratulations upon the matchless success you have achieved for America by the short, sharp, and decisive war which the whole world fully understands was conducted directly by you. The result is everywhere felt by us abroad, as hats are raised considerably higher than ever to Americans and the power of our country and the great qualities of our people have been impressed upon other nations as never before. If some people are cavilling about the want of perfection in the administration of some Departments during the hurried organization of improvised armies, they resemble those who spend their time in criticizing the spots on the sun instead of praising the light it sheds and the warmth it bestows. The negotiations for the cessation of hostilities took the shape which I believed they would finally assume, and all diplomatists are loud in praise of the prompt and thoroughly admirable manner in which they were conducted. They took place, so far as our country was concerned, at just

about the right time. The French are immensely pleased
with the idea of so important a body as the Peace Commission meeting in their Capital. They will do everything to
make it socially agreeable for the Commissioners, and there
is an openly expressed intention on the part of the French
Ministry not to make any suggestions or do anything directly or indirectly which might have even the appearance
of giving any promptings to those engaged in the negotiations.

The final disposition of the Philippines naturally occasions much anxiety in European diplomatic circles. There
is a growing belief that if the United States should control
all the islands, while it would be a gigantic task to undertake, it would be the most likely means of preventing the
great powers of Europe from coming into collision over the
question of "island-grabbing," which most people think
would be begun by Germany and followed by the others
in case any portion of the islands were left in weak hands.
However, we shall no doubt be governed by what we want
to do ourselves and not by what others want us to do. You
have appointed peace commissioners so able as to defy
criticism, and I feel sure that their work will be well done.
I shall be delighted to welcome them to Paris and to extend to them every assistance which it may be in the power
of the Embassy to render. The information conveyed in
my despatches at the outset of the war and afterwards,
that there would be no attempt whatever on the part of
European powers to interfere with us, has been fully
verified.

There is a general rejoicing in the American diplomatic
corps over the appointment of Colonel Hay,[14] since it has
lost as its chief Mr. Day, whom everyone had learned to
admire. The appointment is an ideal one, and with his
large experience, rare qualities, and absolute devotion to
you, I am sure you could not have found his equal as a
successor to Mr. Day. You remember in one of our conversations in Canton I advocated his original appointment
to that place, and I am very happy personally and officially
to see that he is now to take the portfolio.

Russia has just startled the world by an unexpected call

for a general disarmament.[15] She did not consult any power beforehand, not even her ally, France, which was very disappointing to the French. The only concession in her favor was that the French Ambassador was notified of the invitation twenty-four hours before it was made public. I think the nations will generally attend the Conference out of politeness to Russia, but feeling that the details both as to armies and navies will be so difficult of adjustment that no practical result will be reached.

While the sympathies of certain classes of the French, not the Government, ran away with them at the outbreak of the war, they soon quieted down, and now that we are to have the Peace Commission meet here and have passed the bill providing for a handsome participation in the Exposition of 1900 they are manifesting a very kindly feeling.

I trust sincerely that during your vacation you may enjoy a relief from the unparalleled strain which has so long been upon you.

If you could hear the unmeasured praise which people of all countries and of all conditions bestow upon you, and their intelligent estimate of the skill with which you have worked out the great problems forced upon you, you would feel in some measure compensated for all your labors. One very intelligent man made the remark to me, after discussing the silver movement, the tariff, the war, etc., "The Lord seems to give to your President the most difficult problems in statesmanship just because he knows he can work them out and likes to see him do it." [12]

A passage from a letter to President McKinley written fourteen months later sums up the results of the Spanish-American War as it was interpreted by the statesmen of Europe.

Horace Porter to William McKinley

November 14, 1899.

. . . I often wish some of our non-expansionist citizens at home could once take a look at the Philippine question from a stand-point farther off, one which is nearer the true focal distance. It is said that a Wall Street operator can speculate better when far enough away to be out of the immediate influence of the hourly fluctuations than when hanging over the "ticker," and one can take a less circumscribed view sometimes of public questions when on the other side of an intervening ocean. I have frequently heard a number of public men in Europe express the opinion that we did in three months what the great powers of Europe had sought in vain to do for over a hundred years, in having secured a chain of island posts in the Pacific, secured the Philippines, captured their trade, paved the way for a Pacific cable of our own, virtually taken possession of that ocean and occupied a position at Manila easily defended, only a couple of days in time from the Chinese coast, with no fear of Chinese or Russian armies at our back and yet near enough to protect our interests in the Orient. So that while some of our citizens of "mental malformation" are bemoaning our unlucky fate, the most experienced statesmen here envy our transcendant achievements and see clearly the future benefits.[12]

Such was the European point of view, concerning which we needed enlightenment. But it must not be forgotten that Europe stood in quite as much need of enlightenment as we on the point in question. It was the aim of McKinley and Hay that these "transcendant achievements" should not bedazzle us; that in our new state of power and opportunity we should act strictly in accordance with the best traditions of our history. To explain our integrity of purpose to his skeptical colleagues was Porter's constant effort, both at this time and throughout the much more perplexing diplomatic complications that came with the succeeding years.

CHAPTER XVII

FRANCO-AMERICAN ENTENTE

THE working-day of an Ambassador is not confined to the hours that he spends in his own office or the office of any one else; it may last as long as he is awake, and often has as its most important accomplishment something achieved while he is apparently amusing himself. The giving of a formal dinner may count for more than an interview at the Foreign Office; the omission or canceling of it may provide enough material for the gossips of the press and the chanceries to create an awkward international situation. The dinner to preside at which I was prematurely removed from the convent is a case in point: if, at that critical moment, when sympathy for Spain was being loudly expressed, the American Ambassador had canceled a dinner in honor of the President of the Senate and the Minister of Foreign Affairs, the whole diplomatic world would have given his act an interpretation which he could not possibly have explained away.

As it turned out, I was frequently obliged, during the next few months, to take my mother's place at official dinners. I was only eighteen—too young to enjoy the opportunity of talking to some very clever middle-aged men next to whom I was placed; in general, I was frankly bored, and so was my neighbor. Girls were not supposed to have any ideas of their own, and subjects of conversation were so limited that we often lapsed into silence. Wherever I went I heard discussion of the Spanish-American War, and it was an immense gratification to me when the battle of Manila and the destruction of Cervera's fleet stopped all talk of the inadequacy of the American navy. I also observed a certain

224

look of "sitting up and taking notice" on the faces of the diners when Father made any remark. I decided we were beginning to count for something.

But a topic far more absorbing than the Spanish War was the Dreyfus case. Every one took sides: Dreyfus was either a saint and martyr, or the most abominable rascal on the face of the earth. If you happened to be seated between two gentlemen of the opposing parties, you heard some lively conversation. I ate my dinner, but I cannot say as much for my two neighbors.

In arranging our official and private dinners we found the seating, as Father had found it even in the simple days of the Grant Administration, sometimes very complicated. We could have only two ambassadors at a time: they sat one on each side of my mother, for it was not according to etiquette to place an ambassador elsewhere, unless there were present members of the French cabinet, who went ahead of everybody. If ambassadors were at the table, we seldom invited ministers, who would have to take second place. If you invited royalty it was much easier, for you asked them in advance whom they would like to have invited; it was always the representative of their own country and some personal friends. These friends, to be sure, sometimes made a difficult situation for my father. He, being accredited to the republican government, could not be on too friendly terms with the members of the different deposed—or reigning—royal families. We had at dinner the Infanta Eulalia of Spain, the Prince and Princess Ferdinand of Bulgaria, the Duchess Paul of Mecklenburg-Schwerin; the Infanta and the Duchess were at swords' points over some domestic affairs, and as they had both announced themselves for the same evening and both wanted to dine with us we had some difficulty in keeping their engagements separate. Father managed it through diplomatic channels without offending either of the royal ladies. It was also difficult to see just the right number and the right kind of French people.

Several of our American friends had married into the old aristocratic French families and they and their relatives were strong monarchists. Some of these aristocrats had joined forces with the republicans, which made matters easier for the diplomats; but there was an equal number on both sides who did not wish to know each other. So entertaining in Paris was not always the easiest thing in the world.

Intermingled with the official dinners were many more enjoyable entertainments for our American friends visiting Paris and for the resident American colony. To counterbalance the stiffness of the large balls my mother, remembering her own love of dancing, organized at the Embassy informal parties for the American girls and boys. On these occasions Mother and Father waltzed with us to their hearts' content, and the ball ended with a Virginia Reel.

Altogether I found that I was kept pretty busy helping my mother entertain her guests. At her Monday afternoon receptions the number of callers often ran over a hundred and fifty. We had all sorts and kinds: the lady of the Faubourg St. Germain, generally with a son, grandson, or nephew in tow; always some members of the diplomatic corps, intermingled with French officers and under-secretaries of the government; and a large showing of the American colony and visiting Americans. One gentleman arrived with his small son and persisted in making the boy shake Father's hand because he had shaken hands with Grant and Lincoln. A certain girl had been especially recommended to Father by a senator from some Western state. She was so embarrassed and shy that Mother took pity upon her and handed her over to my special charge. I gave her some ice cream and cake and chocolate, after which she brightened up and became quite talkative. And then, after saying good-by, she rushed back and, pulling her purse from the pocket in her petticoat, asked me how much she had to pay!

MRS. HORACE PORTER

By Mlle. de Merbitz.   Premier Prix de Miniature, Paris Salon, 1900.
Exhibited at the Royal Academy, London, 1904

Another of our guests, from a very different America, was Miss Mary Custis Lee of Virginia. When Father heard she was coming, for she had informed us of her intended visit, he stationed Captain Mott, also from Virginia, at the foot of the stairs; he was to meet the lady at the door and give a signal to Father, who was at the door of the salle d'armes, and who would then come down the stairs, give her his arm, and escort her to the drawing-rooms. It all worked out as planned, and Miss Lee was highly pleased, for she knew that only royalty was treated in this manner. After informing me that Father "was the best dancer at West Point when I was a girl—nobody ever waltzed as well as he—and, my dear, he was so handsome," she turned and told him in the same breath that there was no Yankee's house she would enter except his. To which he quietly replied, "But, Miss Lee, it's your own Embassy."

Other frequenters of the Embassy who played eminent rôles in the Paris of that day were Massenet, the composer, Benjamin Constant, the artist, William Dannat, the American artist who later painted my father's portrait, Alexander Harrison, Eugene Vail, Augustus St. Gaudens, Calmette of the *Figaro,* and Madame Marchesi, famous teacher and singer, whose position was unique. On the occasion of her golden wedding Marchesi presented me with her lace fan. King George of Greece, whom my father saw from time to time at Aix, used to come in a fiacre and leave his card,— "Le Roi des Hellènes." Years afterward his grandson, the present ex King of Greece, told me that on his twenty-first birthday King George presented him with a cigarette-case, saying, "It was given me by a man I greatly admired,—an American, General Horace Porter."

Our house was carefully run according to certain old-fashioned rules of economy. The staff of servants, which, as I have said, Father insisted on having smaller than those of other embassies, was under the guidance of Emily, our German housekeeper. She was thrifty, a hard worker, a good organizer, and greatly resented the waste of time, money, and food to which the maître d'hôtel and the cook were especially addicted. She never took the trouble to learn French properly (she thought English and German good enough); her ear caught some word which sounded right and straightway she used it, never asking its meaning. Thus she startled Father one day by coming into his sitting-room and informing him that the footmen needed to have some new "cocottes." Father, quite surprised and scandalized, asked her what she really meant, and told her she must not use words she did not understand. "Oh, vell, General, you know vot I mean. It's de oder word dat sounds like it." "I suppose," replied Father, gravely, "that you mean 'cocade'—the word you used has an entirely different sense." He also tried to persuade her to say "culotte" instead of "cutlets," in speaking of the footmen's knee-breeches. She presented her book to Father every Saturday afternoon and was never satisfied until he had added up her long columns of figures. In the same way he kept track of all other household expenditures.

The other half of our social life consisted in attendance at the dinners, balls, and soirées to which we were invited, with the consequent round of calls. The big official dinners given by the President at the Élysée, in honor of some special guest, generally royalty, were very gorgeous and very dull. We were often over a hundred persons at table. After dinner the guests proceeded to take their places in one of the salons before a small stage. The dignitaries sat with Madame Loubet in large gilt armchairs in the front row, the second row had smaller armchairs, the lesser fry sat on wiggly satin and gilt chairs, and the small fry stood. The best French artists appeared from the Opéra, the Opéra Comique, and the Comédie Française.

My father took me to my first French ball, at the hôtel of the Duc de Grammont, one of the finest in Paris, on the corner of the Champs Élysées and the Rue du Chaillot.

The ballroom was crowded. The girls were seated beside their mothers, waiting to be asked to dance. A young man came up, put his heels together, made a deep bow, and asked me to honor him with this waltz. He seized me round my waist, and literally twirled me around on a space about five inches wide, keeping me carefully before my father, and then, depositing me on my little gilt chair, bowed again, murmured something, and walked off. The next dancer did about the same. I decided there was not much in French balls.

We spent what seemed to me an endless amount of time making and returning calls. The enjoyable side of the function was that it enabled us to see so many of the historic houses of Paris. For instance, the Austrian Embassy was at the splendid Hôtel Galliera. Count Wolkenstein, the greatest stickler for etiquette in Paris, always received with his wife on her day at home. He stood at the head of the steps leading to the drawing-room door, and if an ambassadress arrived descended, crossed the space between the staircase and the steps leading to the front door, and escorted her to the drawing-rooms. If royalty came, he went all the way to the door. A person of minor importance like myself was met only at the drawing-room door. He once upbraided my father for having called on the King of Sweden first, during his stay in Paris, after a lunch given for him by M. Delcassé. The old count declared that the American Ambassador, representing the President in person, should not make the first call on a visitor to Paris, even if he were a king.

Another interesting hôtel was the German Embassy, which had once belonged to the Reine Hortense. The ballroom was very fine, but in great need of repair. I remember that once, at a big soirée there, upon being asked by a resplendent young officer to go for the third time to the buffet, I was forced to tell him that I really couldn't eat another thing. Whereupon he whispered to me in German, as his

French was rather faulty, "I have orders from the Ambassador,—but please don't tell on me,—to have as few people as possible in this room and to keep them moving, because the floor is not so strong as it should be, and we are always rather afraid of an accident. Whatever you do, keep away from the chandelier, for one of the wax candles dropped on a lady's back the other day and caused her great pain." I never had a better success with Father than when I told him that story.

The British Embassy, situated in the Faubourg St. Honoré, was by far the largest in Paris and had an old garden quite as fine as the Élysée. The official dinners there, few and far between, were celebrated for the magnificent display of old English silver and gold plate and the bad food. Father always professed to envy the resourceful gentleman who once whispered to him in the dressing-room before dinner, "J'ai diné avant de quitter la maison."

Our official calls of course included the wives of the cabinet ministers, and as during the Dreyfus affair old ministers were forever giving place to new, we found the process of making calls a never-ending function. The wife of one minister said to us, "I have kept our apartment, and I come to the hôtel of the ministry only for my days at home. One never knows how soon my husband may fall (*faire la chute*), and then we shall at least have a roof over our heads."

My father soon found out that by frequenting certain salons he could not merely pass a most agreeable afternoon but also hear many interesting details of the inner workings of French political life. He also learned how to play his part with the ladies by making pleasing conversation and saying nothing. His usual tactics were to take me with him on these visits, having trained me, as it were, to keep watch while I talked sedately with the other *jeunes filles,* and to give the signal for departure when I saw he needed it. Often he repeated the conversation to me afterwards, winding up with the remark, "But when you hear this question discussed later you are to know nothing about it."

One form of ambassadorial responsibility that was closely connected with all this social life had to do with international marriages. A cosmopolitan city like Paris was bound to have the usual titled fortune-seekers. These men were generally so notorious that no self-respecting Frenchman would have allowed his daughter to marry one of them. It seemed incredible to French parents that American fathers permitted such marriages and were also willing to pay the price. To the thrifty Frenchman it seemed as if the American were not getting his money's worth!

Naturally Father was always having his advice sought by anxious French and American parents, the American mother wanting to know the exact position and title and ancestry of the French suitor, and the French mamma equally anxious to know the exact number of millions possessed by Miss X's parents. I am not sure that Father did not find compensation for the infinite trouble and annoyance these people caused him in the fun of making a tale out of their ridiculous predicaments. For example: one young man called himself Prince Colonna (it transpired later that Colonna was his grandmother's maiden name), and we had the greatest difficulty in persuading the girl in the case that he had nothing to do with the noble family of that name. "Just think how nice it would sound," she argued to me, "in the town I come from, to have on my visiting card 'Princess Colonna.'" If Father mimicked this artless statement to perfection, there is no denying that he even made a slight improvement in the phraseology of the conscientious mother who, so he declared, put her problem and request to him as follows: "Well, General, I just want to know if this fellow really is a count or if he's no 'count." The obliging Ambassador generally managed to find encouraging references for the families on both sides, reminding them from time to time, however, that the United States Embassy was not a matrimonial agency. To those of them who were shortly at his door again, anxious to get out of the marriages so blithely made, and especially during the Gould-Castellane affair, when one side called on him one day and the other the next, he might well have added that neither was it a divorce court.

Another item in the list of ambassadorial concerns gave my father endless trouble, to wit, applications for decorations from the French Government. These came from people of all sorts,—for some reason artists and dentists were the most persistent,—and the applicants all regarded themselves as good one hundred per cent Americans. Again and again General Porter explained that the Ambassador was "prohibited by custom and regulation from recommending or even suggesting the name of any one for a decoration by France." He knew well the embarrassments of European governments in this respect. They were, he wrote to one inquirer, "particularly averse to giving any details as to the number of decorations awarded, as the lists are very large, and to expose the numbers might cheapen the value in the eyes of the people." But this information did not avail to cheapen the value of the decoration in the eyes of the endless stream of applicants.

Of the means possible for expressing to Frenchmen of all classes and in all places the good will of the United States, incomparably the best were the speeches which the Ambassador was constantly making. One of his after-dinner jests touched upon the extravagance of the United States in sometimes sending to a foreign country a man familiar with the tongue of the land to which he was accredited. It would be much more thrifty, he argued, to appoint a man ignorant, and so give him the opportunity to learn.* It is hard to say with sufficient emphasis how

* Another after-dinner speech began as follows (the occasion was the welcome at Rouen of the *Prairie,* the first United States destroyer to go so far up the Seine): "J'estime que le plus grand mérite de l'orateur est d'essayer d'être agréable à ses auditeurs; dans ce but, je ne ferai, ce soir,

much it meant to the French, of all people, to have the United States represented to them by a man skilled as an orator and speaking their own language. Fully conscious of his unique opportunity, General Porter not only disregarded the stereotyped instructions of the State Department discouraging speech-making on the part of diplomats,[1] but in fact spared no pains in making the most of his chances. He accepted invitations not only for Paris but for other cities; he prepared himself carefully; and after a little experience he could put himself in touch with a French audience as quickly as with an American one.

The summer of 1900 was the busiest period of Porter's whole ambassadorship. It was the year of the Boxer Rebellion; it was also the year of the Paris Exposition, which, during its five months of existence, involved at least a doubling of the usual number of unavoidable fêtes, dinners, and balls, and an incessant demand upon his time on the part of visiting Americans. The troubles began long beforehand with delays in Washington over the question whether the United States should or should not be represented. When the appropriation bill for the American exhibit had at last been passed, General Porter sent energetic messages to Washington urging the necessity of at once retaining whatever good space might be had on the left bank of the Seine. He laid still more stress on the supreme importance of selecting as commissioners men with a knowledge of French and of the country and its government.

Accordingly Washington replied by sending over, as Commissioner General, a gentleman who spoke no French, brooked no interference, and seemed confident that ideas and methods of doing business in Paris would prove to be little different from those of his native city of Chicago. The exposition officials were soon complaining about the

que des remarques fort courtes. Je n'oublie pas que les anciens mettaient un squelette dans leurs banquets pour indiquer que l'homme est mortel; les modernes y mettent le plus souvent des orateurs à perte d'haleine pour indiquer que l'homme peut quelquefois être éternel."

off-hand methods of the American Committee; the latter were exasperated at the red tape of the French; and Porter had much work to do in smoothing the ruffled feathers on both sides.

One incident is enough to illustrate the humor of the situation. As soon as the building of each country was ready, the French President visited it on a tour of inspection. When word came that he purposed to be at the United States building at ten on a certain morning, the Embassy staff begged the Ambassador just to happen to be on hand when M. Loubet, who spoke not a word of English, made his appearance. Though he protested that it was none of his business, my father finally yielded, and with his staff arrived at the building not long before ten on the appointed day. There were attendants about, clearing up at their leisure in complete ignorance of the Presidential visit, but no officials. On the stroke of the hour the President drove up in his open landau, surrounded by a detachment of his never-absent Garde Républicaine. Too polite to remark on the absence of the Commissioners, Loubet exchanged banalities with Father, inspected the building (there was really nothing to inspect), and took his departure. Ten minutes later came the American Commissioner, regarded the Ambassador with surprise, and asked whether he knew that the President was expected, adding that he was apparently going to be late. "No," answered General Porter, "he was on time, as he always is. I happened to be here and showed him round. He has come and gone. Good-by." [2]

By the middle of May the first Americans made their appearance, and before the end of June they were in such predominance that even the hordes of English and Germans seemed insignificant by comparison. To the tourist the Embassy was the happy haven of refuge from all troubles and anxieties: one lady wished to store her sealskin coat with us; another wanted to leave her trunks in our care. Shortage of money was, of course, a very common reason for appealing to the Ambassador. Some of these unfortunates confessed to a night on Montmartre and in consequence the disappearance of all their worldly goods; others, especially the "Americans" who sported the stars and stripes in their buttonholes and spoke broken English, put Father to a deal of trouble when he tried to get to the bottom of their stories; but one and all appeared to expect him to provide for them somehow, to help the efforts of the Paris police in their behalf, to get in touch with their families, or to send them home. They were a very different sort from the boys and girls who, for various reasons, had simply reached the end of their money,—students whose trip to Paris had cost them more than they calculated, and a number of girls who had spent their savings on the journey, expecting to find positions as stenographers, or secretaries, and so see Paris and the Exposition. In fact, so many instances of Americans genuinely stranded in Paris came first and last to my father's attention that he finally gathered up a fund solely to meet such cases.[3]

Of course he became an expert in detecting swindlers, not without having sometimes paid dear for his wisdom. One story that he used to tell afterward was of a fellow who passed himself off, within an hour, first on the Ambassador and then on the Consul General, as the newly appointed consul to Pekin, who had unfortunately lost his letter of credit and needed to borrow a few hundred francs to pay his hotel bill. If ever there was a clever and well-informed swindler he was the man, but Father always said that the moral of the story was simple: the Embassy should have a telephone!

Even in that bewildering summer, with its continuous stream of entertainments, Sousa's band stood out as conspicuous. For the first time the French heard Americans playing American two-steps and marches. Their astonishment over, they took to it all like ducks to water: Sousa, his band, and his music became the rage in Paris and the two-step and even the "Boston" made their way into chic parties.

It was an American, too, who scored the other great success of the season in Paris. Father took the keenest interest in the first appearance there of his old comrade, Colonel Cody; he facilitated his arrangements with the city, and for the opening day of the Wild West Show he saw that boxes and seats were sent to the principal members of the Government and to the ambassadors and ministers. Buffalo Bill, on his side, responded by meeting us at the door of our carriage in full cow-boy regalia,—spurs, pistols, bowie-knife, and all,—walked between us across the tan bark of the ring to the middle box, decorated with the American flag, where he and Father were greeted by a storm of applause, and then, when he had deposited us, stood there a moment, bowing and waving his hat while the audience apparently went crazy.

Exposition year also produced an extra crop of statues to be dedicated. On July third Washington's statue on the Place d'Iena was unveiled before M. Delcassé and a large crowd of French and Americans; at ten the next day we drove to the Place du Carrousel and drew the white cloth from the shoulders of General Lafayette.[4] Of course this ceremony was attended with all the circumstance and *mise en scène* the French love and understand so well. The seats that had been erected around the statue between the broad wings of the Louvre were gracefully draped with bunting and flowers, the official boxes having a special covering of canvas in the tricolor, hung with the arms of America and France; the entrance was arranged with long, heavy canvas curtains, before which was drawn up a detachment of the Garde Républicaine. To the strains of the Marseillaise, played by Sousa's band, President Loubet was escorted to his box by the American Ambassador, who then made the opening speech, first in English and then in French. He was followed by Archbishop Ireland,[5] who eulogized Lafayette in good French with a strong Irish accent; President Loubet answered for the French Government, and my father read a letter to him from President McKinley.

At intervals the program was interrupted and prolonged by the gay music of Sousa's band. By the time the gallant Marquis was actually uncovered the July sun was making itself felt; however, its brilliancy rendered the scene all the more impressive, for it intensified the colors of the French uniforms and the shimmering lightness of best summer dresses, especially among the large group of American women. Many men of note were seated near us: Fallières, Millerand, and Deschanel, three future presidents of France; Delcassé; Caillaux, then Minister of Finance, who has been before the public for good or evil during so many years; General Brugère, governor of Paris; Brunetière and Jules Claretie, the writers; besides a number of the descendants of Lafayette, the Marquis de Chambrun among them.

On this American holiday all Paris seemed to display the feeling of good will toward the United States which had been steadily growing for at least two years. The American flag was hoisted on the Eiffel tower, carried by all the boats on the Seine, and hung from many windows. On his part, Father had issued a general invitation to all his fellow citizens to a reception at the Embassy. Since word had got out that Sousa had promised to play in our garden, people came in throngs to the number of fully two thousand, till at last our big rooms could hardly hold them. The strains of the music drew many listeners to the windows of the neighboring apartment houses and to the sidewalks; and whenever Sousa stopped the entire throng burst into applause.

Doubtless there were some dissatisfied Americans in Paris that summer, but the testimony that made itself heard was voluminous and unanimous in praise of the Ambassador, especially for having so completely won his way to the hearts of the French. Well might he himself refer to that Fourth of July as the day when America "captured all Paris." [6]

CHAPTER XVIII

KINGS AND COURTS

AN important part of my father's program for himself as American Ambassador was as much first-hand knowledge of Europe as he could manage to get in his brief leaves of absence from Paris; his scheme was to travel as a private person, to make a few informal visits, and everywhere to see for himself the people, their country, and their customs.

Of these trips perhaps the most interesting was the one which we made in the summer of 1899 through Denmark, Sweden, Norway, Finland, and Russia. Our stay in Denmark was made memorable by a visit to Oalholm, a castle on the Baltic belonging to Count Raben. The old moat was still there, and neither the numerous wings added at different periods nor the complete "modern improvements" had obscured the character of the ancient buildings.[1] Of the castles we visited in Europe, we always agreed that in its combination of comfort and beauty none was finer than Oalholm.

After other memorable experiences we reached Russia. Besides seeing the usual sights in St. Petersburg and Moscow, my father wished to form opinions of his own about the Russians themselves, who had always greatly interested him. The first of these opportunities came at a luncheon given to him by Admiral Kasnakoff, whom he had helped to entertain six years before in New York. This led to other invitations of the kind that he desired, and he had many conversations about the state of the country, its political and business conditions, and its relations with the other nations of Europe.

The members of the aristocracy seldom seemed to take much interest in their estates, or the people on them, leaving the management to agents who lined their own pockets. Responsible positions in business and industry were held mostly by foreigners,—Germans, Englishmen, Swiss, and Americans,—whose first interest was naturally that of the companies they represented. This fact in itself Father considered a bad omen for the future of the country.

As for the poor, we were constantly confronted with the evidence of their hard lot. One night in St. Petersburg, coming back from the theater to the Hôtel de l'Europe, the largest and best in the city, we saw lying along the walls of the dimly lighted corridor what seemed to be long rolls of rugs. When we stumbled against one of these bundles, it turned over and grunted. They were in fact the hotel porters, valets, and other lower men-servants, who were provided with neither rooms, beds, nor even mattresses, but slept fully dressed on the floors of the corridors. The peasant was even worse off: most of the villages we saw consisted of wooden huts with one room, bare ground for floor, and in the middle of the roof a hole for a chimney. Under this hole was a sort of oven of bricks, and in the warm ashes and around the oven slept the whole family, as well as the domestic animals.

Much earnest discussion between my father and myself of the whole subject of Russia is summed up in this passage from my journal, written after our return to Paris:

> All humanity seems to have been pressed out of these poor Russians by years of degradation, but this is only for a time. I pity the poor emperor who is ruling Russia when these animals are aroused and avenge all these hundreds of years of oppression. Some people declare that by gradual stages Russia will receive her constitution and in the end become a people's monarchy; but I believe that only a great upheaval of the present state of things can make Russia a civilized nation.

The upheaval has come, but Russia is no better off.

By far the most picturesque of my father's excursions in foreign lands was a stay of several weeks in Constantinople

during the autumn of 1901. This visit was unofficial, like
the others, but was seized upon by Abdul Hamid, some of
whose more troublesome subjects had lately captured an
American missionary (Miss Ellen Stone), and were holding
her for ransom, as an opportunity to show his good intentions towards the United States. As soon as he heard of
the arrival of General Porter and his party, the Sultan sent
an aide-de-camp to attend them as guide and interpreter,
and put at their disposal court carriages and, for their excursions by water, a royal caique; from then on he could not
do enough to entertain and honor them. My mother did
not quite appreciate the privilege of having the Sultan's
carriage standing at her call all day in front of the hotel.
She wanted to buy some rugs, "and," she used to explain,
"think what those rugs would have cost if I had entered the
shop from the steps of the royal carriage!" Her remedy
was a shopping expedition on foot, with results that were
altogether satisfactory.

The Sultan's envoy also brought the information that
the visitors were to be granted an audience directly after
the weekly ceremonial of His Majesty's going to Mosque.
To witness this they were invited to the diplomats' reception room in the palace. On the appointed day, Father and
Mother and their friends, Mr. and Mrs. Edward Dodd,[2]
were escorted thither by Munir Bey, the Turkish Ambassador to France. Taking their stand at the windows with the
other members of the diplomatic corps, they waited for the
procession to pass below.

Preceded by an escort of cavalry and officers of his household, by closed coupés bringing the ladies of the harem,
and by three of his younger sons on horseback, Abdul Hamid
was driven slowly in his little victoria down the hill from
the Yildiz Kiosk. He entered the mosque accompanied by
his sons and followed by his ministers and members of the
court, the ladies remaining in their carriages outside. After

an interval of half an hour the monarch reappeared; seating himself in a small phaëton he picked up the white reins and started the two white stallions at a quick trot on his two-minute drive. Then occurred, according to Father's account, the strangest scene imaginable: crowding round the Sultan ran the throng of his courtiers, old and young, fat and thin, their orders and their swords jerking and jumping with the motion of their bodies, and perspiration streaming down their faces in their efforts to keep up with the quick pace of the horses and thus show their devotion to their sovereign. In a few minutes the courtyard was cleared.

After a long wait the American party was summoned by the grand master of ceremonies, who led them through rooms and a long passageway, in which guards were posted, to the foot of a low flight of steps. At the top stood Abdul Hamid. Here is my mother's description of her introduction to the "terrible Turk."

"I found myself looking at the keen eyes and black dyed beard of the Sultan of Turkey. After much bowing, he seated me in a comfortable armchair, not far from his own, saw that your father and the rest of the guests were seated, and then retired to his throne chair. He talked to us in Turkish (though he spoke English fluently), using the master of ceremonies, who spoke French, as interpreter; etiquette required that 'the shadow of God' should not be directly addressed by common mortals. As he talked, I had plenty of time to observe him. In spite of his short stature he had great dignity of bearing. Suddenly he got up and offered me a cigarette—(I had never smoked in my life)—and then tried to light it for me. Of course I blew his match out. Then he tried again and I heard him earnestly adjuring me, *in English,* 'Pull, Madame, pull! don't blow!' I laughed so hard that the match went out again. Then he saw what an absurd position he had put me in and laughed as heartily as any of us."

Later the Sultan expressed his desire to present to General Porter one of the high Turkish decorations; when he learned that, while holding office, an American must refuse all such gifts,[3] he announced his intention of bestowing upon Mrs. Porter the Grand Order of the Shefakat—a star composed of diamonds, emeralds, and rubies which Mother, who never took royalty very seriously, always referred to as the Chief of the Cats.

Evidently General Porter's personality had made a great impression on the Sultan. A dinner party was arranged at the palace to which Mother and Mr. and Mrs. Dodd were also invited; the Master of Ceremonies informed the ladies that they must not appear before His Majesty in the usual European dinner-gown, which was considered highly improper, but with arms and neck well covered. After a long promenade through an endless number of rooms, with guards at the doors and lining the halls, the party was finally ushered into the drawing-room where the Sultan was awaiting them. He proved extremely cordial and was evidently delighted to welcome his American guests. He gave Mother his arm and under the blaze of a thousand lights led her towards the banqueting hall; in front of them, to my mother's great agitation, the Grand Master of Ceremonies walked backwards. After the dinner, which was more noteworthy for the splendor of the table appointments and the sumptuousness of the food than for the conversation, the party moved on to the palace theater. The variety show provided was also witnessed by the royal ladies from behind latticed windows; the length of the acts the Sultan regulated by clapping his hands when he had had enough.

Although after that night the Americans saw no more of Abdul Hamid himself, further courtesies made it plain that he wished to show his respect for the United States by honoring the man whom he considered its leading representative in Europe.

Outside of the term of my father's vacation leaves, he rarely spent a night away from Paris. We had a good many invitations to visit at French country-houses but we seldom accepted them, as Father did not like "one-night stands." The only short trip we took together was an August visit to the chateaux of Touraine. From Blois and Tours we drove in a little victoria for miles over dusty roads under the broiling sun, Father all the time telling me stories of the local history. At the little auberge at Amboise, to my great delight we were addressed as "Monsieur et Madame." I recall vividly, too, the long drives that he and I used to take, on a Saturday afternoon or a Sunday, to charming estates not far from Paris. The most beautiful chateau we visited was farther away; it belonged to the Marquis de Lasteyrie, a lineal descendant of Lafayette, who, as an ardent partisan of the Orleans family, had been exiled with the Comte de Paris and only recently allowed to return. He was a typical French nobleman, distinguished in looks, courtly and gracious in manner.

During the winter of 1901, we received an invitation through the American minister at the Hague to attend the Queen of Holland's wedding. Court functions did not especially interest Father, "but," he said, "we may as well see them as long as there are any of them to see; when you are an old lady there won't be many kings and emperors left."

We found the Hague in holiday attire, the houses decorated with evergreens, and showing the national banner of orange and dark blue. The route from the palace to the Groote Kerk was hung with ropes of myrtle twined with orange blossoms, and many of the Hollanders who thronged the streets were in their quaint peasant costumes. In contrast to all this color, the interior of the church was startlingly bare of flowers and decorations. Even the music was scanty and mournful, and the bridal procession literally straggled in. The Queen-Mother was short and stout ("but," Father says, "most charming to talk to"); her youthful escort, the Grand Duke of Mecklenburg-Schwerin, unsuitably tall and thin; the Queen's diamond crown, with its orange blossoms and tulle veil, was unsteady, and at the moment of the benediction, when the bridegroom rose too soon, the Queen seized him by his coat-tails and forced him again on his knees.

The audience was brilliant, the women in hats and light dresses, with fine jewels, the men in uniform and jeweled orders, and all glittering in the morning sunlight that poured through the plain glass windows. Late that afternoon, from the British Legation, we saw the royal couple drive away in an open carriage with postillions and bodyguard, the Queen bowing and smiling in acknowledgment of the wavings and hurrahs of her people.

In January, 1902, we attended a court in Berlin and, what I cared still more about, enjoyed three weeks at St. Petersburg in the height of the season, for during our first visit to Russia I had longed to see the great empty halls of the Winter Palace filled with the gorgeous assembly for which they were intended. In Russia, since there were no drawing-rooms like those in England, it was difficult for Americans who were not directly accredited to be presented to the Emperor and Empress. At Berlin the case was very much the same: there was one evening presentation at the beginning of the winter, and afterwards only the court balls. The court had always been very exclusive, and it was only within the last six years, since the Kaiser had suddenly taken it into his head to cultivate Americans, that they had been welcome at the "schleppencour."

The arrangements for our visits were made by the two embassies, and during our stay in Berlin we were indebted to the first secretary, John Brinckerhof Jackson, and his wife for many courtesies. According to etiquette, our party, which included my friend Catherine Eddy [4] and Reynolds Hitt, was first of all presented by Ambassador and Mrs.

White [5] to the Grand Mistress of the Robes, the lovely Countess Brockdorff, in the comfortable drawing-room of her apartment at one end of the palace. Mother was asked to be seated on the sofa, the place of honor; Father made the acquaintance of the other ambassadors, ministers, and government officials; to Catherine and me were presented numerous tall, slender, fine-looking young men in immaculate uniforms. I saw Father eyeing them, and as we drove away he commented on the folly of a caste pride which closed a business career to these representatives of the best blood of the country and left the development of its commerce and resources at the mercy of men greedy for money and power and caring little about the good of the Fatherland. "These fellows are a fine-looking lot of men; they have a good education and seem intelligent. It's a pity they are wasting their lives standing round clicking their heels, clanking their swords, and drilling soldiers. The day will come when they'll have to do something else, and the sooner it comes the better it will be for them and their country."

A few evenings later, in our white satin court dresses, with four yards of train, we squeezed into three landaus, and were driven at full gallop, accompanied by two cavalrymen, down Unter den Linden to the old palace. Having entered through the courtyard reserved for the diplomatic corps, we were for a moment almost blinded by the brilliant scene within. We were standing in a large hall, with a ceiling higher than the second story. The incline before us which served as a staircase, having been built by a Prussian king so that he could ride up to his rooms, was filled with ladies in evening dress and men in uniform moving slowly upward. The English and the Russian ladies wore their own court dresses, their tiaras, red or blue sashes, and jeweled orders; each carried her train over her arm like a big package. At the top we were escorted along a brightly lighted corridor hung with tapestries and posted at intervals with tall guards wearing the uniform of the time of Frederick the Great. Father drew my attention to one man even taller than the rest and whispered in my ear, "First cousin to the fellow I pulled out of the water at Fort Pulaski!"

At last we were ushered into a very large, square room, rapidly filling with Government ministers and the diplomatic corps. Here the American Ambassador to France was immediately surrounded; I watched Baron von Richthofen of the Foreign Office talking with him, and saw Mr. White engaged in hunting up Prince Bülow, the Chancellor. But at that moment appeared the Master of Ceremonies, asking in polite language that the ladies of the diplomatic corps line up and get ready for presentation; the men were to take their turn later. First came the wife of the doyen of the diplomatic corps with the ladies of her embassy, then the other embassies, and after them the legations, all in order of seniority. Each lady spread out the train of the lady in front of her, so that there was about six yards of space between them. When the Master of Ceremonies, after a great deal of fussing and hurrying about, considered us presentable, the doors of the throne-room were opened and the procession began to move slowly forward.

From where I stood waiting for my turn, I had the whole picture before me: the high, brilliantly lighted room, the young pages in white satin and crimson and gold forming a line from our door to the far end of the room where, between two high doors, on a raised dais of crimson velvet and under a canopy of crimson and gold, was the throne.

On the dais, very erect, immovable as a statue, his hands folded on his sword, stood the Kaiser, his face expressionless and like marble. As each lady passed him he bowed politely but seemed thoroughly bored. When I came nearer, I remarked the intellectual power of his brow and eyes. Beside him stood the Empress, sweet-faced, gentle, and high-bred, with a figure that any young woman might envy; her jewels were very fine, and on her soft gray hair she wore a thin lace veil and her diamond crown. A clever chamberlain manipulated my train with his staff, and when I had finished my courtesies I backed out of the door which led through a long gallery into the ballroom. As I leaned forward to gather my train, a gentleman entering in a great hurry bumped suddenly against me, and then, as he could not jump over those voluminous folds, rolled my train up, deposited it, package-wise, on my arm, and with a deep bow and a muttered "gnädiges fräulein," was gone. "I suppose you are the only American girl," remarked Mrs. Jackson, "who can boast of having a Chancellor pick up her train!" The gentleman was Prince Bülow.

Through diplomatic channels Father received the suggestion of a private interview with the Kaiser, but this he had decided against before he left Paris. So, as the court was in half-mourning for the Empress Frederick and there were no official balls, we none of us saw Emperor or Empress again. The further gayeties of our few days' stay we owed to the Jacksons. Their crowning effort in our behalf was a ball which served admirably its serious object of affording Father a further opportunity of meeting the high German officials; but I am not sure that he himself did not value it quite as much for the supremely good time it gave to Catherine and me.

The three weeks that followed in St. Petersburg were a wonderful succession of amusements: in the afternoon sleighing parties and teas; in the evening dinners, dances, "picnics" (a coasting party and supper at a primitive little clubhouse in the country), and the opera. The music and the ballet were an astonishment and a delight to us; we began to understand something of Russia's contribution to the world of art.

But what Catherine and I had come to Russia for was the first court ball of the season, to which three thousand people were invited and at which the presentations to the Empress were made. At the very last moment Mother was not well enough to go; so we had to set forth without her, we girls in ball dresses, this time without trains, Father in his uniform, which on this occasion he could not escape wearing, though it was against his custom. Again the diplomatic corps was admitted to the palace by a private entrance; in a large round room, at the top of a winding staircase, the Marquise de Montebello, doyenne of the diplomatic corps, who presented all foreign newcomers, gathered us together as a hen gathers her chicks. In her wake we entered the great ballroom of white and gold.

How different was my feeling, as I followed along, an invited guest, from the sensations with which I had scrambled across the polished floors as a tourist! The sight before me was as gorgeous as a tale of the Arabian Nights. The room was so enormous that three thousand people did not begin to crowd it. To the right stood the Russian ladies, to the left the ladies of the diplomatic corps, across the end of the room the diplomats, the Russian officers, and the gentlemen of the court. The men were all in uniform, with an inconceivable display of gold lace and bejeweled orders and swords, of which the most conspicuous of all were the belts and daggers of the Cossack officers.

The arrival of the Grand Dukes and Duchesses created quite a stir, and never in my life have I seen such dresses and such jewels. The Grand Duchess Vladimir wore a Worth dress of cloth of gold with a long train, and on her head an "all-round" crown composed of emeralds so magnificent that they hardly seemed real, surrounded by diamonds and tipped with enormous brilliants; another amazing ornament was a garland of flowers worn by the Grand Duchess Serge, sister of the Empress;[6] it stretched from her shoulder to her waist and proved to be made entirely of diamonds and rubies.

When all the guests had arrived the doors of the ballroom were closed; then, after a breathless hush, they were opened again, and two chamberlains with their rods[7] entered and stationed themselves one on each side. After them came walking backwards Prince Dolgorouki and a frumpy little old lady, Princess Galitzine, grandmistress of the robes; they, too, moved aside. Framed in the doorway, stood the Emperor and the Empress. They made a deep bow, which was answered by a unanimous curtsey and bow so profound that it seemed that the whole room had gone on its knees.

The royal couple walked around the room, bowing to right and left, and then the Emperor proceeded to speak to the various Ambassadors and Ministers, while the Empress turned her attention to the Marquise de Montebello. I was so near the Empress that I had time to study her face before she spoke to me; I thought her extraordinarily beautiful. Compared to the Grand Duchesses, she was simply dressed, wearing several large jeweled orders on her broad light-blue ribbon, and a pearl necklace. On her head was a characteristic Russian crown, set with diamonds and tipped by magnificent pear-shaped pearls.

I had been told that should she offer to shake hands with me I must remove my glove; as I made my curtsey I saw her proffered hand and actually managed to get rid of the glove in time. She "made conversation" with me, asking the usual questions that royalties ask; then suddenly inquired for my mother, regretted not seeing her, and questioned me as to whether we should stay long enough in Petersburg for the next court ball. This ball was a comparatively small affair, like a big dance in a private house, and one from which we, as outsiders, had thought ourselves excluded. My face must have told her how eagerly we would accept an invitation, for she immediately said: "Give my regards to your mother and tell her to bring you to the next court ball; I will send you an invitation to-morrow morning." She was as good as her word.

As the Empress moved away, I looked down the long line of expectant faces and saw, standing apart, two men conversing: the tall man in the uniform of an American general I realized was my father; the small man, looking up into his face, was the Tsar of all the Russias.

After the presentations, a quadrille was danced by the Emperor and Empress, the Grand Dukes and Duchesses, the Ambassadors and their wives, and higher court officials. The gentlemen had a terrible time keeping off the train of the Grand Duchess Vladimir, who, as Father said, moved with supreme indifference to their antics.   General dancing followed, and then, at twelve o'clock, the Emperor and Empress led the long procession of guests, walking two by two, through a series of apartments to the dining-room. At the door stood a master of ceremonies who without hesitation actually told each lady where to find her place-card (her partner took the next chair).   On a raised dais, at a table triangular in shape, sat the royalties, and with them the Ambassadors and Ministers and their wives.

In striking contrast to the white walls of the room was the gold and black worn by the army of lackeys, one to every second guest, who served us with incredible speed to a long succession of all the delicacies imaginable,—among them fresh asparagus, in the middle of winter! Meanwhile the Emperor himself, according to old Russian custom, walked around among his guests and saw that they were properly served. Suddenly I perceived that he was behind my chair, bowing gravely, but etiquette required that I remain seated and simply return his greeting. After the supper there was only a little dancing, for the Empress left early and that seemed the signal for the party to break up.

Two days later my father's leave was over and he went back to Paris, but he urged us to stay for the second court ball; indeed, we could not very well have gone with him after receiving the invitation from the Empress. The ball was held in a comparatively small room, round, with white marble pillars; from it opened the malachite room, into which the Empress could retire with a few ladies whom she

PORTRAIT OF HORACE PORTER BY FUNK
Owned by the Union League Club

invited for tea. All through the evening she was like a
hostess at her own private party, speaking to her guests,
and several times leading the figures in the old-fashioned
cotillion; when her young sister-in-law, tangled in the long
train of the Duchess of Marlborough, fell violently to the
floor, her diamond tiara over one ear, it was the Empress
who pulled it straight and arranged her hair; seeing my
mother standing, she went over to her and brought her to
a seat next her own, motioning the Grand Duchess Vladimir to join them. I did not know at the time that the
source of her sympathy was that she herself was suffering
from the heart-trouble which would have eventually killed
her. Later, when I looked about for Mother, I discovered
her in the malachite room, seated between the two august
ladies, chattering in her vivacious way, enjoying, like the
Empress, the privilege of speaking English. Mother was
wearing gold and white brocade, sable-trimmed, with pearls
across the corsage and diamonds about her neck and in her
hair; handsome and animated, she held her own, in looks
and carriage, with the beautiful sovereign beside her.

Life as we had seen it this time in the Russian capital had
fascinated us all, but, instead of camouflaging, it had intensified our old sense of its terrible contrast to the life of
the poor and of its insecurity. A government that tolerated
such extravagance among its upper classes and such misery
among the people, my father kept saying, was bound to col-
lapse, and with a pretty hard tumble. The country was
rich, taxes were high, revenues enormous; what became of
the money? For the roads were bad, the railways inadequate, and the school-system far behind the times. Why
were foreigners allowed to get control of the vast resources
and business interests of the country? Because the average
intelligent Russian likes to write and to talk,—especially
talk,—but does not like to work, "and you've got to work
if you want to get anywhere in this world."

The Tsar had impressed my father as a ruler having little

force of character or sound judgment. "They need a man like old Peter the Great, and I don't believe that even he could keep this country together." For these reasons he believed that the alliance between Russia and France would prove unfortunate for France. He could hardly understand why the French, usually cautious in money matters, had invested their millions in a country utterly different in ideas and ways of thinking, and with a government which, sooner or later, must meet its day of reckoning.

CHAPTER XIX

"THE FLOUNDERING EUROPEAN POWERS"

AS General Porter indicated in his official dispatches during the Spanish-American War, from the point of view of world-politics the contest was significant chiefly in its effect on the action of the European powers in the Far East. With it the center of diplomatic gravity began to shift from the Atlantic to the Pacific. The fame of John Hay rests largely upon his recognition of this fact, the vision which showed him that the United States, by virtue of its new responsibilities, was the nation to take the lead in this new and confused state of affairs, and the courage which prompted him to summon the nations of Europe to fall into line behind the young power of the West. If as Secretary of State he was acutely conscious of the treaty-blocking power of the Senate, he was also inspired in this course by the support of such chiefs as McKinley and Roosevelt.

It so happened that the most important events of this period,—the negotiations concerning the policy of the "open door," the Boxer rebellion, and the Russo-Japanese war,—fell within the term of Porter's service as Ambassador, and that Paris was a capital at which, in this succession of crises, he could be of great use.

By the summer of 1899 the action of the European powers in China was taking such a turn that the United States, with no sphere of influence of its own, saw its trade seriously threatened. Moreover, the hostility of the Chinese to foreigners was gaining ground; indeed, on account of the activities of the Boxers, it soon became necessary to send a marine guard to protect our legation at Pekin. By

253

this time it was clear to Hay that we ought to take action not only to protect our own interests but also to preserve the integrity of China, threatened from both without and within. He accordingly, on September 6, addressed a note [1] to Great Britain, Germany, and Russia, the purpose of which was to obtain from these powers a joint declaration to the effect that privileges granted by China were not to be used by the favored nation as a weapon for excluding commercial rivals. This was to apply to tariffs on merchandise landed or shipped to ports in leased territory, to harbor dues, and to railway rates within the spheres of interest. The current designation to cover the various items of this policy was the phrase "the open door." Within a few weeks Secretary Hay included in his request France, Italy, and Japan, and Porter was asked to take the matter up with Delcassé, the Minister of Foreign Affairs. [2]

As the dispatches that follow make clear, France, by the nature of her undertakings in China, could with advantage accept the policy of the open door as defined by Hay. Nevertheless, Delcassé hesitated about including the spheres of interest, either from excessive caution or because of France's relations with Russia. At any rate, the number of interviews that Porter had with the Foreign Minister on this subject within a short period of time shows that he had a considerable task to perform and was expected to produce results. Delcassé was learning, as Hanotaux had learned before him, what it was to be the object of "systematic work" on the part of the American Ambassador.

Horace Porter to John Hay

November 10, 1899.

. . . I had a long talk with M. Delcassé about the situation in China and the interest which all commercial nations naturally have in the observance of the policy of the "open door" in the ports of that Empire. He talked very freely on the subject and is exceedingly well informed thereon, as he is indeed upon all subjects pertaining to foreign relations, which he watches closely and studies personally with great care.

The trade which France has with the different Chinese ports, while not large in comparison with that of several other nations, is one which the French Government aims constantly to increase, and this fact gives the country no small interest in the maintenance of the "open door" policy. The Minister clearly expressed this view. He evidently believes that this principle will continue to be observed by the several foreign powers controlling Chinese ports by lease or treaty, and seems to feel that it would be unwise and impracticable on their part to adopt any other line of policy.

Of course, this Government at present aims under all circumstances to be in accord with Russia on the matter of foreign relations, but in such an effort France would not sacrifice any portion of her trade. The Government evidently believes that Russia will maintain the policy of the "open door" in China. Judging from this interview with the Minister and from conversations with others who keep well advised as to the policy and purposes of France, I am of opinion that her Government would not look at all unfavorably upon any effort on the part of other powers to secure a definite agreement with the countries which have leased ports in China pledging a maintenance of the "open door" policy.

I may say, while writing upon this subject, that there is much apprehension felt by all diplomats in Europe regarding the possibilities of serious complications in China which may some day make it a storm centre involving many of the great powers. There is the growing ambition of foreign nations to secure as large a share as possible of the great trade of that nation, the increasing influence of Russia, the undefined claims to "Spheres of influence," the numerous grants to foreigners of concessions for railways connecting with or interfering with each other, the foreign control of many ports, the weakness of the Central Government, the political intrigues at the Capital, etc., etc. It is feared that, perhaps not in the near future, the Spheres of influence may become Spheres of hostilities and that the great powers will be led either to sustain and strengthen the Chinese Government to enable it to enforce its treaties and agreements, or to bring about a partition of the Empire which would probably result in a general scramble for territory, with the nations already there standing the best chance in such a contest. Of all this feeling, however, you are, I am sure, fully aware and are watching the course of events there with your usual care.[3]

Horace Porter to John Hay

November 22, 1899.

I received your cable * yesterday morning and in the afternoon had a long interview with the Minister of Foreign Affairs, in which we discussed, in an informal way, the subject of what action France might be expected to take in reference to securing a definite declaration from the powers controlling leased ports in China, pledging a maintenance of the open door policy. I handed him a copy of the form of declaration prepared by you for submission to certain powers, and also a French translation of it which I took with me to facilitate the discussion. The Minister read it carefully and was evidently struck by the comprehensive manner in which it aimed to cover all the points which might become questions of controversy in Chinese territory.

His impression was that the first and second sections might be agreed to without difficulty by the powers holding leased ports and claiming certain spheres of influence, but that it would perhaps be more troublesome to secure the adoption of the third section † from the fact that it embraces so many important matters, the details of which are hard to express in an agreement covering for a period in the

* Asking Porter to obtain the adherence of France to the policy of the open door.—*Foreign Relations of the United States,* 1899, p. 129.

† Covering equality of treatment in the spheres of interest as to harbor dues and railroad charges.

future the conduct to be observed in these "spheres of interest," which will perhaps be always loosely defined. That is, that an assent to the provisions of this section might require considerable thought and study before a conclusion could be reached. However, this was only a first and immature impression. He stated that the subject had never been discussed in the Cabinet, but that he would bring it up in that body and urge attention to it. I gathered from what he said that he, personally, was rather pleased to see amicable steps being taken through diplomatic channels to ensure an observance of this policy. Although he does not think that there need be any fear of the abandonment of the present attitude of the leasing powers as to the recognition of the "open door," I endeavored to impress upon him the advisability of his Government declaring itself in favor of securing a declaration, fixing definitely this policy for the future and even joining in an effort to obtain it. It being a subject which he had never discussed with his colleagues of the Cabinet, he could not now give an intimation of what view would be taken by his Government as to such action. He will talk it over with them and I shall then see him again about it.

I may mention in this connection that the Bay of Kwang Chan [Kwangchow] in China, which France leased from that country some time ago, and about which there has been a controversy as to whether by the terms of the lease certain islands in the harbor were included in its provisions, has now come into undisputed possession of the French. It is not a treaty port, in fact not a port at all, only a bay. There are two islands at its mouth with poor channels between them and the main land. I think it would require four or five hundred thousand dollars to make a fair ship channel and a practicable harbor for a naval station. I do not believe that France expects to make much use of it and I doubt whether the work requiring such expenditure will be undertaken, at least in the near future.[3]

Horace Porter to John Hay

December 1, 1899.

After the Minister of Foreign Affairs had delivered his speech in the Chamber of Deputies, [Nov. 24] in which he openly expressed the interest felt by France in the maintenance of the "open door" policy in Chinese treaty ports etc., I took occasion to see him again on the subject of his aiding, as soon as possible, in obtaining a definite declaration of that policy.

He had been so busy preparing his speech and attending the somewhat exciting sessions of the Chamber for the purpose of looking after that portion of the Budget which pertains to his Department that he had not yet had time to take up with his colleagues the subject we have been discussing. He has been giving it further thought, however, and is now considering seriously the idea of asking from England, Russia, and Germany, very soon, a declaration about like the one proposed by our Government in reference to maintaining the open door policy. I am inclined to think that this intention will be carried out in some form or other unless the Cabinet opposes it vigorously, and I cannot see any reason why it should do so.

I suggested the following as an argument he might use. Notwithstanding the fact that the powers leasing Chinese commercial ports adhere at present to the open door policy, if the trading nations make no formal expression of what they propose to insist upon in regard to its continuance, in case any of the powers should change this policy and a trading nation should then protest, it might receive answer that it was rather late and be asked why it did not present its demands before, and request, formally, a declaration to that effect. It would seem, therefore, necessary that, if only for the sake of the record, a trading nation should at once put its demand on file, make known officially its attitude, and secure, if possible, a declaration in writing of its rights for the future. I shall follow the matter up closely.[3]

Horace Porter to John Hay

December 15, 1899.

The substance of your despatch of the 13th instant *
was discussed at great length with M. Delcassé. He expressed himself as anxious to aid in any project which
would tend to preserve the general peace and establish
good relations in China, and was entirely in favor of giving
some general declaration as to the intention of France to
maintain the open door policy; but he stated that he feared
that "spheres of influence" or "interest" was too vague a
term to use, and even if definitely understood the scope of
the declaration submitted might be open to great differences of opinion. Some would interpret the declaration
as meaning that in a so-called sphere of interest all nationalities were to receive treatment equal to that of the leasing
nation as to port dues, tariffs, railway rates, etc., while
others would contend that it went much farther and permitted the people of all nations to secure vested rights,
build railways, and possess and work mines, water powers
etc., in such spheres. He could see that it was definite as
to commercial privileges, but not as to industrial privileges.
In a parliamentary Government, he would be closely questioned by the Chamber of Deputies as to a declaration thus
voluntarily given, and called upon to define explicitly
spheres of interest and state precisely what rights were
granted to foreigners.

I reminded him that "spheres of influence" had become
a term generally understood and recognized in diplomacy,
and used, for instance, in the treaties defining the territories
in Africa over which European nations exercised a certain
control, and stated that no one had yet devised a better
term and that it would no doubt always be fairly interpreted. He said that he would willingly bring the subject up before the next cabinet meeting on Friday the 15th
and recommend and advocate strongly the giving of a
declaration in substantially the form we desired; but that

* Announcing that Great Britain and Germany had signified their acceptance, and instructing Porter to renew his efforts with Delcassé.

if approved by his Government he might want to reserve the right to have the term "spheres of interest" more clearly defined, and possibly some further explanation given as to what we exactly understood as to industrial and property privileges which would be accorded to people of nationalities other than those of the leasing nation. He wanted to know the wording of the declarations which would be given by England and Germany.

I showed him that your telegrams mentioned that they would accept "the proposals," and that I understood from that that it meant the declarations which had been presented to them by our Ambassadors. By the time this reaches you, you will have heard more by cable. I send this to let you know the chief obstacles which have presented themselves to M. Delcassé's mind in case we have to cable about them later.[3]

Horace Porter to John Hay

(Telegram)

December 18, 1899.

Received from the Minister of Foreign Affairs in a letter marked private the following: The Government of the Republic desires throughout the whole of China and, with the quite natural reservation that all the powers interested give an assurance of their willingness to act likewise, is ready to apply in the territories which are leased to it equal treatment to the citizens and subjects of all nations especially in the matter of customs duties and navigation dues as well as transportation tariffs on Railways.

My despatch No. 589 of the fifteenth will explain his hesitation about mentioning spheres of interest till that term and extent of control which might be exercised by nations possessing them can be more clearly defined, but France being hardly interested as possessor of spheres is evidently in favor of open door and equal treatment in broadest sense throughout China.[3]

With this partial victory Porter was not satisfied. Bent on obtaining from the Foreign Minister a declaration which, following those of Great Britain and Germany, should include the spheres of interest in the open door policy, Porter sought another interview at the Quai d'Orsay. In the meantime, Russia had come into line (Dec. 18).

Horace Porter to John Hay

December 21, 1899.

I spent nearly an hour with the Minister of Foreign Affairs yesterday and in the interview argued the desirability of his adding to his statement, as to France's policy in China, the words "spheres of interest" in addition to leased territory.

I urged that this wording be inserted for what it might be worth, as even if France did not possess any tangible sphere it would show her good intentions as to the future in case she should hereafter claim any such territory. As to his objections that such spheres were not clearly enough understood to be embraced in specific declarations and that he would not be able to define them satisfactorily in answer to interpellations in the Chamber of Deputies, I again showed him how conspicuously France had employed the term in the Treaty of June 14th, 1898, with Great Britain in the delimitation of their "spheres of influence" in Africa. He answered very pertinently that these spheres were definitely fixed geographically by accurate boundaries, and the scope of the rights to be enjoyed was clearly defined.

I feel that it is pretty well settled in the minds of the government here that to pledge anything definitely regarding a sphere of interest is unnecessary and would in fact be an attempt to make a declaration as to the policy to be carried out in territory they did not possess or control.

France has expended large sums of money in purchasing coal mines, petroleum wells, securing interests in railway concessions, etc., at several points in the interior of China, and she is, naturally, on the side of preserving the open door policy and equal treatment for all in China so that no one claiming spheres of interest may interfere with her vested rights or the transportation facilities for reaching the field of her industries.

This with my recent despatch and telegrams will give you fully the whole situation up to the present time.[3]

In the course of the negotiations for making the conditional acceptances formal, however, France receded from her extreme position, and when, on March 20, 1900,[4] Hay made announcement to the six powers concerned,—Great Britain, Germany, Russia, France, Italy, Japan,—of their mutual agreement to observe the principle of the open door, the spheres of influence as well as the leased territory were included.

Formal adherence to a general and idealistic statement of policy is one thing; the practical execution of it by nations bound by age-old traditions of aggression is quite another. The United States showed its hope that conditions would improve by withdrawing the legation guard at Pekin;[5] but events were destined to follow the old, familiar course. Encroachments here and encroachments there under the protection of European powers only stimulated Chinese hostility to foreigners; finally, in June of 1900, the Boxer Rebellion was fully under way in Northern China. The foreign ministers were besieged in the legation quarters of the capital, the German minister was murdered, and for a month the outside world had no knowledge of what was going on at Pekin.

Hay's first aim, when communication was interrupted, was to get the European powers to agree if possible not to send forces into parts of China where there was no disorder,[6] but when Porter presented this suggestion, Delcassé's reply was characteristic of the European point of view. The French policy, he said, was to allow "the greatest latitude" to commanders in China.[7] As his speech in the Chamber of Deputies a few days later made plain, he considered that France was displaying unusual toleration in not declaring war against China.

On July 3, in another circular telegram,[8] to our representatives in Europe, Hay set forth the aims guiding the policy of the United States, which may be summarized as follows: opening communication with Pekin, protecting Americans and American interests, preserving the territorial and administrative entity of China, guarding treaty rights, and safeguarding the principle of equal and impartial trade. A clew to his method of obtaining these ends is to be found in the last dispatch which he had been able to get to Minister Conger at Pekin: "There must be no alliances." [9] In other words, he sought to play the part of a disinterested outsider, endeavoring by moral suasion to bring about agreement for their own good amongst parties having conflicting interests and accustomed to rely on force and intrigue as the chief means for settling international problems. The method, it may be remarked, opens to an American Secretary of State a field of action in which he can not be thwarted by the Senate.

This purpose of Hay's General Porter understood and furthered with all his skill. As has already appeared from the story of the Exposition, it was America's year in France; Porter's knowledge of the official world and his personal popularity everywhere gave him prestige which he could employ throughout this perplexing summer. During the siege of the legations, he at Hay's request tried to communicate with Pekin through the Chinese minister in Paris, and he transmitted to Washington the meager information that came from the same source. When, however, after the relief expedition, commanded by the German general, Count Waldersee, had accomplished its purpose, and the Powers were hesitating as to the next step to take, Porter's frequent dispatches reporting his conversations at the Quai d'Orsay followed each other thick and fast. One confidential communication on this subject is sufficient to indicate the bewilderments of the shifting scene.

Horace Porter to John Hay

September 28, 1900.

The diplomatists of Europe seem to be all at sea regarding the Chinese Question, and the jealousy, suspicion, and want of confidence in one another is increasing. Germany's aggressive action, with an apparent attempt to dominate the situation, awakens distrust. Russia's recent move in the direction of annexing territory in northern China after her declaration to the contrary is a disturbing act. The Russian diplomatists explain it by saying that it is only a temporary military necessity, and that when tranquillity is restored this territory will be relinquished. I am pretty sure that France was not previously consulted as to this movement and had no notice of it until it was publicly announced. The belief here is that the Russian Emperor was not only the first to consent to the appointment of Waldersee to the command of the allied forces in China, but that he suggested him.[10] Reports which seem based on pretty good foundation represent that active but unsatisfactory negotiations are taking place between England and Portugal about the Boers in Portuguese territory in Africa and a desire to pursue them there with English troops, and some believe that this is coupled with the long-pending desire on the part of England to get Delagoa Bay, and that there is some secret understanding with Germany that she will not oppose such a transfer. I do not believe, however, that the Delagoa Bay matter is being pressed just now.

The straightforward, manly, and sensible decision taken by the United States not to remain in China for an indefinite period, with the danger of becoming embroiled with the floundering European powers, but to negotiate independently if necessary, was a surprise, but is looked upon and really appreciated as good statesmanship on our part.[11]

In the meantime the State Department pursued its efforts to get the Powers to formulate their aims towards China and their demands upon her, to agree upon a plan for withdrawing their troops, and to start negotiations for a treaty.

A letter written by Porter some months later indicates the slow rate at which the negotiations proceeded. His guarded comments about Russia show what an uncertain element she was in the problem, and that, in his conversations at the Foreign Office, he constantly kept in mind the possible influence that Delcassé might have upon Russian diplomacy.

Horace Porter to John Hay

January 17, 1901.

I can inform you better in a letter not to go upon the official files as to the feeling and action here regarding the negotiations in China and my talks with French officials. After receiving your cable on the 4th suggesting the advisability of calling a Conference of Plenipotentiaries of the Powers to meet in Washington or some European Capital, M. Delcassé discussed the matter with me at some length, asked many questions in regard to the proposition, and said he felt anxious to unite in any action in that respect to which the other Powers might agree, said he had no preference as to the place, and in any case he would not ask that such a conference be held in Paris. He telegraphed to the French Minister in China for his views. The reply, which was not unanticipated, favored conducting all negotiations in Pekin, at least until some crisis was reached which would show some other plan to be necessary. The disposition here was evidently to await some indications from other powers before giving a definite answer. When, in obedience to instruction, I informed M. Delcassé that we would not press the suggestion as to the Conference, but that we were extremely anxious that the negotiations be hastened, he assured me that his earnest desire is to adopt almost any practicable means that will expedite them. He talks very freely as to this and sees that a longer continuance of the forces in China adds to the indemnities to be claimed, and increases the danger of some serious disagreement between the Powers. As I cabled you to-day, he showed me a telegram he had sent to the French Minister at Pekin, urging him to use his best efforts to hasten the negotiations.

M. Delcassé and the Minister of Foreign Affairs of Russia are in close touch and frequently confer, and the impression given me here is that Russia agrees fully as to the advisability of concluding the negotiations as soon as possible. But as to that, you are doubtless already fully informed.[12]

What with the blundering and intrigue in which these negotiations at Pekin were involved, it was September 7, 1901, before the final protocol was signed. By that time the stage was set for the next scene of that tragic drama in the Far East in which greed was involving the European powers. By the end of that year it was well understood in diplomatic circles that China, as the result of persistent and intolerable pressure, was about to sign a treaty granting, in a measure, not only Russia's territorial ambitions in Manchuria but also important commercial concessions to her there.

It was at this point, January, 1902, that General Porter took his family to St. Petersburg, ostensibly to attend the Tsar's annual court ball. In his interview with the Emperor the two men conversed on the benefits that their countries would derive from the completion of the Siberian railway and other harmless topics of international interest; but it is obvious that in the course of his visit at the Russian capital and at Berlin, where he had interviews with Prince Bülow, the Chancellor, and Baron von Richthofen, the Secretary of State for Foreign Affairs, he must have picked up information which would help him to grapple with the intricacies of the European situation at that moment. On his return to Paris he found energetic dispatches of protest addressed by Hay to the American representatives at the European courts. From Porter's reply it is plain that the French Minister of Foreign Affairs was standing stoutly by his ally.

Horace Porter to John Hay

February 20, 1902.

I duly received your despatch of February 3, inclosing a copy of a memorandum which had been telegraphed to our representatives at Pekin and St. Petersburg, regarding Russian negotiations with China to secure extensive concessions in Manchuria.

I gave a copy, as directed, to M. Delcassé, who appeared not to have received information of any steps on the part of Russia looking to a departure from the principle of the open door and equal treatment in China to all commercial nations. He said in all his talks and communications with officials of the Russian government there had been repeated declarations made regarding that country's determination to maintain the policy of the open door and to adhere to the previously expressed intention to withdraw from Manchuria as soon as it could be safely done. I do not give his exact words, but it is evident that he believes in the good faith of Russia regarding these matters. He did not say whether he knew any of the details regarding negotiations looking to exclusive concessions.[13]

Indeed, Delcassé could not well take any other position. Simultaneously with Hay's protests, the astonished diplomats of Europe received the news of the Anglo-Japanese treaty of alliance (January 30). The agreement was a threat at Russia and through Russia at France. The two nations on the defensive responded promptly (March 16) with a counter-declaration which reaffirmed their alliance.

Another dispatch of Porter's shows the cross-currents of world politics at the time, and the way in which an adroit politician in power would seek to steer a course advantageous to his own country by setting two nations at odds with each other. Possibly Germany was seeking to organize a commercial combination against the United States; possibly it was only a "floundering" which Delcassé for his own ends exaggerated into something more sinister.

Horace Porter to John Hay

February 6, 1902.

I had the honor to send you a telegram to-day (copy enclosed) in reference to the action taken in France regarding the proposed commercial combination of European nations against the United States.

I have been watching with great interest, and at times with a little anxiety the efforts of the statesmen of several of the powers to organize a combination to take united action with a view to counteracting the effect of the commercial prosperity of our country upon the trade of Europe.

I have always believed that while such action, under any circumstances, would be exceedingly difficult, without the cooperation of France and Russia it would be impossible. M. Delcassé told me yesterday, very frankly, what had occurred as far as his country is concerned regarding the recent steps in this direction. He was approached by Germany * for the purpose of ascertaining the disposition of France and to learn whether his Government would join with Germany and the other Powers in the proposed combination. He informed me that he gave a prompt and emphatic refusal, saying that France would not be a party to such action; that the relations between his country and the United States were of the most friendly character, that the trade between them was increasing and that there was every desire on the part of France to continue her harmonious intercourse with the American Republic. He made no objection to my communicating this to you, but as it might be embarrassing to him to have these details of our conversation given publicity, at least for the present, I have communicated them in a confidential despatch.[3]

* It is interesting, in this connection, to remember that the date of Prince Henry's visit of friendship to the United States was in the early months of 1902.

Horace Porter to Grenville M. Dodge

February 12, 1902.

I received your very gratifying letter just as I was starting with my family to take a couple of weeks' vacation in Russia,—we having been invited to the Emperor's annual ball,—as I had promised my family for several years that we would go and see that wonderful court ceremony.

I had an interesting talk both with the Emperor and Empress. He is very anxious for the rapid completion of the Siberian Railway, and looks forward to our being good neighbors and increasing our trade largely when there shall be only the Pacific ocean between us. I am back here fighting tariff legislation and arranging the manner of carrying out some of the details still hanging along regarding the agreements made for the settlement of the Chinese question, etc.

I had been watching anxiously the commercial combination which certain countries in Europe have been trying to form against the United States. A definite proposition was made to France; but she has promptly and absolutely refused to take any steps in that direction or do anything to rupture her amicable relations with our country which she fully appreciates.

With Russia refusing also to go into any such combination, it will be a miserable failure. . . .[12]

The terms of personal friendship which Porter was able to establish with two German ambassadors in succession enabled him to understand better the hidden motives that gave rise to such incidents, or "gestures," as this. What befell these two representatives of the Kaiser in Paris is worth mentioning, for it illustrates the growing tension between France and Germany.

Prince Münster (1820-1902), previously Ambassador to Great Britain and since 1885 Ambassador to France, was an experienced and able diplomat. During Hanotaux's term as Foreign Minister, when England stood as the "enemy"

of France and Hanotaux desired to cultivate peaceful relations with the growing empire to the east, Germany was
fortunate in having in Münster a man of high character
and knowledge of the world who was acceptable to the
French Government. But the old Prince had slight respect
for the ill-considered policies of "the young man at Berlin,"
as he always called William II, and protested against a
measure effecting more stringent passport regulations between Alsace-Lorraine and France. This act afforded the
authorities in the Foreign Office in Berlin an excuse for retiring him from the service. His personal misfortune he
could take philosophically; but the event was a straw showing the set of the current, and this disturbed him. "Politi-
cally speaking," he wrote to General Porter in reply to the
latter's letter of regret at his departure, "it was a mistake to
take me away at this moment, as I feel sure that a new crisis
in world politics is coming on." [14]

His successor, Prince Radolin (1841-1917), whose wife
was connected with the Talleyrand-Perigord family, was the
first German ambassador since 1870 to be welcomed in the
Faubourg St. Germain, and there were not lacking many
open and hopeful comments upon this "esprit nouveau."
Yet he, no less than Münster, was destined to find himself
in a difficult situation. Early one morning in the last weeks
of Porter's stay in Paris, Radolin appeared at the American
Embassy in truly agonized distress over a speech delivered
by Delcassé the day before. The Moroccan crisis was at
its height, and the Minister of Foreign Affairs, like many
another statesman on such occasions, had, in making his remarks palatable for home consumption, gone beyond the
point of safety as regards his audience across the Rhine.
Prince Radolin saw himself making a hasty departure for
Berlin.[15] General Porter, beholding the gulf that was
widening between the two nations, needed all his American
tact to smooth down the troubled servant of the Kaiser.
However, the tension was eased for the moment by the

forced retirement of Delcassé. Not yet was Prince Münster's prophecy of a "new crisis in world politics" destined to be fulfilled.

Meanwhile events had been taking shape in accordance with the alliances announced in the early part of 1902, and were drifting on towards the Russo-Japanese conflict, which in crippling Russia weakened France. When the outbreak of hostilities was imminent, and Delcassé, now after five years in office a seasoned diplomat, was making final efforts to preserve peace, Porter, in writing to Hay, gave a clear statement of the point of view and methods of the French minister.

Horace Porter to John Hay

January 21, 1904.

M. Delcassé is laboring earnestly in the cause of peace. His opinions and judgment are much respected in diplomatic circles and I feel that in certain directions he is accomplishing some good. He has not taken any action in regard to a communication sent him by the Peace Bureau similar to the one received by you, and does not intend to do so. He feels, like most people in Europe, that any joint action by the Powers, even under the provisions of the Hague agreement, might be misunderstood and produce a source of irritation, and that therefore individual efforts would be more effective. He and the Russian Ambassador here have had numerous conferences since Russia received the last Japanese note, and M. Delcassé is as optimistic as ever and still feels that the Czar is tenaciously for peace and hopes that he will be able to bring about a peaceful solution of the dispute. However, all opinions now are merely conjectures.[3]

When it became plain that war was inevitable, Hay again stood forth as champion of the principle of the integrity of China. He proposed that the neutral powers should use their good offices with Russia and Japan to induce them to respect China's neutrality, "and in all practicable ways her administrative entity," by localizing the area of hostilities. Porter was to make this proposal to Delcassé and to ask him, if he approved this course of action, to send instructions to the French representatives at St. Petersburg, Tokio, and Pekin. All the signatories to the protocol of Pekin would then be consulted.[16] This dispatch to Porter was dated February 8, only two days before war was declared. The Ambassador, replying on February 12, stated that Delcassé himself took "the common-sense" view of Hay's circular. "The issuing of the circular," he went on to say, "has certainly been very timely and is directly in the interest of all the powers. It has again brought the practical diplomacy of America to the front, and given it great prominence." [17]

Japan acceded to the proposal promptly, but Russia as usual was dilatory. Then followed brisk communication between Washington and Paris, in Hay's effort to obtain action on Delcassé's part which would have effect at St. Petersburg. On February 18 Porter was able to tell the full story of what he had been about.

Horace Porter to John Hay

February 18, 1904.

I handed in person to M. Delcassé yesterday your cable of the 16th expressing the gratification of the President at the prompt and cordial co-operation of France in the movement to assure the neutrality of China. He was exceedingly gratified and wished me to convey to you and the President an expression of the great pleasure it has given him to unite in securing this much desired object.

I received your first despatch upon this subject on Tuesday the 9th, and fully appreciating from the start the importance of securing at the earliest possible moment the co-operation of France, I took the subject up the same day with M. Delcassé and had repeated interviews with him during all the rest of the week, in which I presented every possible argument to show that the movement was not inimical to but largely in the interest of Russia, France's ally, as well as of the other powers. Unfortunately the press here misquoted the text of your note and took an entirely erroneous view of the matter, and for a couple of days misled and disturbed the public. The Cabinet could not give the note proper attention immediately, as the Ministers were absorbed in the discussion of a very important treaty with Siam which they were anxious to and did settle that week.

The true purport of your note soon became fully understood by the press and in official quarters, and in my last conference on Saturday 13th the matter was settled favorably and a definite reply given. As M. Delcassé accompanied his assent by certain qualifications I asked him to write down the exact terms in which his Government gave its adhesion. This he did and I immediately cabled you a careful translation in English.[18] He naturally communicated fully with Russia and I believe his action will contribute largely to securing or at least to hastening the assent of that Government for, as I cabled you, information was received by him that Russia will accept very soon.*

Mr. Iddings at Rome telegraphed me that Italy was awaiting the answer of certain powers before giving assent. I telegraphed him the acceptance by France and other countries and he informed me the next day that Italy had accepted, which I was very glad to know.

French sympathy, as you know, is very generally with Russia, but nothing has been done so far to give it practical expression except to open a subscription in Paris for the Russian wounded which has reached so far the sum of about 160,000 francs and will be largely increased.

It is still the impression of well informed bankers here that Russia cannot secure another loan in France, at least not at any reasonable rate of interest.[12]

* She accepted on Feb. 19.

One more letter dealing with the embroilments of the European powers remains to be quoted; before the Russo-Japanese conflict was concluded, my father had resigned his position as Ambassador and had returned to the United States.

*Horace Porter to Robert C. McCormick** *

April 7, 1904.

I have read with great interest your interesting letters advising me of the state of feeling in Russia. I am not at all surprised but not a little annoyed at the course pursued from the start to the present time by the press and people of the country mentioned [England]. While all well meaning diplomatists in Europe were laboring by every honest means to prevent the present deplorable struggle, the machinery referred to was intensely active in goading Russia and arousing the war spirit of her people. So many despatches have been published in London *dated* from America, insisting that there is an inimical sentiment in the United States towards Russia ready at any time to take some active shape, that I do not wonder at the feeling against us which prevails there, the result of which may be to destroy our large and profitable trade with that country and make an enemy of our old friend.[19]

President Roosevelt has, as usual, hit the nail on the head in issuing his notice impressing upon all United States officials the importance of observing a strict neutrality in the present struggle, and refraining from either expressing sympathy for or criticizing adversely either of the two friendly powers that are unfortunately at war. It would be the easiest thing in the world for us to retain the friendship of all the powers, and why not do so as long as we are not parties to their wars? I believe that very grave questions will arise when the terms of peace have to be settled, and that it may then require a supreme effort on the part of diplomatists to secure the just rights of the great com-

* Ambassador to Russia.

mercial nations. America should so shape her course that
she could appear in the light of a friendly nation in order
that her potent voice might be heard with a feeling that she
was acting in a disinterested manner for the best interests
of general commerce, with no suspicion of hostility to any
one nation.

The so called entente* between France and England
was promoted principally by the representatives to the
Hague Peace Congress. The treaty of arbitration, though
limited to only five years, was a very good step to take.
France suggested a willingness to make a similar treaty with
us, but Mr. Hay replied that there were several treaties
before the Senate now and as the session was drawing to a
close he thought it an unauspicious time to send to that body
another treaty. He appreciates fully the friendly feeling
which dictated the suggestion.

None of the negotiations between France and England
can in any way disturb the excellent relations of the former
power with the United States. Traditions of friendship
and the recollection of successful alliances are much more
potent than general treaties and the exchange of visits on
the part of chiefs of State.

With the good work you are doing at your post now of
such great importance, I trust and believe that present misunderstandings will in time be cleared up and the present ill
feeling removed.[12]

This letter, at the same time that it concludes the story
of one aspect of General Porter's diplomatic work, intro-
duces another. One of the activities undertaken by Delcassé, by way of insurance against the perils of the general
European situation, was the negotiation of treaties of arbitration limited to a term of five years. Great Britain was
the first country with which he signed such an agreement
(October 14, 1903), and he naturally turned next to the
United States.[20] In view of Porter's later work in the cause
of arbitration, especially at the second Hague Conference,

* Announced on April 8, 1904.

in 1907, it is interesting that even before he heard from
Delcassé on the subject he had proposed the negotiation of
a similar treaty between the United States and France.

Horace Porter to John Hay

November 26, 1903.

I sent you by the last mail the French Yellow Book giving
the text of the recent arbitration treaty made by France
and Great Britain, together with the correspondence which
led up to it. This treaty was for some time urged upon
both Governments by Chambers of Commerce, Boards of
Trade, and other commercial bodies, as well as by the delegates to the Hague Peace Congress and the groups advocating a peace policy generally. It was regarded as somewhat experimental and that is why it is not made more
binding, contains so many exceptions, and is limited to five
years. It has been received with very general delight by all
classes of people, and has proved to be a very popular act
on the part of the Government here. As the relations between our country and France have never been more cordial
than at present, and as the Government is certainly anxious
to further cement this good feeling by every means possible,
it might be a fitting opportunity to consider the question of
our making an arbitration treaty with France. Although
I have never mentioned such a thing to any official here
and would not, of course, do so without instructions from
you to that effect, I am of opinion that it could be brought
about, if desirable, very readily on the basis of the treaty
with England, and no doubt in a form more comprehensive and more carefully considered if we should prefer.
If the present Cabinet should change, the conditions might
not be so favorable. Such a treaty would bring about a
"rapprochement" which might help us in our contests over
the tariff questions which often arise, and as European
nations entertain the erroneous notion that we are rather
belligerent in our policy such an act would furnish another

proof that we are practical advocates of the policy of pacification.

One reason why Mr. Cleveland's arbitration treaty with England was rejected was because it was considered too comprehensive and too binding in its terms.

France has begun with a rather restricted treaty with England, which it is supposed will educate the public mind in the right direction. It will probably be followed in time by one more comprehensive in its provisions.

I merely throw out these suggestions for your considera- tion.[12]

Although, as Porter's letter to McCormick discloses, Hay, ever sensitive on the subject of treaties and the United States Senate, rejected the plan at the moment, he took it up after the next fourth of March and on November 1, 1904, signed with Ambassador Jusserand at Washington a treaty along the lines proposed. Even although the Sen- ate of the new Congress ran true to form and rejected it, the fact that the treaty had been drawn up and signed was hailed as auspicious in both countries.[21] Porter, of course, had no active part in the final negotiations, but his work for seven years had helped to build the foundations that made them possible.

During his term of service as Ambassador, General Porter was required to act in many diplomatic situations of great delicacy. The information which he needed for his guidance he obtained through travel and contact with the right men all over Europe. His personal prestige came as the result of unremitting attention to his social duties and opportunities. But the chief element of his great success was the cordial and complete understanding between him and the three men with whom he had principally to deal,— Hay, Hanotaux, and Delcassé. When Porter expressed to Ambassador McCormick his belief that in international relations traditions of friendship and the recollection of successful alliances were much more potent than general

treaties and the exchange of visits, he was doubtless thinking of the temper in which he and these men had worked
shoulder to shoulder. Time has justified the wisdom of
their method and the two countries whom they served will
long have reason to remember them and their deeds with
gratitude. For this period of history the "traditions of
friendship" existing between France and the United States
means the work done together by Hanotaux, Delcassé, Hay,
and Porter.

JOHN HAY

CHAPTER XX

AN AMERICAN IN EXILE

AFTER all, a diplomat is a man condemned to exile. No matter how happy and successful he may be in his work, if he is a man of as many ties as General Porter his isolation from them all,—his own fireside, his friends, his clubs, his business, public affairs,—is bound to bring now and then a pang of homesickness. "The life of a diplomat is the life of a vagabond," he said once, and few men have in them less of the vagabond than he had. The letters assembled in this chapter dealing with affairs in America show something of the genial and sympathetic side of his nature,—the side which made men care for him as a companion and friend.

Horace Porter to William McKinley

November 12, 1900.

Let me convey to you less briefly than in my telegram how sincerely I congratulate you upon the crowning glory of your public career, your triumphant re-election by a majority in the Electoral College never before equalled, all things considered, in the history of the Republic. . . .

This election has been looked forward to by statesmen, and in fact by all classes of people abroad, with an interest never before manifested, not only because you have made our country far better known in other lands and given it a status for the first time as a world power, but for the reason that your mastery of the great public questions which have been thrust upon you has wrung praise even from supposed enemies, convinced statesmen that you are fostering amicable

279

relations with other powers, cultivating the arts of peace instead of the science of destruction, and that in your re-election the tranquility of the world has received an additional guarantee. The true sentiments of President Loubet were gracefully expressed in his telegram of congratulation. During the campaign, M. Delcassé, the Minister of Foreign Affairs, asked me repeatedly and anxiously my forecast of the election, and the day the result was known, the 7th, when I carried the news to him he was enthusiastic in his felicitations and requested me to convey to you his profoundest congratulations and best wishes for your continued success. . . .

One of the greatest disappointments that I ever experienced was not being able to leave my post here at such an important period and go home to take part in the electoral compaign, the first one in which I have not participated actively in thirty years. I felt like a hound struggling in the leash, and the homesickness from which we all suffer over here was largely increased every time I read of the activity that was taking place "at the front." [1]

Horace Porter to John Hay

September 20, 1901.

I have received the various cables of the Department informing me of the attempt upon the life of the President and, subsequently, of his death [on September 14], accompanied by instruction to acknowledge in suitable terms the expressions of condolence and of sympathy tendered in France, an instruction which was carried out with as little delay as possible.

Expressions of sorrow and abhorrence of the crime were numerous; they came from all quarters and all classes of people. The President of the Republic called on me in person, as well as all the members of the Government and high officials at present in Paris. A vast number of persons inscribed their names at the Embassy [Chancery] and at my house.

The American Chamber of Commerce of Paris, the British Chamber, and the Belgian Chamber met and adopted Resolutions expressing their profound sorrow and condolence. The city councils of Paris, of Aix-les-Bains and of Vendôme, the home of the Rochambeau family, voted addresses of the same character. Emblems of mourning are visible in many places and at the Palace of the Élysée the flag is at half-mast. Manifestations of grief have been shown in so many forms that I am confident that the death of Mr. McKinley has evoked in France such expressions of sorrow as have rarely been experienced before in this country.

A large meeting of Americans residing in Paris took place at the Embassy on the 17th instant and, after hearing addresses from Senator Lodge and myself, adopted resolutions of sympathy, copies of which I was requested to transmit to Mrs. McKinley, to President Loubet, and yourself. The request was complied with in regard to the President of the French Republic and I enclose herewith copies intended for Mrs. McKinley and the Department. I also enclose copies of the telegrams, letters and addresses referred to in this despatch, with newspaper clippings upon the same subject.

Yesterday, at three o'clock, a memorial service was held in honor of the late President in the American Church of the Holy Trinity, Avenue de l'Alma, all the American and English speaking clergymen in the city participating in the ceremony. Notwithstanding the large seating capacity of the church, it could not hold the vast crowd of people desirous of attending the service. The President of the Republic, then in the North receiving the official visit of the Emperor and Empress of Russia, was represented by an officer of his household. All the members of the Cabinet then in Paris attended, as well as a great number of other high officials of the Government. Nearly all the members of the Diplomatic Corps were also present in uniform. There was every manifestation of sympathy on the part of those who participated in the service.[2]

Horace Porter to John Hay

December 9, 1901.

Two things have occurred which move me to send you my heartiest congratulations,—the arrival of the full text of your Chamber of Commerce speech and the unanimous approval by the Senate Committee of the Hay-Pauncefote Canal Treaty. The speech in both matter and manner was thoroughly admirable. It has attracted much attention in Europe as well as at home, and, as we would say of an actor, you made a hit. The subject carries me back to the many years when, as Vice President of the Chamber, I was chairman of the dinner committee and used to line up the Demosthenes and Ciceros of the land at the annual feast, and recalls the scene when a former Secretary of State— Bayard, backed up against a gas jet, and for exactly an hour and five minutes mumbled forth the contents of a manuscript which for all we could understand might have been a discussion of the intuition of the absolute or the mutability of human affairs. It was as great a failure as was yours a success. In fact, in looking through all those days I can recall no speech from a member of a Cabinet which was so complete in itself and did so much good all round. You can go up head!

As to the treaty about which the whole world is talking. After my experience with the San Domingo Treaty when before the Senate in the days of Grant, I came to the conclusion that the "white man is unsartain" and that one cannot find many tribunes of the people who size up to a full hundred per cent, and nothing can surprise me in the process of treaty ratifications. But you are pretty sure now, I should say, to win, and I know what a satisfaction it will be to you and all your friends. It is of great moment to the country. . . .[1]

Horace Porter to Theodore Roosevelt

November 7, 1902.

Dear Mr. President:

Now that we know definitely the result of the election, I cannot forego the pleasure of sending you a word of cordial congratulation.   The off year between presidential elections has always been so doubtful that I had at one time great apprehension about the House of Representatives. My first encouragement was when you made your thoroughly admirable series of speeches in the East, dispelled the existing apathy, and took a bold stand in favor of the rights of the people.   Then came the coal strike, which recalled the Homestead strike in the second Harrison campaign, which really cost our party the loss of the election. At that time there was no leader who had enough grasp and vigor and who possessed to a sufficient degree the confidence of all classes to end the strike.

All persons of political experience realize fully that our success now is due to your well directed efforts and the effects of your personal popularity, and it is not too much to say that the saving of the party from defeat may be attributed entirely to you.   I believe that if your contemplated tour in the West had not been interrupted by the results of the frightful accident which gave us such a genuine scare, the enthusiasm that you would have aroused and the clear and forceful way in which you would have presented the salient issues of the campaign would have changed a number of Congressional Districts and considerably increased our majority in the House.

With an earnest expression of delight at your recovery from your wound and renewed congratulations upon the elections, I remain,

Your attached friend and well-wisher,

HORACE PORTER.[1]

Horace Porter to Elihu Root

March 12, 1903.

I was delighted to receive your letter sending me the copy of the new army Bill. I was rejoiced to see that it had passed, and I congratulate you heartily upon your success in the matter. It is safe to say that no one else could have secured this much needed law against the opposition which came from interested parties. It will do a big work for the army and make a splendid epoch in your administration of the War Department.

I was glad to see that you are a member of the Alaska Boundary Commission, because it will do much to ensure success, and yet sorry to see that the Government is loading you with every delicate problem that comes up. However, you will always be the wheelhorse as long as you are in the public service, and you will have to make up your mind to this.

The best news in your letter was the information that you will come to Europe this spring. You must come prepared to spend as much time in Paris as possible, where we shall have some riotous old times together.[1]

Horace Porter to George B. Cortelyou

July 12, 1904.

. . . Unless my thirty-five years of experience in active politics fails to constitute me a prophet, President Roosevelt will be elected by an overwhelming majority and will have the most vigorous, honest, independent and truly American administration that has ever blessed the Republic. One does not have to go around with a portable search light to see where he stands or use an ear trumpet to hear the annunciation of his principles. While sitting at breakfast the other day beside Count Goluchowski, Prime Minister of the Austro-Hungarian Empire, he said, "How is that remarkable man, your President? He is perfectly

well known everywhere in my country. Everyone is talking
about him, reading his books and admiring his great qualities. His personality is something extraordinary and I
am always delighted to hear about him." This enabled me
to recount many personal traits which endear him to the
people but which do not get into print. This greatly interested the Minister. This is a specimen of the interest
which attaches to the President in all Europe. I should
feel more at home if I were personally in the midst of the
campaign fight even if I could not do any good, but my
political friends, upon whose judgment I rely, and I cannot
help agreeing with them, think that the too conspicuous
appearance of office holders serving abroad would lead to a
repetition of the occurrences of President Grant's second
campaign when some of our representatives abroad came
home and attempted to stump parts of the country. They
met with a howl of criticism and the opposition hurled
questions at them, wanting to know whether they were
drawing pay from the Government, and why they were not
at their posts, and charged that the Republican campaign
was so weak that it had to be bolstered up by paralyzing
the service abroad, etc. The experiment proved a source
of weakness and the representatives had to be hauled off and
sent back to their posts. These are facts which we have to
consider.[1]

Only once during his eight years of service did Porter
return to the United States. In connection with the cen-
tenary celebration, in June, 1902, of the United States Military Academy, he, unquestionably its most distinguished
living graduate, was chosen orator. It was an invitation
which he could not resist; coupled with it was the opportunity to speak at the dedication of the Rochambeau statue
in Washington. Leaving France early in May, he was,
from the moment of his arrival in New York, plunged into
a round of reunions and festivals. Dinners and speech-
making were the order of the day. Mingled with jests
about his duties as Ambassador was always a serious note,
—the importance of good will among nations, and specif-

ically the value of fostering our good relations with France.
The arrival of the military and naval mission sent by President Loubet to take part in the Rochambeau dedication
made his remarks of special timeliness, and that event itself,
an unusually brilliant occasion,—one of the first of many
such during the Roosevelt administration,—brought to the
attention of the entire country the traditional and existing
bonds of friendship between the two Republics. At West
Point old comrades were present to greet him, younger men
looked up to him with pride as a man who had carried out
the lesson of service to his country not only in the professional field for which the School had prepared him but in
other fields as well. The story of the French boy and his
touching act of recognition which formed the closing passage of the oration was all the stronger in its appeal because
it came from the lips of one who, from the day that he
entered the Academy, forty-seven years before, had lived
his life in the spirit of that deed.*

One incident of Porter's visit to America is worth mentioning because it proved the spring for starting in him a
characteristic piece of activity. While in Washington he
encountered his old friend, Elihu Root, then Secretary of
War, who proposed to him that he prepare a formal statement of his action on the memorable day at Chickamauga.
In Root's opinion, what Porter had then done well deserved
the award of the Congressional medal of honor on which is
inscribed the word "Valor." Thanks to the Secretary's
good offices, this all came to pass in due season. The next
summer, when Root was visiting Porter in Paris, they fell
into conversation on the subject of the medal itself,—a
shockingly inartistic and tawdry piece of metal. On the
Secretary's suggestion, Porter undertook to study the lore
of medals and to have prepared designs of a decoration
that would be adequate in beauty and appropriateness to its
commemorative purpose. The investigation carried him

* The address is given in full in the Appendix.

into a curious corner of learning which he explored with zest and thoroughness, and the form of the medal used at present is largely the result of these labors.

I have spoken of my mother's health, which failed a little, year by year. She never would slight her official soirées or her Monday afternoons, which meant many hours of standing; she was determined to entertain all classes of Americans, for, as she once remarked to Father, "that's what we're here for." After the Fourth of July reception in the Exposition summer, she was completely prostrated. In 1901, father sent her to Zurich to be under the care of the famous Swiss physician, Théophile Mende. His rational treatment, the quiet living, the walks in the Dolder woods, always greatly helped her; but a few months of Paris life seemed to undo any benefit she had derived from her stay at Zurich or Marienbad. During the spring and early summer of 1902 my aunt, Mrs. Wheeler, and my brother Clarence with his lovely young wife were with us; and Mother, in their company, regained to a certain extent her health and spirits. But in the following winter she grew worse; even Dr. Mende's skill could not save her. On her way back to Paris from Zurich she took cold; her case was pronounced an attack of grippe. For the next few days my father gave up his regular daily walk and spent most of his time at her bedside; then, on April 6, she seemed so much better that, putting on his hat and coat in her presence and kissing her good-by, he started to go out. Before he had left the house he was called back by the frantic voice of our faithful Tante Marie, and rushed to his wife's room just in time to catch her in his arms and feel her head drop on his shoulder.

The death of his oldest son twenty years before had left a great void in my father's heart. The new grief was such that for a time I feared he would never rally. He, the man of iron determination and self-control, sat for hours in his mother's old chair, buried his face in his hands, and cried softly to himself. When I tried to comfort him, he kept telling me of Mother's beauty, and of the first time he saw her; then he spoke of his dead son.[3]

Hardly was my mother laid to rest than Father talked of sending in his resignation, and wrote to the President asking to be relieved. More than ever he longed for America. Again it was only a sense of duty that made him yield to Roosevelt's request that he remain till the end of the administration. He had no zest for his work. The great house in Paris depressed him: he wandered through the rooms, repeopling them with the brilliant throng that had passed through our doors so many times within the last six years. He had the reception rooms closed up, and they were not opened again for any entertainment until my wedding, two years later. My brother and his wife joined us, and we took Father to Italy, for he spoke of wanting to see Venice once more. When we were leaving to return to Paris, he kept looking back at the Piazza, and in answer to some remark of mine, said, "I am saying good-by to all this beauty: I shall never see it again." With a shock I remembered that he was nearing seventy, which for most men means old age.

The summer of 1903 we spent in a cottage by the sea at Dinard. Father had lost his old buoyancy of spirit, and this time forever. The next winter in Paris he refused all invitations, even to the houses of his friends. He wished to see no new faces. But before the close of our Paris life we had one more happy trip. He had often spoken, even in the bygone days of my childhood, of traveling with me to Greece: "We will see the Parthenon together." Athens appealed to him at this moment especially, because his old friend from the Embassy at Berlin, John Brinckerhof Jackson,[4] had been appointed Minister to Greece. Father considered Jackson a most valuable man in our diplomatic

service, "one of the few men we have whose training, traditions, and character fit them to serve as Ambassador."

True to his word, Father and I together saw the Acrop-
olis for the first time. The lectures I had followed at the
Sorbonne made the site of ancient Athens keenly interesting
to me, and Father, his mind again very alert, was steadily
talking, explaining, and discussing with me as we wandered
from one lovely spot to another. It was an afternoon in
early May; the splendid façade of the Parthenon, as we
stood before it, was lighted by the rays of the setting sun.
We both knew how beautiful it should be, but it far sur-
passed our imaginings. Those hours spent in study and admiration before it were a fitting end to the last trip my
father and I took together.

The Ambassador's eight years of service in France were
coming to an end. The resignation which he would send to
Washington, to take effect on March 4, 1905, at the beginning of President Roosevelt's second term, was to be
more than a form. Knowing his intention of returning to
America, the French Government was anxious to show its
appreciation of his distinguished achievement by conferring
upon him the highest decoration in its gift—the grand cross
of the Legion of Honor. Porter's letters to Hay tell the
story of the incident and likewise of the proposal of the
same honor to the Secretary of State. It was a graceful
act to recognize simultaneously the work of these co-
laborers in the field of international good-will; unfortunately some of Hay's opponents in the Senate made objection, and in June of 1905, only a few weeks before his
death, he requested that the resolution permitting him to
receive the decoration be withdrawn.[5] In my father's case
there was no difficulty.

Horace Porter to John Hay

June 18, 1904.

. . . M. Delcassé notified me that he was coming to the Embassy to see me this morning. When he arrived he said that the President had instructed him to come and offer in person to me the Grand Cross of the Legion of Honor, and he tendered me the insignia, saying that it was perfectly understood that as long as an American official remained in office he could not give a definite acceptance until the constitutional provision had been complied with which requires the authorization by Congress, and that it was only expected that I would receive the decoration subject to such conditions. Under the circumstances I could not refuse it without my motives being misunderstood and possible offence given to those who have been aiming to confer a high honor. Besides, coming from a sister Republic, it is different from the offer of some monarchical insignia. Of course it is intended not as a compliment to me but as a means of honoring the country. The French have been very much touched by the marked courtesies shown to their recent Ambassadors in America, and especially the action of the great universities in conferring upon them the highest degree known in our country—that of LL.D. As Congress does not meet for some time, I shall write you later upon the subject of its sanction. The chief satisfaction to me is that this testimonial came without the slightest suggestion from any outsider and was given entirely upon the initiative of the Government.

The anxiety of the President and M. Delcassé was again expressed in the warmest and most complimentary terms to confer upon you this highest grade of this famous order. Your marvellously successful direction of what they call the "American diplomacy," and your timely efforts in taking the initiative in the important steps looking to the world's peace, and your disposition to co-operate in a friendly way with other powers when great good can thereby be accomplished, all prompt this strong desire to confer upon you some testimonial; and the highest in the gift of France is "La Grande Croix de la Légion d'Honneur," rarely given, as you know, except to chiefs of State and particularly eminent officials. M. Delcassé and I are so intimate and so much together that we can talk very freely on such a subject. The only question was whether it would embarrass you to send you the decoration immediately. I explained again the deep appreciation which I know you entertain of all their kind thoughts of you, but intimated that until I talked the matter over further with them it would not be well to take such action.

Both the President and M. Delcassé understand and appreciate perfectly all the circumstances which control you in the matter at present. I can say to you positively that if at any time I may be authorized to "remove the embargo" the decoration will be sent to you the very next day. You know best what to do. My advice would be that if you do not assent before, you should do so at the time you retire from the public service, as you could then have no hesitation about accepting. It would be one of the pleasant souvenirs of your diplomatic life to hand down to your children. I hope, however, that the date of such retirement may be postponed for many a year, for the sake of the country and the diplomatic corps.[1]

The days that terminated my father's service as Ambassador brought also the parting between him and me. The most impressionable years of my life had been spent in Europe, and in the end the bonds that kept me there were stronger than those that bound me to America. Once again and for the last time the great rooms of the Embassy were opened,—on the occasion of my marriage to Edwin Mende, the son of the Dr. Mende who had attended my mother. The ceremony took place at the Church of the Holy Trinity on the fourth of March, 1905, the anniversary of her birthday. My father was to return as soon as possible to New York; I was to live in Berne, where my husband was already well started in his professional career. After the first shock from the idea of our separation, Father turned with his old zest and energy to giving me "the finest wedding that ever a girl had." Amongst the innumerable details to which he devoted his attention, I remember the vexed question of the automobile. No bride from the diplomatic corps had as yet driven to church in a motor, but I was determined to do so, "Protocol or no Protocol." For the last time, accordingly, the Ambassador sent in a formal request and received a note of official sanction from the hand of the mounted messenger.

When I left the Embassy with my husband late in the afternoon of our wedding day I knew my father was happy to have me enter on a simpler existence than that which he had given me during the last eight years. I had also the comfort of knowing that for the next few weeks his thoughts would be fully occupied in bringing to a close one of the most extraordinary undertakings of his whole life.

ELSIE PORTER MENDE

CHAPTER XXI

JOHN PAUL JONES

THE story of General Porter's second crusade on behalf of America's heroic dead was widely known at the time and is on record in great detail.[1] It is given here more briefly, but still largely in his own words. The bare facts of the search for the body of John Paul Jones are interesting and unusual enough to warrant their reappearance here, but the most interesting and unusual aspect of the narrative is to be read between the lines. Richard Watson Gilder, printing my father's article in the *Century,* comments upon it thus:

Few readers of General Horace Porter's account of his recovery of the body of our first naval hero will marvel so much at his success as at the audacity of the attempt. Other men of public spirit have put their hands in their pockets to aid some enthusiast in the prosecution of a practical object of national interest; but when before have the means and the enthusiasm proceeded from the same person to accomplish a doubtful and distressing task, calculated at the most to satisfy a sentimental craving?

Yet sentiment is the soul of patriotism, and this unique achievement, begun in a desire to atone for a people's neglect, is certain to result in the founding of one of the noblest and most lasting of human influences—a national shrine.

It was a task that called for belief in the value of heroic example, confidence in the logic of facts, and courage to face difficulties that would daunt anyone but a soldier bred to the rigid pursuit of duty and success. The needed qualities were found in a West Point graduate, trained as an engineer officer, tried at Chickamauga, where he won the medal of Congress for distinguished services, and polished in the finishing school conducted by Ulysses S. Grant between the Wilderness and Appomattox. Yet something more was required, such as a knowledge of men gained in the conduct of public affairs and the experience of a diplomat, who by the application of tact often removes obstacles all the more difficult because they are elusive.

Nor does it seem accidental that the man who has restored to the nation the relics of its first sailor-hero should have been he who led to success the movement which resulted in the shrine on Riverside Drive, where the body of the nation's great soldier-hero rests as a comfort and stimulus to future generations. The earlier service probably was the incentive to the later one. In the light of the plain recital in the preceding pages, and the impressive illustrations, can the reader picture a man of different training and experience entering on such a self-appointed service, much less pursuing it to complete success?

Gilder's analysis of the elements that were necessary to make up a man capable of this "unique achievement" is true to the letter. I would add to it only one thing. Gilder justly uses the word "sentiment"; I would have the reader of this abridgment of my father's *Century* article stop to consider how deep, how ardent, how insistent that sentiment must have been.

"Upon assuming charge of our embassy in Paris and finding myself among the old landmarks" which are associated with John Paul Jones, "I felt a deep sense of humiliation as an American citizen in realizing that our first and most fascinating naval hero had been lying for more than a century in an unknown and forgotten grave. . . . Knowing that he had been buried in Paris, I resolved to undertake personally a systematic and exhaustive search for the body. The investigation began in June, 1899."

A search for the certificate of burial brought out the fact that the register containing it had been burned by the Commune in 1871; the first copy of the certificate found (in the Bulletin of the Society of the History of Protestantism) fixed the date of Paul Jones' death, concerning which historians had differed, as July 18, 1792, but it did not mention the place of burial. Luckily the principal verb of the principal sentence,—the verb, indeed, of which "Jean Paul Jones" was the subject,—was missing, and this fact suggested that the copy was imperfect, and led to further search.

"In the Bibliothèque Nationale was at last found a copy of a magazine called the 'Correspondance Littéraire,' containing an article by Charles Read, giving the correct copy of the certificate of burial, which he had made from the register" in 1859. This copy supplied not only the missing verb, "was buried," but also, immediately following it, "the all-important phrase," "in the cemetery for foreign Protestants." "The article expressed the conviction of Mr. Read that the cemetery for foreign Protestants was the long since abandoned and almost forgotten cemetery of Saint Louis, situated upon a street formerly called L'Hôpital Saint Louis, at present Grange-aux-Belles."

In the course of a long search "to verify the grounds upon which Mr. Read had based his belief," it was found that in 1720 the government "had set aside a lot for the burial of foreign Protestants near the Porte Saint Martin," "which was closed in 1762. The Saint Louis cemetery for foreign Protestants was opened about that time and officially closed in January, 1793." The fact that the custodian of each of these cemeteries was named Corroy and that certain old documents showed that the position had descended from father to son "was evidence tending to show that the Saint Louis was the immediate successor of the Porte Saint Martin cemetery." And afterwards, indeed, there came to light a copy of a decree of 1781 which confirmed this fact. Then followed a search, lasting several months, through "all the journals and periodicals obtainable of about the date of the funeral," but still no reference could be found to any other cemetery for foreign Protestants nor yet to the burial-place of the admiral. As certain records in Paris showed that it was the Dutch ambassador who had got the government to set aside the cemetery for foreign Protestants and that "all the burials of such persons could be made only upon certificates issued by the Dutch embassy," records were searched in the Dutch legation and in the foreign office at the Hague, but no copies of such certificates had been preserved."

In following up every possible source of information about the burial there was "brought to light for the first time the mortifying fact that the hero who had once been the idol of the American people had been buried by charity, and that the payment of his funeral expenses was the timely and generous act of a foreign admirer." It seems that Gouverneur Morris, then American Minister to France, who was on intimate terms with Paul Jones, refused to spend on "such follies" as a public funeral "either the money of his heirs or that of the United States," and "told the person at whose house the Admiral lodged to cause him to be interred in the most private manner, and at the least possible expense." But M. Simonneau, the Commissary to whom this person was obliged to apply for a Protestant burial, was indignant "at the order given by the Minister," and said that if America "would not pay the expense of a public burial for a man who had rendered such signal services to France and America he would pay it himself." Whether or not Simonneau actually paid the funeral expenses out of his own means was the next question, and further investigation revealing that he did so, to the amount of 462 francs (the franc being then worth more than $.60), and that he was not reimbursed out of Paul Jones' estate, when it was settled, a search was at once instituted "to see whether any needy lineal descendants of . . . the generous Commissary could be found, with a view to paying to them the amount, with interest, expended by their worthy ancestor, as a tardy recognition of his noble act. Six persons of that name were discovered and communicated with, but no proof could be ascertained that any one of them was a descendant."

The Simonneau incident furnished indirect evidence in favor of the Saint Louis cemetery, since Simonneau would certainly have buried Paul Jones in a well-known and officially designated cemetery; another bit of corroborative evidence was the fact that the person who delivered the funeral oration was in the habit of burying his own parishioners in the Saint Louis cemetery. It was in connection with studying the records of this parish that there occurred "one of the many disappointments encountered during the researches,"—the absence of four pages just at the time of Jones' burial; and also one of the many triumphs, in the tracing of these pages through a collector and through junk-shops and antiquarian stores to the library of the Society of the History of Protestantism.

It now remained to run down a few rumors and traditions to the effect that John Paul Jones had been buried in Père Lachaise, in Picpus Cemetery, and near Dumfries, Scotland, and to disprove them all in turn. "All doubt having been removed as to the place of burial the next step was to make a personal inspection of the ground beneath which the long since abandoned cemetery was located and to endeavor to ascertain its history and its condition at the time of Paul Jones' death. It is situated in an uninviting section of the northeastern quarter of Paris at the corner of two streets now known as Rue Grange-aux-Belles and Rue des Écluses Saint Martin, and covered with buildings, principally of an inferior class." Two old maps of the property, 1773 and 1794, and a report, 1804, all three discovered only by long search, showed the cemetery as occupying a garden on Rue Grange-aux-Belles, behind and some eight feet below a courtyard, containing a house and a shed, which fronted on Rue des Écluses Saint Martin. "Thirty years later the grade of the street had been changed and the garden had been leveled up even with the courtyard, and the fact seemed to have been lost sight of that there had ever been a cemetery beneath."

"The next question was whether the dead have ever been removed from this abandoned cemetery, as had been the case in many others." Evidence, both positive and negative, was finally secured from various sources which established the fact that no body had ever been removed from Saint Louis cemetery except that of Lady Alexander Grant. There remained only the very remote possibility that the coffin might have been illegitimately removed by the revolutionary armies in order to turn its lead into bullets.

It was on the fact of the coffin's being lead that the chief hope of success now depended. "If the admiral had been buried in a wooden coffin hardly a vestige of it would have been in existence and only the mere skeleton of the body would have been found. Fortunately, however, the authentic letter written to Mrs. Janet Taylor, Paul Jones's eldest sister, by Colonel Blackden contained the following valuable information: 'His body was put into a leaden coffin on the 20th, that, in case the United States, which he had so essentially served, and with so much honor, should claim his remains they might be more easily removed.' The bill of 462 francs paid by M. Simonneau . . . would have provided for an unusually large expenditure and would have amply covered the cost of a substantial leaden coffin, a thorough preparation of the body to insure its preservation, and an elaborate system of packing, with a view to its transportation by sea."

"After having studied the manner and place of his burial and contemplated the circumstances connected with the strange neglect of his grave, one could not help feeling pained beyond expression and overcome by a sense of profound mortification. Here was presented the spectacle of a hero whose fame once covered two continents and whose name is still an inspiration to a world-famed navy, lying for more than a century in a forgotten grave like an obscure outcast, relegated to oblivion in a squalid corner of a distant foreign city, buried in ground once consecrated, but since desecrated by having been used at times as a garden, with the moldering bodies of the dead fertilizing its market vegetables, by having been covered later by a common dump pile, where dogs and horses had been buried, and the soil was still soaked with polluted waters from undrained laundries; and as a culmination of degradation, by having been occupied by a contractor for removing night-soil."

At this point, just as negotiations were about to be opened "with the proprietors and tenants who occupied the property with a view to purchasing the right to enter upon the premises and make the necessary excavations in order to explore thoroughly the cemetery . . . unfortunately the news of this intention became publicly known through the indiscretion of persons who had been consulted on the subject." Stories began to go round "regarding the prices that were to be paid for the property, the whole of which it was said was going to be bought by a rich government, at any cost. . . . Such representations . . . rendered negotiations on a practicable basis entirely impossible. This was altogether the most discouraging episode in the history of the undertaking. There was then but one course to pursue, however reluctantly, which was to drop the matter entirely for a couple of years in order to let the excitement subside.

"At the end of that time negotiations were quietly opened upon the basis of purchasing the right to explore the abandoned cemetery by means of subterranean galleries, provided that all damages to houses should be repaired, any victims of disease caused by foul emanations from the disturbed soil indemnified, and the property restored to its former condition. After a series of prolonged and tedious negotiations, appeals to the public spirit of the occupants of the property and an assurance that the government had made no appropriation nor taken any action in the matter, and that the work was simply an individual undertaking, I at last succeeded in procuring options in writing from all concerned granting the right for three months to enter upon the premises and make the necessary excavations.

"President Roosevelt, whose patriotic sentiments are among his strongest characteristics, upon learning of the undertaking, had asked for information regarding it, and upon receiving my reply giving an account of the project, sent an urgent message to Congress in February, 1905, recommending an appropriation of $35,000 for carrying out the work. It was late in the short session and no action was taken. It would not have been altogether unnatural, however, to regard the scheme as too Utopian in its nature to receive serious consideration, the remains of the admiral having been long since relegated to the realms of mystery and given up as lost beyond recovery.

"The Prefect of the Seine kindly permitted M. Paul Weiss of the service of the carrières (quarries) of the city of Paris to direct the work, which was begun on Friday, February 3, 1905. . . . The project presented serious difficulties from the fact that the filling of earth above the cemetery was composed of the dumpings of loose soil not compact enough to stand alone, and the shafts and galleries had to be solidly lined and shored up with heavy timbers as the excavations proceeded. The drainage was bad in places and there was trouble from the water. The walls of one of the buildings were considerably damaged. Slime, mud, and mephitic odors were encountered, and long red worms appeared in abundance."

The very first excavation "proved clearly that the dead had never been disturbed"; it also confirmed a statement in the report of 1804 to the effect that most of the bodies were buried in trenches, and "led to the conclusion that there would be very few leaden coffins found, as they could be afforded only by persons in easy circumstances." In all five shafts were sunk, to a depth of eighteen feet. "Day and night gangs of workmen were employed. . . . The excavated earth had to be carried to a distance of two miles. . . . Galleries were pushed in every direction, and 'soundings' were made between them with long iron tools adapted to this purpose, so that no leaden coffin could possibly be missed." Within the area enclosed by the cemetery wall,— approximately 120 by 130 feet,—there were excavated "80 feet in length of shafts, 800 feet of galleries, and about 600 feet of soundings."

"On February 22 the first leaden coffin was discovered. . . . The outer wooden coffin had nearly disappeared and the inscription plate it bore had fallen on the lid of the leaden coffin. . . . It was so corroded and incrusted that no portion of the inscription could be read," so it was taken "to Messrs. André & Son, the well-known decipherers and restorers of ancient enamels and art objects, who . . . promised to report the next day." The coffin plate proved to bear the name *M. E. Anglois,* but already "a reporter with a lively imagination . . . invented a highly dramatic story and gave it to the press, stating that there was such certainty entertained that this leaden coffin contained the body of Paul Jones that I had summoned the personnel of the embassy and others to the scene, including the Commissary of Police, who attended ornamented with his tricolored scarf; that the coffin was opened with great ceremony and solemnity, and the group, deeply affected, stood reverently, with bowed heads, awaiting the recognition of the body of the illustrious sailor, but that it was evident that a serious error had been made, and that, to the sad disappointment of all present, it had to be acknowledged that the body bore no traces of being that of the admiral. This pure fabrication was copied in America and France, and in some quarters commented upon in a manner to give the impression that the projector of the exploration was simply guessing as to the identity of the object of the search.

"On March 23 a second leaden coffin was discovered, with a plate easily read, bearing the words 'Richard Hay, Esq., died in Paris the 29th January 1785.'

"On March 31 a third leaden coffin was unearthed. . . . It was much superior in solidity and workmanship to the others. A thorough search was made in the vicinity, but no inscription plate could be found. It was decided to open this coffin, but as the odors were so disagreeable in the unventilated gallery the examination was postponed until a connection could be made with another gallery, so as to admit a current of air.

"On April 7 the coffin was opened in the presence of Colonel Blanchard, M. Weiss, M. Géninet, superintendent of the work, the foreman, several workmen, and myself. The lid was so firmly soldered that it was removed with some difficulty. There was a strong alcoholic odor. . . . The body was covered with a winding-sheet and firmly packed with hay and straw. A rough measurement indicated the height of Paul Jones. Those engaged upon the work had been furnished some time before with copies of the admiral's Congressional medal showing his bust in profile. Half a dozen candles were placed near the head of the coffin, and the winding-sheet was removed from the head and chest, exposing the face. To our intense surprise the body was marvelously well preserved, all the flesh remaining intact, but slightly shrunken and of a grayish brown or tan color. The surface of the body and the linen were moist. The face presented quite a natural appearance except that the cartilaginous portion of the nose had been bent over toward the right side, pressed down, and completely disfigured by its too close proximity to the lid of the coffin. Upon placing the medal near the face, comparing the other features and recognizing the peculiar characteristics—the broad forehead, high cheek-bones, prominently arched eye-orbits, and other points of resemblance, we immediately exclaimed, 'Paul Jones'; and all those who had gathered about the coffin removed their hats, feeling that there was every probability that they were standing in the presence of the illustrious dead—the object of the long search."

That night the coffin was taken to the Paris School of Medicine that the body might be scientifically examined by experts in anthropology and pathology for the purpose of complete identification. During the six days consumed by this examination the digging went on in the cemetery and two more leaden coffins were found, in separate graves, like the others, near the walls and away from the common trenches. One of these bore a plate inscribed with the name of *Maidison;* the other, which was unmarked, contained the skeleton of a man considerably over six feet in height. All the coffins except the one containing the remains of the admiral were left undisturbed in the places where they had been discovered, and the shafts and galleries were refilled and the property restored. . . .

"There now took place one of the most scientific, painstaking, and conscientious examinations conceivable for the purpose of verifying beyond all doubt the identification of the body submitted for this purpose. . . . Twelve American or French persons officially took part in or witnessed the work of identification, and their affirmative verdict, after six days passed in the application of every possible test, was positive and unanimous, and was formally certified to under the official seals of their respective departments." The scientists who made the examinations "were not employed experts; they cheerfully gave their services gratuitously, purely in the interest of science, and as an act of comity between two friendly nations in solving an important historical problem. . . .

"Two circumstances combined to render the identification of the remains comparatively easy: the remarkable state of preservation of the body and the abundance of accurate information in existence descriptive of the dead." In addition to the Congressional medal, there were two busts by Houdon, said to be excellent likenesses, one of which was life-size and furnished reliable measurements; there was also "a mass of authentic information regarding the admiral's chief characteristics, appearance, size, color of hair, age, etc."

The records examined had led to the expectation that no uniform, medal, or sword would be found in the coffin, and so it proved. The body was clothed, under the winding-sheet, in a "shirt of fine linen, handsomely made, with plaits and ruffles corresponding with the historical description of the admiral's fondness for dress." The only other article of clothing was the linen cap into which the long hair had been gathered at the back of the head; this was marked in thread with a small letter,—a "J," or, when reversed, a "P." All the anthropometric measurements tallied with those of the life-sized bust, the greatest difference being two millimeters: the arch of the eye-brows was the same, the contour of the brow, the width between the eyes, the unusual shape of the lobe of the ear, the high cheek-bones, the muscles of the face, the distance between the hair and the root of the nose, between the sub-nasal point and the lips, and between the lips and the point of the chin. The height of the body, five feet seven inches, corresponded to record (three-eighths of an inch is the difference allowed by anthropologists between a person standing and the same person lying down); so did the color of the hair, which was a brown so dark that it might be called black; tinges of gray in a few places and the condition of the teeth indicated a person between forty and fifty years old, and John Paul Jones was forty-five when he died.

"Then came one of the most interesting features of the verification—the autopsy, doubtless the only one in history ever made upon a body that had been buried for a hundred and thirteen years." It disclosed a spot or rather, a scar, on the left lung, "clearly the result of an attack of pneumonia or broncho-pneumonia"; this corresponded to the accounts of Paul Jones' contracting pneumonia when he was in Russia. It further proved that he had died of chronic interstitial nephritis, the disease which would account for the various pathological symptoms presented by him at the close of his life.

"No mark of a wound was discovered on the body. Paul Jones was never wounded. History is in abundant possession of the most detailed records of every fight in which he was engaged, and there is nowhere a single mention of his ever having received a wound."

After the examination had been brought to an end in due form, the body was prepared and packed again for transportation to America, the old coffin placed in another leaden coffin to which was affixed the seal of the American Embassy, and the whole set in "an outer coffin of oak provided with eight silver handles, the lid of which was secured by sixteen silver screws." On April 20 General Porter, his secretaries, the consul-general, Mr. Gowdy, and M. Weiss escorted this coffin covered with the American flag, to the American Church of the Holy Trinity, where it was left to await transfer to the United States.

Upon receiving the "official certification of the American Embassy and Consulate of the identification of the body of Admiral John Paul Jones" and the "official certification of the participants and witnesses," President Roosevelt had ordered a squadron of four battleships, commanded by Admiral Sigsbee, to proceed to Cherbourg and convey the body to Annapolis, where it was to be interred in the crypt of the new chapel then under construction. The French Government took advantage of the arrival of the Americans to pay every possible courtesy to them and every possible honor to the memory of John Paul Jones. On the sixth of July Admiral Sigsbee brought five hundred bluejackets to Paris, and that afternoon the ceremonies attending the transfer of the body took place in the Church of the Holy

Trinity, before one of the most distinguished audiences that had ever been drawn together in Paris. Eight American sailors of over six feet in height carried the coffin. It was placed on a French artillery caisson and escorted down the Avenue des Champs Élysées and across the bridge of Alexander III to the Esplanade des Invalides in a procession made up as follows: "the famous French cavalry, the Garde Républicaine, five hundred American sailors,[2] the body of John Paul Jones, Admiral Sigsbee and staff, the American ambassadors[3] and Senator Lodge, the personnel of the American embassy, the high officials of the French government and of the diplomatic corps, delegations from the American Navy League and from the American Chamber of Commerce in Paris," and members of various American patriotic organizations, all on foot. "Then came a battalion of French horse-artillery and a battalion of French infantry with their famous bands." On the Esplanade des Invalides the coffin was placed on a catafalque beneath a tent of purple velvet and gold. Here the troops filed by and rendered the highest military honors to the dead. "Paris had that day witnessed a pageant entirely unique in its way and of surpassing beauty and solemnity. The weather was superb, and the streets and houses appropriately decorated. The vast crowds . . . uncovered reverently as the coffin passed."

With the closing paragraphs of this story, my father also closed the story of his own life in France.

"The next day, July 7, I went to Cherbourg to sail for home. A cordial invitation had been received from the government and Admiral Sigsbee to take passage on board the flagship. While this was deeply appreciated, it was declined, as I felt that it would be in better taste to return by the ordinary lines of travel now that the subject of the mission had been formally placed in the hands of the navy and I could render no further useful service.

"The fleets of the two nations lay side by side in that

picturesque military harbor, discharging their peaceful and sympathetic mission, our phantom-colored vessels presenting an interesting contrast to the black hulls of the French warships. There I took a last look at the coffin which contained all that is mortal of the hero, the search for whose remains had furnished a congenial task for the past six years."

As my father sailed out of the harbor, the squadron honored him with a parting ambassadorial salute.

BOOK IV
LAST YEARS
1905-1921

CHAPTER XXII

PEACE OR WAR?

GENERAL PORTER had looked forward not only to coming home but also to the time when he could be free from responsibility. That time had now come, and in his old home in New York he determined to live as he wished during the few years life still had in store for him. Though nearly seventy, he seemed in looks, mind, and health a decade younger. Nevertheless the numerous proposals that he received for reëntering the business world made no appeal to him. What he wanted was to renew old friendships, and also to impart to his fellow countrymen, either by writing or by speaking, some of the conclusions that he had formed as the result of his eight years abroad.

With the advent of the winter season he found himself in as much demand as ever as an after-dinner speaker. Old friends were eager to welcome him to the Lotos Club, the Lambs' Club, the Chamber of Commerce; at the New England dinner, the Pilgrims' dinner, the dinner of the Bar Association, and at many others he was warmly received. The ease, the genial wit, the sparkle that had always charmed his listeners were still there unchanged; but the serious note was new. In earlier days he had been wont to look to the past for his inspiration; now he turned to the future.

His study of the "floundering powers of Europe" had given him a sure insight into the years ahead. He had witnessed at close range the fall of Delcassé, driven from office by the Kaiser; he had seen King Edward acclaimed in Paris as a new friend and ally; he knew in detail the story

311

of the mad race in armaments to which the Great Powers had committed themselves. Indeed, hardly a day of his experience as Ambassador had failed to supply him with evidence that the great problem for the next decade was the peace of the world. Toward its solution he could now contribute his warning and his wisdom. "Law and Diplomacy,"' "Foreign Policy," "The Peace of the World," "Arbitration," arguments for a permanent court of international justice,—these were the topics to which he responded at the toastmaster's call. His skill in this form of oratory kept him from pushing his seriousness too hard or too far; for that very reason his message counted at its full weight.

Although the body of John Paul Jones had reached our shores in July, 1905, it was not until April, 1906, that the Government, by formal exercises at Annapolis, paid due tribute to its first great naval commander. Nothing was omitted to make the ceremony worthy of an historic occasion, and, as was most fitting, to Porter was entrusted the honor of giving the oration of the day. As in writing or speaking of Grant Porter had striven to present his character in such a way that he should seem a real man, a rounded character, alive with purpose and feeling, so in his address on John Paul Jones he used the same method to the same end.

Impressive though this recognition was, Porter was not satisfied with such an ephemeral tribute. He desired a permanent memorial to the hero, and so pressed upon Congress a bill appropriating a considerable sum of money for the construction of a crypt under the chapel at the Naval Academy, in which the body of John Paul Jones should rest. To obtain action upon the bill proved a matter of some years; but the beautiful memorial now at Annapolis is as much the embodiment of one of Horace Porter's dreams as is the tomb on Riverside Drive in New York.[1]

It was through such activities as these that Porter came

to the next event in his career, his service as delegate to the second Peace Conference at the Hague in 1907.

The first Peace Conference, initiated by the Tsar in the late summer of 1898, was in a way an open recognition of the nervous state in which the European powers found themselves on the outbreak of the Spanish War. Not only were they under the strain of competition in armaments; their plans as to China were upset by the advent of the United States in the Philippines, and they were at a loss as to how to deal with the new Power which, by means of a swift and successful war against one of themselves, had so unexpectedly disturbed the balance of world affairs. When the Conference assembled in the summer of 1899, it used the traditional methods of diplomacy, and attained, as Porter had foreseen, the inevitable negative results. Armaments were not limited, and no effective means were taken to prevent or delay the outbreak of armed conflicts.

Soon after the dissolution of the conference, the peace of the world was broken by the Boer War. The Boxer rebellion made another continent the scene of arms, and then followed the Russo-Japanese War. As the appalling contest in the Far East dragged on from month to month, Roosevelt, as President of a strong neutral power, felt called upon to use his influence to turn the thoughts of the world toward peace. The immediate cause of his action was the resolution adopted by the Interparliamentary Union, which had been holding its annual session at St. Louis. Accordingly, in October, 1904, Secretary Hay addressed to the signatory powers of the acts of the first Hague Conference a note proposing that the nations reassemble to carry on to completion, if possible, the work which the gathering of 1899 had left unfinished.[2]

This note it had been Porter's duty as Ambassador to discuss with Delcassé. If it was the general opinion of European diplomats that the assembling of the conference must wait upon the conclusion of the war, it was recognized also that the United States might play an important part in hastening that day. A few weeks later at the banquet of the American Club in Paris on Thanksgiving Eve, the significance of Roosevelt's leadership in world affairs was recognized by Baron d'Estournelles de Constant, long known as a steadfast advocate of peace; Porter's speech on the occasion was a tribute to the glory of our navy and a plea for proper support of it as essential if we were to make good our claim to leadership.

Upon the signing of the treaty of Portsmouth in 1905, President Roosevelt courteously waived, in favor of the Tsar, any privileges that his initiative may have given the United States as to the calling of the proposed conference, and in due season it was agreed that the second Peace Conference should assemble at the Hague in June of 1907.

To the President and his Secretary of State, Elihu Root, who had succeeded to that office after the death of Hay in June, 1905, the purpose of the United States in participating in this international assemblage was to present and to urge a positive and yet reasonable program which might serve as a step toward a real organization of the world. If we were to do this effectively we must be represented by our best, by men who, through their high international standing, could command the attention and respect of the diplomats of Europe. America's two most distinguished ex-ambassadors were Joseph H. Choate [3] and Horace Porter, and it was natural for Roosevelt to nominate them as first and second delegates respectively. The third delegate was Uriah M. Rose, of Arkansas, a Democrat, at one time president of the American Bar Association, and the author of articles on American and European jurisprudence.

Although my father after his return to America had frequently averred in his speeches that he had come back to stay, and that he would never again quit his native shores unless the sheriff drove him out of house and country, he

JOSEPH H. CHOATE AND HORACE PORTER

was not unwilling to accept the appointment, mostly because
of the chance it offered him for further service in a field
in which he was entirely at home, and in which he could
foster the spirit of conciliation among the Great Powers
before it was too late; but also incidentally because he was
glad to visit me in Berne and make the acquaintance of his
grand-daughter. I met him in Paris in May and stayed
with him while he was completing the arrangements for
obtaining the services of the devoted Bailly-Blanchard.
Since the proceedings of the Conference would be in French,
it was necessary to have a secretary familiar with that
tongue and the ways of diplomacy, and no one fitted these
requirements better than he. The two traveled to the
Hague, arriving in good season for the opening of the Conference on June 15.

The second Hague Conference was an international assemblage in the true sense of the word; indeed, it was the
first of its kind. Whereas in 1899 only twenty-six nations
had sent delegates, in 1907 forty-four nations were represented, the increase being mainly accounted for by the presence of representatives from all the countries of North,
Central, and South America except Costa Rica and Hon-
duras. Although the members assembled with varying degrees of hope or skepticism, all recognized the fact that the
possession by Russia of the presidency of the Conference
gave that country an undue preponderance of influence.[4]
It was a diplomatic rather than a parliamentary body; that
is, the vote was by nations; and any resolution passed with
less than unanimous support was recognized as having little
more than the status of a pious and therefore negligible
wish.

Under these rules of the game,—the rules of old-world
diplomacy,—the delegates of the new order for which the
United States stood must play their hands. As has been
said, they were far from being novices, but over and above
their practical knowledge they were inspired by a sincerity

and intensity of purpose derived partly from their own natures and partly from the instructions that they had received from Washington. As Americans they had practiced ways of thought and action in public affairs which they believed to be applicable to a wider sphere than their own country and of which they knew the world as a whole stood in need. They had been intrusted with the duty of advocating before the assembled nations of mankind such proposals as a permanent court of arbitral justice, the immunity of private property at sea in time of war, abstention by a government from force in collecting contract debts due to its nationals from another country, a general arbitration agreement among nations, the establishment of machinery for calling future conferences without waiting for the action of any one nation.[5] If they were to have good fortune in advocating this idealistic program, it must come from an uncommon blend of judgment with idealism.

Socially, the four months of the session was a period of much pomp and circumstance. There were receptions, dinners, luncheons, and many informal affairs; but during all this coming and going the serious purpose of the Conference was not lost sight of, and many matters of business were discussed and agreed upon in these hours of apparent relaxation. To Porter and Choate they supplied valuable opportunities for finding out how the land lay in respect to the proposals that they were instructed to advocate.

With many of the delegates my father was already on friendly terms. Nelidow, the Russian first delegate, had been Ambassador at Paris during his years there, and when the Tsar's representative showed too openly his disposition to be domineering it was frequently the American's tactful but none the less vigorous appeals to his "cher collègue" that opened the latter's eyes to the wisdom of a more conciliatory course. With the German first delegate, the huge Marschall von Bieberstein, Porter could also work amicably, in spite of their wide differences of opinion on the subject of arbitration. He considered him one of the most forceful men in the Conference, and the fact that Baron Marschall, like old Münster, was critical of the Kaiser was a point in his favor with my father.

The use to which Porter put his knowledge of diplomatic procedure and his native quickness of wit may be illustrated by one incident. When Germany submitted plans for an international prize court, the Americans were taken by surprise. Not to be left behind, General Porter took a blank sheet of foolscap, folded it, and wrote on the outside "American Proposal for an International Court of Prize." Obtaining the floor, he expressed the interest of his country in the project, and delivered his paper at the secretary's desk. He gravely explained that the sheet was blank, for he did not have the detailed plan with him at the moment, but assured the assembly that it would be forthcoming when needed. The act was a characteristic piece of Yankee bluff, but it gave the Americans the recognition they desired when the matter was discussed in committee. Indeed, in obtaining the adoption of a convention on this subject Mr. Choate rendered important service.[6]

Porter's special duty at the Conference was responsibility for the proposal that a government should not use force in collecting debts due to its nationals from another country. On account of the blockade of Venezuelan ports in 1902 by Germany, England, and Italy, this was a question of vital interest to the countries of Latin-America, and through a dispatch written at that time by Dr. Luis M. Drago, Minister of Foreign Affairs for Argentina, it had been brought to the attention of the entire world. It had also been the subject of a resolution adopted by the Pan-American Conference at Rio Janeiro in 1906. "The question had been a very serious source of controversy for many years. Sometimes nations had almost come to blows, and very bitter feelings had been excited by a resort to force by creditor nations, even in the case of inability to pay, and the first creditor nation that grabbed the customs or territory or other resources of a debtor nation, was deemed to have the preference in any solution or settlement that might ensue." [7]

The arduous nature of the task with which General Porter was entrusted is well brought out by Mr. Choate. "From the moment of its introduction until its final adoption, General Porter, by night and by day, in season and out of season, in public and private, devoted his entire energies to carrying this important measure. It was a work of the greatest difficulty and delicacy, because it ran counter to the settled convictions and practices of many of the nations, and to the general objections to obligatory arbitration in any form, and also because the friends of the principle of the measure were much divided in their views. To reconcile these differences required all the ability of a most experienced diplomatist, and as every word in the convention, as finally adopted, was subjected to close criticism before the actual phraseology finally arrived at could be adopted, the wonder is that he was able to succeed at all." [8]

Of course the real work of the Conference was carried out in the sessions of the commissions and subcommissions into which the body was divided. It was at one of these meetings, held on July 16, that my father made his formal statement in behalf of what was known among the delegates as "the proposition Porter." In the opening portion of his argument he shrewdly made much of the embarrassments to which the foreign office of a nation had been often exposed on account of the importunities of its citizens or subjects that the armed forces of the country should be used to collect money which had been invested in a speculative venture at a high rate of interest. He pointed out that the amounts claimed were often excessive, showing that in thirteen large claims that had been examined by commissions during the past sixty years the highest sum awarded had been only 80 per cent of the amount asked for, while in several cases it had fallen to the absurdly low figure of three-quarters of one per cent. In one instance the United States, after sixteen years of effort and the expenditure of $2,500,000, had obtained nothing.[9]

This recital of facts Porter followed up by reference to the opinions of eminent authorities in international law, and by quotations from our own secretaries of state and from prime ministers of Great Britain. His final sentences were a plea that this Conference, in which both debtor and creditor nations were represented, should take action to put a stop to an evil practice so fraught with danger to the peace of the world.*

Although "the proposition Porter" expressed a policy which was of manifest advantage to the nations of the world and which involved the sacrifice of no cherished rights, there were, as Mr. Choate indicates, difficulties both in principle and in detail which must be overcome before it could be presented to the plenary session of the Conference for final approval. In these labors Porter and the American delegation received great assistance from Dr. Drago, delegate from Argentina. It was not till the very end of the session that the convention was put into the form which ensured its final adoption; as it passed it constituted one of the most important achievements of the Conference. To the nations of the New World it meant that the Monroe Doctrine had "made its first and formal entry into the public law of Europe as well as America."[10] American ports were not to be again blockaded by foreign fleets for the collection of contract debts. Moreover, the informal arguments of Porter and his colleagues in urging the proposal upon the other delegates made it plain to all that the United States stood ready to defend the Monroe Doctrine by force if necessary. Finally, as Mr. Choate pointed out, it was "perhaps the first case on record, of a form of compulsory arbitration, agreed to by all the nations of the earth except five, who abstained from voting."[11] Since, owing to the

* The English translation of his speech will be found in the Appendix.

vigorous opposition of Germany and Austria, it had been found impossible to obtain more than an abstract "declaration" in favor of general compulsory arbitration, the acceptance of the principle in a restricted form in the convention was a triumph of which the American delegate who brought his "proposition" into safe harbor may well have been proud. From that time to this the convention has been accepted without question by all the nations of the world.

Although, except for Porter's accomplishment, the proposals for world organization to which the United States was committed made little progress at the Conference, it was quite otherwise with the part of the program which had to do with war. The subject of limitation of armaments was virtually prohibited; but there was a great variety of topics, covering the rights of neutrals and the employment of different methods of warfare, concerning which definitions might be framed and regulations of more or less binding force made. Considering the debate that went on as to these points day and night, the gathering might almost be called a War Conference.

Of this phase of the discussions my father had much to say when in September, shortly before the close of the sessions, he visited me in Berne. I confess his views of what the future held in store appalled me. "The next war," he said, "will be under the water and over our heads. Nothing will be immune from it." Besides these terrors, there would be poison gases, and long-range guns that would render useless the fortifications of such cities as Paris. The controversy over the employment of aircraft gave him particular concern. "If those delegates at the Hague don't come to a definite decision about the use of airplanes in war time," he remarked, "they'll be dropping bombs on every town they see." To my suggestion that only fortifications and large garrison towns could properly be bombarded, he answered: "How are you going to distinguish? Nearly every town in Europe has a wall or tower of some sort, and a few soldiers can constitute a garrison." His informal talks on the subject with the representatives of the leading European nations revealed great diversity of opinion. England and France were non-committal, and my father received the impression that the English felt themselves safe across the Channel. Marschall von Bieberstein, a Rhinelander, was apprehensive of the fate of frontier towns. There was, however, so little knowledge of what aircraft could and could not do that the Conference could not be brought to express more than a conventional "voeu," or opinion, on the matter.

With his mind full of these subjects, he attended with me the maneuvers of the Swiss army. Believing, as he did, that the large standing armies of the great European nations would surely lead to war, he was greatly impressed by the military system prevailing in Switzerland. He considered it an ideal method of giving those essentials of training that he believed desirable for the citizens of his own country, and he was confident that it would supply a force adequate for defense; yet, unavailable for aggression, it would never arouse jealousy and suspicion; and it kept at a minimum the professional officer class whose only hope of promotion within a reasonable time lay in war.[12]

In all these armament discussions I saw that my father's training and practical experience as a soldier made him impatient with the point of view of the professional diplomat. "If some of those fellows at the Hague," he said to me, "had been through four years of battles like the Wilderness and Cold Harbor, they'd be mighty anxious to stop war at any cost. They don't know what war means."

On his return to America Porter naturally took advantage of every opportunity to give to his fellow countrymen his recent impressions of the state of the world as regards war and peace. It was not a merely academic report that he presented; he was convinced that, if the sinister forces of which he had had such clear revelations continued to work,

America could not afford to go her old way regardless of it all. She would need the services of a trained and able diplomatic corps; she must have the power to defend herself both on land and on sea. Concerning these problems the ordinary business or professional man was little informed, little interested, and inclined to dismiss the whole subject with a skeptical or cynical remark. With peace societies, the International Law Association, and the Navy League, it was a different matter; here Porter had eager listeners.

Of all the many aspects which this complicated question presented, the one which happened to engage his interest most deeply and which gave him opportunity for the practical work which he enjoyed was that of a naval program suitable for the needs of the United States. The American Navy League had been founded in 1902 upon the model of similar organizations in England and Germany. Porter had been one of the early members, and upon his return to New York in 1905 had joined the small group of men who directed its fortunes. It was a modest organization, issuing bulletins, sometimes publishing a magazine, holding dinners, and striving to bring into its ranks men who would be influential in putting its program before Congress and the country. When in 1909 Porter accepted the office of President he had little notion of the importance that the League would assume within the next six years.

Nevertheless, certain signs of the times had a message for those who could read them. Shortly after the close of the Hague Conference President Roosevelt had started our fleet on its spectacular trip around the world; Germany was building rapidly; in England a "naval scare" was about to burst forth. When, on February 22, 1909, our returning vessels steamed into Chesapeake Bay with a reception which in its impressiveness made a fitting close to the Roosevelt administration, Porter, as he watched the stately procession pass, saw in the event something more than a mere cause for national pride. That evening he was to preside at a dinner given by the Navy League to the officers of the fleet. "Speak with authority in pleading for peace and justice when nations rush wantonly into useless wars," was the note he had made as the theme of his remarks. This was again his text at the dinner given a few weeks later at the Lambs' Club to Admiral Sperry.

To the censorious it might appear that Porter's attitude on the subject of war and peace was two-faced. This criticism was openly made of him a little later in the spring of 1909, when, at the annual meeting of the Peace Society of the City of New York, he was elected one of its vice-presidents. Calling Porter a "Dr. Jekyll and Mr. Hyde," one ardent peace advocate protested against the election of the President of the Navy League to office in their organization. The presiding officer, Andrew Carnegie, calmed the storm by the genial remark that "General Porter is a many-sided man. No doubt it is one of his better sides that has been elected here this afternoon." [13] If he was inconsistent, the best justification for his course was furnished in Carnegie's address on the same occasion. "Never in our day," he said, "has the world's peace been so seriously threatened, never were nations so busy as to-day in the hopeless task of becoming 'too powerful to be attacked.' Britain has just discovered in Germany a menace to her existence. Germany, having equal rights upon the sea, fails to recognize the right of Britain to be 'mistress of the seas.' But even if a collision be miraculously avoided, the guiltless, peace-loving nations of the world in turn will have been compelled to embark upon the building of excessive navies, many of these obtained and maintained only by extorting millions from people already bordering upon starvation."

Of this inconsistency General Porter was of course fully aware. I give his defense in his own words taken from a speech delivered a few years later, in 1913, at the annual dinner of the Navy League. It shows how strikingly the experience of the soldier and the wisdom of the statesman enabled him to interpret the course of events.

"Now I have been on both sides of this question of peace and war. I began my career by helping to make man 'downright,' and afterwards in diplomacy I took up the more difficult task of trying to make him upright. At the second Hague Conference, which was the first great international peace assembly in the world, the first one in which every nation in the world was represented, and represented by very able men, we labored in the interests of peace for four months and a week, in season and out of season, by day and by night. What did we accomplish? Why, before we got there we were notified in writing by the Great Powers that if the question of reduction of armaments was mentioned they would leave the conference. Russia at the conference eight years before had made that one of the paramount topics to be discussed; now it could not be mentioned. And after all our labors we had hardly turned our backs when this flame of war was seen in every direction, leading finally into this destructive war in the Balkans. Well, this taught us many lessons. It taught us that in the great emergency a nation may be saved by guns but never by tongues. It was said by many that the only peace that the powers there knew of was how to get a piece of another country's territory, and that the peace conference was composed of delegates who discussed the subject of peace in the brief intervals between wars. It taught us that you cannot go without an armament and say to a nation, 'Please don't shoot.' You cannot get down on your knees and apologize. You can never gain ground by eating dirt. You can make treaties. Well, we have a good many instances of treaties that did not hold, and they seldom hold longer than the necessities which brought them about. Treaties in fact are like sausages; the more you know about how they are made, the less you are apt to like them."

No less strongly than my father insisted on the need of a

suitable army and navy for defense did he stress the importance of the right organization of our foreign service. His eight years in France had made him thoroughly familiar with the defects of our system, if system it could be called; and the article which he wrote for the *Century* (March, 1909) entitled "Should the Government Own Its Embassies?" contains a vigorous statement of existing faults, together with praise for the reforms in the diplomatic service initiated by Secretary Root. The course of events in the next few years only increased the ex-Ambassador's conviction that the management of foreign affairs is a field in which ignorance and inexperience are more than usually harmful.

Besides these activities, mention must be made of the honors bestowed upon General Porter by various colleges. The degree of LL.D. was given him in 1906 by Princeton, in 1908 by Williams, in 1910 by Harvard.[14] He served as President of the Board of Visitors at both West Point and Annapolis; for his services in recovering the body of John Paul Jones he received the unanimous thanks of Congress and was given the privilege of the floor of both houses for life.

During the years between 1907 and the outbreak of the Great War I visited my father at Bar Harbor with my family in two different summers, and we spent the winter of 1908-1909 with him in New York. I found him leading in New York much the same life as in former years, but at a less strenuous pace. His house was managed by his secretary and companion, Miss Emma Foster, a niece of General Longstreet's. Dinners there and at the houses of his friends were his chief recreation, interspersed with frequent visits to the theater and the opera. How much people enjoyed him is well expressed by one of his old Southern friends: "I especially recall his wonderful kindliness of spirit, sense of humor, and spontaneity of wit, which always left one invigorated and mentally refreshed."

In spite of his advancing years he was very independent. He was contented to spend many hours a day by himself and when he went out in the evening he usually chose to walk home or hail a taxi rather than to order out his own car. One evening, when he was over seventy-five, the taxi in which he was riding collided with another motor, the door gave way, and my father was thrown out upon the sidewalk. All that he asked of the policeman who helped him to his feet was to brush his coat and call another taxi to take him on to the Metropolitan Opera House.

During the last of these visits, at Bar Harbor during the summer of 1913, I realized with a heavy heart that the infirmities of age were rapidly gaining upon him; but I could not then imagine how much he had yet to live through.

The Great War burst upon the world; both in its coming and in the method used in conducting it my father saw the confirmation of all his prophecies and all his fears. The work which he had put into the Navy League had fully justified itself, and though he was in his seventy-eighth year he was ready to give one more term of service as its president. His last public appearance in this capacity was at its annual banquet in New York on May 14, 1915. That date had been chosen on account of the presence in the Hudson River of the North Atlantic squadron. On the subject of naval preparedness public opinion was no longer indifferent, and the League was receiving increased support for its bold program that the Government should authorize a bond issue of $500,000,000 for a larger navy. In the first week of May came the sinking of the *Lusitania;* excitement in New York was intense, and the morning papers on the day of the banquet contained President Wilson's first note to Germany. General Porter's remarks in introducing the toastmaster, Colonel Robert M. Thompson, were brief, but they were no less fervent than the speeches that followed from Assistant Secretary of the Navy Franklin D. Roosevelt, Dr. Lyman Abbott, and others. At the plate of each guest was a copy of *The Seven Seas,* the new official organ of the Navy League, to which Porter had contributed an article entitled "Living in a Fool's Paradise." The fact that he had overcome a growing distaste for writing sufficiently to prepare an article shows his sense of the crisis in which the United States found itself.

The appalling war waging at present in Europe [he wrote] warns us to take counsel as to the means of saving our country from ever being involved in such a calamity. We assume that every right-thinking person in this nation is an ardent advocate of peace. It would be a bloodthirsty creature who would be in favor of war for war's sake. The only difference between certain classes of our citizens is as to how best to secure the blessings of peace. The peace-at-any-price faction insist upon destroying the national defense, and depending entirely upon the execution of treaties forbidding wars, which might be called the "coaxing method."

The vast body of patriotic Americans—those who take a practical and not a mere sentimental view of the case—believe in maintaining an adequate military force to defend the life of the nation against invasion so that we may not invite attack by demonstrating to the world our inability to resist it. The whole country has recently received a severe shock in learning from official sources our condition of absolute unpreparedness. Those who have studied the history of wars and their causes and have had experience in international negotiations are firmly convinced of the peril of the situation and believe that it is not only dangerous but criminal. Our thoughtful people do not urge the maintenance of an unnecessary, a large standing army and navy, but they insist upon an adequate force on land and sea and particularly a supply of war material so essential to the national defense. There is a realizing sense that we have assumed the proportions of a world power with our colonies extending around the circuit of the globe, with intricate international questions constantly occurring; and at a time when the rivalry, jealousy and faithlessness of nations are made more manifest every day, patriotic Americans believe that the Republic should be able to speak with some authority when she lifts her voice in defense of the right in the numerous disputes which constantly arise between nations. The ultra-pacifists believe that international peace can be secured by treaties. Unfortunately they are leaning upon a broken reed. A supreme effort in this direction was made at the second Hague Peace Conference. The work performed by it was the most important in the history of international negotiations.

It was the only congress ever convened in which every nation on the face of the earth was represented. The ability of this assemblage, composed principally of trained statesmen, diplomats, and jurists, was noteworthy. Every delegate felt himself sent by his Government to apply all his experience and best talents in framing the most solemn and binding treaties that could be devised. They labored assiduously and devotedly for more than four months to discover what could possibly be done in favor of the world's peace. Their labors finally terminated in the making of twelve comprehensive treaties, which were executed by virtually all the powers of the world. Only about half a dozen delegates, principally from some smaller powers, abstained from voting, Not a negative vote was cast.

It is discouraging to realize that our backs had scarcely been turned upon The Hague when the most desperate and uncalled for of wars broke out and that the treaties were ruthlessly violated. It made all feel that mere treaties had failed to secure the great objects hoped for and that some other means must be resorted to in preserving the world's peace. No one performed nobler work in this great congress of peace than my distinguished and brilliant colleague, Joseph H. Choate, who gained title deeds to honor of which he can never be dispossessed and to whom the country owes a debt of gratitude which it can never pay. He voiced the general sentiments of the delegates when he said in a public lecture on his return in speaking of the maintenance of our Monroe Doctrine—"Its maintenance in the future, especially after the Panama Canal shall have been opened, will depend wholly upon the strength of our arms to maintain and enforce it. For one, I am decidedly of that opinion and ardent as is my advocacy of peace I believe that it would be the height of folly for us to expect to maintain peace without the maintenance of an adequate navy ready and able in any emergency to resist any attack upon our cherished national doctrine."

The first peace conference at The Hague was called by the Emperor of Russia and in the programme of measures to be discussed he made prominent an effort to reduce or limit armaments. In the second congress this matter was stricken out and the delegations were forbidden to introduce and discuss such a measure. It is just as well to continue to make certain treaties for what they are worth, but not to let them blind the people and destroy the national defense. The extreme pacifists rely upon our ability to create a large army and navy upon sudden notice and dwell upon our large population to recruit great numbers of men, but do not reflect that they would be without sufficient ships, arms, munitions and discipline and lacking in sufficient drill masters to instruct them. Confronted by a well appointed and disciplined foreign force they would be as sheep going to a shambles. It would not be war, it would be slaughter. When a wolf enters a sheepfold he is not deterred from his excursion by the number of sheep he expects to find there.

. . . It is a grave error to suppose that the maintenance of a competent army and navy for defense is provocative of war. No power in this country can declare war except the representatives of the people assembled in Congress. Increasing the police force of a city does not invite mob law and bloodshed in the streets. . . .

It is wise in looking to the safety of the Republic to take time by the forelock as he is very baldheaded behind. A well-disciplined and well-armed defense of the nation is the cheapest policy of insurance. Trained battalions and battleships are cheaper than battles. The patriotic people will always demand not an unarmed war but an armed peace.

When in the summer of 1919 we crossed the ocean once more, this time in an army transport under many difficulties, I found that my father had been deeply affected by the war.

The fiery spirit of his youth had been roused; but he had followed the conflict with the eyes of a man far from the scene of action. He had little sympathy for any one country except France; had he been a Frenchman he could not have lamented her devastation more. In the newly partitioned countries he had little faith; he still believed in the future of Russia, "when its people are educated, and some proper form of government comes out of all this chaos." Although he deplored and despised the methods of the Bolsheviks, he was not surprised at the revolution; in fact, he wondered that it had not come sooner.

To what we had to say about the war he listened with great interest. I, who had seen the effects of it at close range,—the misery of the wounded prisoners sent to Switzerland to get well or to die, the tragedies in the families arriving from the devastated regions,—could only feel a deep pity for helpless humanity, and a strong resentment for the governments that had not had the courage and the wisdom to make this misery impossible.

Thus we came to speak of the League of Nations, then about to be organized. "The idea of the League of Nations is good," he said; "so was the idea of the Hague Conference. We threshed out there many of the same questions that will come up at Geneva. But the large nations predominate and they are going to have things their own way. They will continue to discuss disarmament and to arm meanwhile, to make speeches and to go to dinner parties, just as we did at the Hague. They'll make their secret understandings and the man with the biggest guns behind him will make his wishes law. America had better keep out of it as it stands to-day. A society of nations can exist in the true sense of the word only when every country is represented. At present the spirit is wrong. Until the delegates from all nations meet in a true spirit of conciliation, talk of self-determination, justice, and lasting peace will be nothing but—talk."

HORACE PORTER AT EIGHTY

A serious operation in 1920 caused my father's health to decline rapidly, and I spent the following winter with him. Severe blows had fallen upon him in the death of his only remaining son, Clarence, and later of Clarence's wife. Each day of that last winter we motored to Riverside Drive, and each time I felt that a silent salute of loyalty was being made at the tomb of his old commander. Only once did he reveal to me there what was in his thoughts. "I have left ten thousand dollars for the upkeep of the monument, for I don't want it to be neglected. Americans forget so quickly." In the late afternoons and evenings, sitting in his mother's arm-chair, in the room that had been his wife's and under her portrait, he talked with me of many things. He seemed to be summing up his long, eventful life. He repeated many stories of his mother and of his boyhood days in Harrisburg; anecdotes of West Point and the Civil War; his stand at Chickamauga; Lincoln, Grant, the scene at Appomattox. Of the twenty odd years spent in New York, his chief memory, besides the building of the Grant Tomb, was the McKinley campaign. He often repeated witticisms from his speeches, or stories of his old associates, of whom he said, "Like Oliver Wendell Holmes, I am the last leaf." His mind reverted much to his life in Paris. He was continually referring to conversations and episodes which bore upon the events that later upset the world. Many of his prophecies had come true; emperors and kings had fallen, and the map of Europe had been carved up anew. His own country had at last taken a place as a world power so strong that its advice and help were sought by the very nations that had formerly resented its appearance in the field of world politics.

Unlike so many men grown old, he never lamented the "good old days" of his youth. He seemed satisfied that in his own long span of life he had wasted few of its precious hours. He had thought much, had worked hard, and had been true to the high purpose of his young manhood. He took a natural pleasure in the honors that had come to him, and in the continued recognition of his work even when he had been for many years withdrawn from public life; "but," he said, "all that doesn't count for so much in the long run. What really counts is to be at peace with oneself. A clear conscience is what is most conducive to sound sleep. I'm sitting here waiting for taps," he added, "and when it is sounded they'll find me ready."

On May 27, 1921, the summons came.

APPENDIX

APPENDIX

ADDRESS AT THE WEST POINT CENTENNIAL,
JUNE 12, 1902 *

SINCE the foundation of the United States Military Academy upon the historic spot on which to-day this vast concourse of visitors is assembled, the dial hands of the celestial clock record a century's flight. Upon the centennial of the birth of this devoted child of the Nation, she stands with outstretched hands to press the cup of greeting to the lips of all who come to pay her homage and, with natural fondness, bids her sons to return to her after the trials and vicissitudes of their life's career and once more repose their heads upon her bosom.

It is in every sense an ideal site on which to have founded an institution to teach the science and the art of war. Here the Academy sits enthroned in the fastness of the legendary Highlands; the cold, gray, rugged rocks which form her battlements are symbolic of the rigor of the discipline exacted of her children; her towering hills seem to lift man nearer to his God; the mist-laden storm clouds may lower above her, but they break upon her crags and peaks as hostile lines of battle have so often broken upon the sword points of her heroic sons. Her abode is incomparably beautiful at all hours and in all seasons. At one time we find her mountains reverberating and her plain trembling with the thunder of her guns, as their volleys rend the air in mimic warfare, or, as with their crimson breath they utter their notes of greeting to an illustrious soldier-President who honors her imposing fête day by his distinguished presence. At another

* Centennial of the United States Military Academy at West Point, Vol. I, pp. 32-45.

time stillness rules her camp; the snowy whiteness of her tents glistens in the golden light of a midsummer moon, the prevailing silence is broken only by the cadenced footfalls of her trusty sentinels, or the rippling of the waters of the noble stream which flows at her base, bearing to the sea those great argosies of commerce which measure a nation's material prosperity.

As we stand here to-day a hundred years of history pass in review before us, and we would fain light the torch of memory and count the brilliant beads of recollection. When our ancestors threw down the gauntlet to the mother country and resolved to conquer the right to form a government of their own, able leaders were found who had gained a valuable experience in battles with savage tribes and especially in the French and Indian wars, but there was a total lack of officers who had received a military education, and drill masters for our troops were eagerly sought among the trained soldiers of Europe. This want led our statesmen, at an early day, to consider the question of establishing a training school for officers of future armies. Washington favored West Point, which had been so closely identified with his military career, as the most appropriate site for such an institution. During his second administration, in 1794, a military school was located here, but in 1796 the building was destroyed by fire and for several years the instruction was suspended. In Washington's Farewell Address, that immortal document, well described as unequaled by any composition of uninspired wisdom, he formulated a memorable maxim in the words:

> To be prepared for war is one of the most effectual means of preserving peace.

Two days before his death in 1799, he wrote to Hamilton a letter, probably the last one his illustrious hand ever penned, saying—

The establishing of a military academy upon a respectable and extensive basis has ever been considered by me as an object of primary importance in this country, and while I was in the Chair of Government I omitted no proper opportunity of recommending it to the attention of the Legislature.

Thus this infant of the State received at its baptism Washington's dying benediction.

The present permanent Academy was founded in 1802. The class that year contained 2 cadets. During the ten years following the average number was 20. We might say of the cadets of those days what Curran said of the books in his library—"not numerous, but select." The instruction was then as meager as the rations, and this newborn child was so poorly cared for that it was scarcely provided with decent swaddling clothes. In fact, the necessity of the school came to be seriously questioned. But then occurred the War of 1812; the institution received greater consideration, was more efficiently organized, and the maximum number of cadets was fixed at 250. The golden age of the Academy, however, began with the advent as Superintendent of a soldier who seemed especially created for the position, that man of honored memory, crowned with the title of "Father of the Academy," Col. Sylvanus Thayer. He brought to his field of usefulness a broad scholarship, a ripe experience, an unerring judgment. In his work it was the very magnitude of the task that seemed to call forth the powers which mastered it. While upon an official mission in Europe he had culled from the most noted war schools of the Old World the best features of their curriculum, and afterwards introduced them here. In the sixteen years of his labors he raised the institution from an elementary school to the grade of the highest academies. Among West Point's graduates a test of fidelity is the veneration in which they hold his name.

After the close of the War of 1812, when the drums had beaten the glad notes of victory and the bugles had sounded a truce, there was a period of some thirty years in which the colors were furled and swords were sheathed. Again a lack of appreciation of the work of the Academy prevailed, and there was much grumbling at the expense it entailed. But then came the war with Mexico. An adventurous campaign was to be undertaken in an unknown land, where skill and science were to play an important part, and her graduates were gladly sought to complete the organization of the expeditionary army. The encomiums passed upon them by their commanders for the practical manner in which they applied their scientific knowledge and their devotion and personal gallantry in that triumphal march from the Gulf to the Halls of the Montezumas silenced all objectors, and convinced the most reluctant that the living had justified their schooling by their deeds; that, if one can barter blood for gold, the dead had amply repaid the cost of their education with their lives.

At different periods campaigns against hostile Indian tribes—the most distasteful of all warfare—tested the powers of our little Army. In 1861 the Temple of Janus again threw wide its portals, and the nation entered upon the most appalling struggle that the New World has ever known. For four years the arts of peace gave way to the science of destruction, blood flowed as freely as festal wine, and the high carnival of slaughter reigned until the record of the carnage staggered humanity. West Point's graduates in that war, from leaders of armies to commanders of companies, by their brilliant feats of arms and conspicuous display of American manhood, challenged the admiration of the world.

In subsequent years an attack was made again upon the Academy. A Representative in Congress proposed to abandon it and sell the property. The answer made to him was in substance:

There never was but one American who tried to sell West Point, and God in his Providence did not permit him to succeed. His name was Benedict Arnold.

In the war with Spain West Point again proved her usefulness. Her officers bore an honorable part in liberating an oppressed people, lighting their watch fires even in the lands of the antipodes, dipping the fringes of their banners in the waters of Oriental seas, setting our country a century ahead in history and raising it to the proud distinction of a world power.

In this contest the blue and the gray of the previous struggle were blended into one harmonious, patriotic color, and men whose opinions had once made them foes again marched shoulder to shoulder beneath the folds of the red, white, and blue, that banner which represents a trinity of colors— a union of loyalty.

The most recent prominent event in the annals of the Academy has been the donation of the majestic building, with its chaste lines and graceful proportions, the hospitality of which we to-day enjoy. The donor, by this act of princely generosity, gained title deeds to gratitude of which he can never be dispossessed. It has been said that gratitude is a debt in which it is left to the debtor to pay in whatever coin he pleases. Alas! we have no coin save the fervent tribute of thankful hearts with which to pay the priceless debt of gratitude we owe to General George W. Cullum.

The system pursued in the conduct of this Academy is in perfect keeping with the spirit of our liberal institutions. The equal participation of all the States and Congressional districts in the nomination of Cadets, their selection without regard to race, religion, color, wealth, or station, and their impartial examinations, in which the names they bear exert no more influence on the result than the numbers which designate them, are methods as democratic as the most liberal-minded could desire. The fact that during the past

century less than one-half of those who entered were graduated shows an instruction as thorough as the most exacting
could demand. Here every Cadet must stand on his own
individual merits. He who would be called Thor must be
able to wield Thor's battle-ax; he who would be called
Ulysses must be able to bend Ulysses's bow.

It has been asked why impart practically the same education to all Cadets, to those destined for the line as well as
for the scientific corps? It is because it is believed that the
mental discipline, powers of investigation, and accurate
methods of thought requisite in solving difficult problems in
the higher branches of science are the same qualities which
are necessary in planning campaigns against wily savage
tribes or conducting battles against trained armies.

An ancient writer has said: "We fatten a sheep on grass
not in order to obtain a crop of hay from its back, but so
that it may feed us with its mutton and clothe us with its
wool." In like manner we train a soldier in science, not with
the expectation that he will use an equatorial in getting the
range of an advancing battle line, or ascertain his own
whereabouts by finding astronomically the longitude of his
post by means of lunar culminations, or frighten away an
enemy by shaking a table of logarithms at him, terrifying as
those figures are, but in order that he may have the general
powers of his brain fully developed, be able to concentrate
his thoughts, to reason logically, to grasp with precision the
difficult problems of a campaign and thus be the better prepared to lead men and to gain battles for the Republic.
The fight may last but a day, the training to win it may require many toilsome years. A bicyclist, with a broken machine, stopped at a country blacksmith's to have it mended.
The workman said his charge was a dollar—twenty-five
cents for the job and seventy-five cents for knowing how to
do it. Battles should be won first with the brain, then with
the sword. Men should be taught not only how to stop
bullets but how to direct them. Where human life is at

stake, we want duels, not butcheries; victories, not excuses. It is quite certain that future successes in war will depend less on numbers and more on discipline, the cultivation of the morale of the soldier, improved weapons, celerity of movements, and an intelligent application of the study of logistics.

It is conceded that no student can successfully master a subject unless his mind becomes duly interested in it. To produce good music an instrument must be in tune. The student who here studies the art of war finds himself in a purely military atmosphere, and feels all the stimulus of his surroundings. About this region, celebrated for its strategic importance, there cluster the most inspiring memories of the war of independence, which constituted the heroic age of the Republic. Here invading armies were checked, hostile fleets were barred, treason was baffled. Here flows the historic Hudson, rich in precious revolutionary reminiscences. From the unequal battle of Harlem Heights to the triumphant field of Saratoga, yonder stream, throughout its entire length, is studded with beacon lights of liberty. Upon the plain are displayed the trophies of former wars; upon the giant rocks are graven the names of victorious battles; pendant on the building's walls are tablets and portraits which recall the record of imperishable deeds and perpetuate names which deserve to be immortal. Here statues are erected to commemorate men who lived believing in their country, who died that their faith might be fulfilled. The mute eloquence of their monuments will plead for equal sacrifice should war again threaten the nation's life, for example is stronger than precept, and patterns are better followed than rules. It would be a recalcitrant cadet indeed who, under such circumstances, could fail to be imbued with an absorbing interest in the study of the profession of his choice.

It may be asked whether an education amid such surroundings may not make men lovers of war and anxious to taste its experiences. There is little fear of such a result. In this country a soldier is no longer respected if he fails to realize that war should be undertaken only in the interest of peace, and that a nation's prosperity depends upon public tranquillity. He knows full well that a people can be military without being warlike—that a government can be progressive without being aggressive. It was one of our most combative commanders in the field who uttered the famous aphorism: "Let us have peace," and whose distaste for war was so pronounced that, in after life, he never attended a review of troops, even when tendered in his special honor by the great military powers of Europe. Washington, after having experienced the horrors of war, fully appreciated the piping times of peace, when soldiers may turn their battle-axes into billhooks and their helmets into beehives, and yet he never failed to put himself on record in favor of the maintenance of an adequate army. For example, when in convention a delegate moved that the size of the Army should never be allowed to exceed 5,000 men, the great Founder of the Republic, with a display of ready wit which surprised his colleagues, killed the motion by offering an amendment prescribing that no foreign power should be allowed to invade the country with more than 3,000 men. An army may be dangerous when wielded by an arbitrary sovereign, but never when directed by a sovereign people.

The true soldier regards an army as serving the same purpose to the country as the lightning rod to the house, which reaches out, not to attract the lightning but to meet it when it strikes, disperse its forces, and stay the ruin it would work. Upon our national arms the American eagle is represented as holding in one talon the olive branch of peace, in the other the shafts of war. He leaves to his adversaries which to choose.

No scholar can claim a monopoly of knowledge or perfection in learning. That would be mere pedantry; and Addison tells us that "Pedantry in learning is like hypocrisy in

religion—a form of knowledge without the power of it."
There are two means of acquiring an education—in the
schools and in the great university of experience.   Fortunately for the prosperity of nations and the peace of the
world, we do not have continual wars in which to instruct
our officers, and so we give an education in the schools,
making it as practical as possible.

In future, as in past wars, the great bulk of our Army
will always be composed of volunteers, those patriotic types
of American manhood who, at the call to arms, quit their
peaceful avocations, sacrifice their material interests, and
rally to the defense of their country's standard.   They
receive their valuable but hard-learned lessons in the field
and even in the presence of the enemy.   The graduates from
their ranks have furnished to the Army some of its most distinguished officers.   The cordial and efficient coöperation
of these two great branches of the Service has everywhere
brought success to our arms.   I have no patience with occasional writers who would make it appear that there are dissensions and discord between these two bodies battling in the
same cause.   It is a common practice for volunteer organizations to apply for Regular officers to command them, while
the Regulars have constantly sought commissions in the
Volunteers.   In the field inseparable ties of true comradeship have been formed among them, for as iron is welded
in the heat of the forge, so are friendships welded in the
heat of battle.   Any one in either of these two honorable
branches of the Army who would be guilty of petty jealousy
or half-hearted coöperation would be unfit for the Service to
which he belonged and unworthy of the name of soldier.

This Academy had its birth and grew to manhood in the
most marvelous century of recorded time, an age in which
the advance of civilization and the triumphs in useful inven-
tions and scientific discoveries inspire us with the grandeur
of events and thrill us with the majesty of achievement.
During this eventful period there were graduated 4067

Cadets. They have displayed their devotion upon countless battlefields and attested their usefulness in all the civil walks of life—in science and art, in trade and commerce, in literature and oratory, in theology, law, diplomacy, and statesmanship, from the modest engineer to President of the Republic. Nearly all who entered the Army have been disbursing officers in some capacity or other, from post treasurer to Paymaster-General, and with such scrupulous fidelity have the hundreds—perhaps thousands—of millions intrusted to them been accounted for that those who have ever been charged with peculation can be numbered on the fingers of one hand. Time does not permit us to recount their services. To select for special comment, even the more illustrious, would be to make invidious distinction; to mention all who have efficiently served the State, would be to call the roll of graduates. They need no eulogist, their services attest their worth. They did their duty and trusted to history for their meed of praise.

Of the total of 4067 graduates, 238 have fallen, killed or mortally wounded on the field of battle. In the trials of the self-sacrificing profession in which they cast their lot, they had to learn that "all hours wound—the last one kills." The record of West Point's heroic dead is inexpressibly sad; it is incomparably glorious. The story of their deeds rises to the sublimity of an epic. They honored the age in which they lived, and future generations will read with pride the inscription on their tombs. The world can better appreciate their services since they have fallen, and the historian has had time to record their achievements. A tree is best measured when it is down. When La Tour d'Auvergne, who by his matchless deeds of valor gained the proud title of the First Grenadier of France, finally fell with his face to the foe, pierced by the enemy's bullets, Napoleon issued an order prescribing that this soldier's name should be carried on the active list, and to this day the sergeant of the company to which he belonged calls "La Tour d'Auvergne," and the color bearer answers "Mort au Champ d'Honneur." If the roll of West Point's graduates were called to-day answer could be made, not for one but for hundreds, "Dead on the field of honor."

I know that I voice the sentiments of every graduate, every officer of the Army, and every patriotic citizen when I express the profound acknowledgments and the deep sense of obligation due to all who have been instrumental in procuring the recent liberal appropriations from a generous Congress for enlarging and improving the Academy, with a view to keeping pace with our growing population, and in order that the efficiency of the institution may increase and multiply and its usefulness be greater even in the coming ages than in the century which is closing. In these names I include those eminent statesmen whose intelligent foresight has been so important in guiding national legislation, the honored Secretary of War, the "organizer of victory," the Carnot of this administration, the able Superintendent of the Academy whose superb courage on the field is matched by his rare powers of administration, and all those associated with him, and the officers of the Army holding high positions in Washington, who, in cases where they are not enrolled as graduates have been as faithful and devoted to the interests of the institution as if they had been reared within its walls. Conspicuous among the latter I would name the distinguished Adjutant-General of the Army.

And now a word to the Corps of Cadets, the departure of whose graduating class marks the close of the first century of the Academy's life. The boy is father to the man. The present is the mold in which the future is cast. The dominant characteristics of the cadet are seen in the future general. You have learned here how to command and, a still more useful lesson, how to obey. You have been taught obedience to the civil as well as to the military code, for in this land the military is always subordinate to the civil law. Not the least valuable part of your education is your service in the cadet ranks, performing the duties of a private soldier. That alone can acquaint you with the feelings and the capabilities of the soldiers you will command. It teaches you just how long a man can carry a musket in one position without overfatigue, just how hard it is to keep awake on sentry duty after an exhausting day's march. You will never forget this part of your training. When Marshal Lannes's grenadiers had been repulsed in an assault upon the walls of a fortified city, and hesitated to renew the attack, Lannes seized a scaling ladder and rushing forward, cried: "Before I was a marshal I was a grenadier, and I have not forgotten my training." Inspired by his example, the grenadiers carried the walls and captured everything before them.

Courage is the soldier's cardinal virtue. You will seldom go amiss in following General Grant's instructions to his commanders, "When in doubt move to the front." Modesty should go hand in hand with valor. Never underrate yourself in a battle, never overrate yourself in a dispatch. When clothed with authority, avoid everything which savors of puppyism, an evil sometimes bred by power, and shun as well a spirit of dogmatism, which Johnson said is only puppyism grown to maturity. When you are sure that you are right, do not be disarmed by unjust criticism. Mankind is divided into two classes, those who go ahead and do something and those who sit back and criticize them for not doing it better. You cannot make all men think alike. You might as well try to synchronize the clocks of Charles the Fifth. Censure is often the concomitant to success. Ostracism was the Greeks' reward for popularity; derision and caricature pursued the recipient of a Roman triumph. Even at the present day, in a land whose boast is justice, and among a people whose patent of manhood is their sense of fair play, while the American soldier, by his fidelity, his manly bearing, his matchless gallantry, has earned the right to stand with head covered and with feet sandaled in the presence of the proudest warriors of foreign lands, at home the envenomed shafts of slander are hurled at him from behind his back, but they have not even pierced the khaki of his uniform. When the authors of these baseless calumnies are moldering in unmarked and forgotten graves, the patriotic American people will be searching for monumental marble white enough and pure enough on which to engrave the names of our heroes in the distant Philippines.

In this institution the flag of your country is kept constantly in view. It is not simply a piece of bunting which can be purchased for a few shillings in the nearest shop; it is not a mere cluster of brilliant colors with which to decorate a window for holiday display; it is the emblem of dignity, authority, power. Insult it, and millions will spring to its defense, resolved that it shall never be dethroned from its proud supremacy. In this free land there is no sovereign, fealty to whom symbolizes national loyalty, no crown to typify inherent authority; our sole emblem of fidelity to country is the flag. Here you are trained to salute it, taught to reverence it. Remember that it is to be your pillar of cloud by day, your pillar of fire by night, that it will wave above you in victory, will be your rallying point in defeat, and if it be your privilege to offer up your life in its defense, its gentle folds will rest upon your bosom in death, its crimson stripes will mingle with your generous heart's blood, its very presence there will write a nobler epitaph than that on the sarcophagus in which the great Sesostris sleeps.

A generous country has with fostering care equipped you for your career. It is entitled to your undivided allegiance. In closing, let me mention, by way of illustration, a most touching and instructive scene which I once witnessed at the annual meeting in the great hall of the Sorbonne in Paris for the purpose of awarding medals of honor to those who had performed acts of conspicuous bravery in saving human life at sea. A bright-eyed boy of scarcely fourteen sum-

mers was called to the platform. The story was recounted
of how one winter's night when a fierce tempest was raging
on the rude Normandy coast, he saw signals of distress at
sea and started with his father, the captain of a small vessel,
and the mate to attempt a rescue. By dint of almost super-
human effort the crew of a sinking ship was safely taken
aboard. A wave then washed the father from the deck.
The boy plunged into the seething waves to save him, but
the attempt was in vain and the father perished. The lad
struggled back to the vessel to find that the mate had also
been washed overboard. Then lashing himself fast, he took
the wheel and guided the boat, with its precious cargo of
human souls, through the howling storm safely into port.
The minister of public instruction, after paying a touching
tribute to the boy's courage in a voice broken with emotion,
pinned the medal on his breast, placed in his hands a diploma
of honor, and then, seizing the brave lad in his arms, im-
printed a kiss on each cheek. For a moment the boy seemed
dazed, not knowing which way to turn, as he stood there
with the tears streaming down his bronzed cheeks while
every one in that vast audience wept in sympathy. Suddenly
his eyes turned toward his old peasant mother, she to whom
he owed his birth and his training, as she sat at the back of
the platform with bended form and wearing her widow's
cap. He rushed to her, took the medal from his breast
and, casting it and his diploma into her lap, threw himself
on his knees at her feet.

Men of West Point, in the honorable career which you
have chosen, whatever laurels you may win, always be ready
to lay them at the feet of your country to which you owe
your birth and your education.

ADDRESS ON THE LIMITATION OF FORCE IN THE COLLEC-
TION OF CONTRACTUAL DEBTS, JULY 16, 1907 *

As delegates of a peace conference we are assembled
here, charged with grave responsibilities, for the purpose
not only of ameliorating the horrors of war, but of endeavoring to prevent wars by removing their cause.

There is a general and growing impression that the employment of armed force to collect unadjusted contractual
debts from a debtor nation, unless restricted by some general international agreement, may become the most fruitful
source of wars, or at least give rise to frequent blockades,
threats of hostilities, and rumors of warlike intentions calculated to interrupt commerce, affect the markets of the
world adversely, create a feeling of uneasiness, and disturb
not only the countries concerned in the dispute but neutral
nations as well.

If the debtor nation resists, war becomes certain.

If so-called "peaceful blockades" are undertaken in order
to force payments, there is an increasing disposition on the
part of neutral commercial nations not to recognize them,
and actual war has to be declared to make blockades effective.

This may lead to the landing of troops, the seizure of
property and territory, and the violation of the sovereignty
of an independent nation. If the occupation be prolonged,
the question even of the balance of power may be raised,
and many difficult, embarrassing, and complicated conditions
may result.

Again, there may be other states having claims against
the same country that would protest against the arbitrary
seizure by a particular creditor of the property of the common debtor.

The case not unfrequently is that of an investor or a spec-

* As printed, in translation, in Scott's *American Addresses at the Second
Hague Peace Conference,* pp. 25-33.

ulator who withdraws his services and his money from his own country to risk a venture in another with the sole object of increasing his private fortune.

If he gains millions, his government does not share in his profits; but if he loses, he demands that it go even to the extent of war to secure sums claimed to be due and often grossly exaggerated.

The onerous rates exacted confirm the belief that he is assuming an extra hazardous risk.

He not unfrequently purchases in the markets bonds of the debtor state at a low figure, and then makes his demand for payment at par.

In fact he is playing a game in which he expects to have recognized the principle of "Heads I win, tails you lose."

His foreign office, to which he appeals, has, generally speaking, no means at hand to make a thorough investigation of the subject, to procure and examine all the necessary documents, to inform itself as to the opposing evidence and form a correct judgment of the true merits of the case.

It has no jury to ascertain the facts, no competent and impartial court to guide it as to the law, no tribunal to pronounce upon the equity of the claim. In giving a decision the minister of foreign affairs must feel that he is violating a primary principle of the administration of justice in admitting that a case may be adjudged solely by one of the parties to the controversy.

If by so serious a means as that of armed force the amount of the claim be secured, the taxpayers of the coercing nations have to bear the expense of enriching an investor or a speculator who has taken his chance of gain or loss in a foreign land, even if the cost of collection amounts to a hundred times the amount of his claim.

Perhaps there are no subjects which confront a foreign office that are more annoying and embarrassing than the pecuniary claims of individual subjects or citizens against a foreign government, stated at their own valuation and pressed for payment even though this may entail the for-

midable question of an act of war. If it were made known
that investors and speculators undertaking financial negotiations with a foreign government were expected to deal upon
the principle of *caveat emptor,* or if it were understood at
least that their home government would not proceed to a
compulsory enforcement of their claims until such claims
had been adjudicated and their true value ascertained by a
competent court of arbitration, and that the debtor nation
had then arbitrarily refused to abide by the award, foreign
offices would be relieved of one of the most vexatious and
perplexing of their duties.

History records the fact that the great majority of such
demands exhibit an exaggeration in the amounts claimed
that is positively amazing.

Statistics show that in the last sixty years mixed commissions and courts of arbitration have examined thirteen large
claims for damages, indemnities, unpaid contractual debts,
etc., alleged to be due to subjects or citizens of one country
by the government of another country. The greatest sum
allowed in any case was only 80 per cent of the claim, while
in some cases the lowest fell to the ridiculous figure of three
fourths of 1 per cent.

On one occasion, one of our citizens having made a contract with a foreign government to perform certain services
for it, difficulties arose in regard to the carrying out of said
contract and it was annulled. The contractor took advantage of this to demand an indemnity of about $90,000,
which was refused. He succeeded in persuading the United
States government to take up his case, and, after much correspondence, many conferences, and tedious negotiations, to
send finally a fleet of nineteen war ships to support his claim.
At last, after sixteen years of effort, our government, without succeeding in collecting a single cent, had spent more
than $2,500,000 to achieve this result.*

We considered this lesson not only instructive, but ex-

---

* The claim against Paraguay. See Moore's *Digest of International
Arbitrations,* Vol. II, pp. 1485-1549.

pensive. To use a familiar expression, "The game was not worth the candle."

It sometimes happens that the citizens of one power succeed in persuading their government to send a fleet to coerce another government, by reason of a default in the payment of interest on securities held by them. The knowledge of such a step causes a rise in the market. The holders take advantage of this to sell their securities abroad at a profit, so that after the claimant power has gone to the trouble and expense of forcing a payment, the benefit goes principally to foreigners.

These examples alone should forever deter civilized nations from resorting to arbitrary coercive measures for the enforcement of unadjudicated foreign debts, which leads to converting gallant soldiers into bailiffs and swapping human lives for dollars.

The resort to force of arms to collect such debts is a recognition of the now universally condemned doctrine that "Might makes right."

Such coercive measures are analogous to the practice formerly in vogue of imprisoning individuals for debt, except that no such action could be taken against the debtor until a competent tribunal had first granted a legal judgment in favor of the creditor. As the prisoner's maintenance became a charge upon the state, and his seclusion prevented him from earning any money with which to pay his debts, and even from providing for his family, so the blockading of a debtor nation's port and the destruction of its property by hostile fleets or armies interrupts foreign commerce, deprives it of its revenues from customs, and compels it, perhaps, to incur the expense of resisting force by force. This only serves to diminish its means of paying its debts.

The imprisonment of individuals for debt came to be regarded as illogical, cruel, and inefficacious, and has been generally abolished. The analogous practice of nations in the treatment of a debtor state should likewise be abandoned.

Coercive collections may result in enforcing payment at once, when the debtor nation may have so suffered from insurrections, revolutions, loss of crops, floods, earthquakes, or other calamities beyond its power of prevention, that it has no means of making immediate payment but could meet all its obligations if given a reasonable time. There are instances of a number of states that, in the past, were at times unable to pay their debts when due, but which, when accorded reasonable time, eventually met all their obligations with interest and are now enjoying a high credit in the family of nations.

Neither the prestige nor the honor of a state can be considered at stake in refusing to enforce by coercive action the payment of a contractual debt due or claimed to be due to one of its subjects or citizens by another nation. There is no inherent right on their part to have a private contract converted into a national obligation. If so, it would be practically equivalent to having the government guarantee the payment at the outset.

The ablest writers upon international law consider that the state owes no such duty to its citizens or subjects, and that its action in such cases is entirely optional.

While these writers differ as to the expediency of intervention, research shows that a majority are of opinion that there exists no such obligation.

The following citations from the written opinions of eminent statesmen, diplomatists, and jurisconsults are valuable and instructive upon this subject.

Lord Palmerston, in 1848, in a circular addressed to the representatives of Great Britain in foreign countries, referring to the unsatisfied claims of British subjects who were holders of public bonds and money securities of foreign states, after asserting that the question as to whether his government should make the matter the subject of diplomatic negotiations was entirely a matter of discretion and by no means a question of international right, said:

> It has hitherto been thought by the successive governments of Great Britain undesirable that British subjects should invest their capital in loans of foreign governments instead of employing it in profitable undertakings at home; and with a view to discourage hazardous loans to foreign governments, who may be either unable or unwilling to pay the stipulated interest thereupon, the British government has hitherto thought it the best policy to abstain from taking up as international questions the complaints made by British subjects against foreign governments which have failed to make good their engagements in regard to such pecuniary transactions.

In 1861 Lord John Russell, in a communication to Sir C. J. Wyke, wrote: "It has not been the policy of her Majesty's government, although they have always held themselves free to do so, to interfere authoritatively on behalf of those who have chosen to lend their money to foreign governments."

Lord Salisbury in 1880 announced a similar policy. In a debate in the British Parliament—December, 1902—during the controversy with Venezuela, Mr. Balfour, the Prime Minister, said:

> I do not deny, in fact I freely admit, that bondholders may occupy an international position which may require international action; but I look upon such action with the gravest doubt and suspicion, and I doubt whether we have in the past ever gone to war for the bondholders, for those of our countrymen who have lent money to a foreign government; and I confess that I should be very sorry to see that made a practice in this country.

Alexander Hamilton, in the early days of the government of the United States, affirmed the same principles, saying:

Contracts between a nation and private individuals are obligatory according to the conscience of the sovereign, and may not be the object of compelling force. They confer no right of action contrary to the sovereign will.

In 1871 Mr. Fish, then Secretary of State of the United States, wrote:

Our long-settled policy and practice has been to decline the formal intervention of the government except in case of wrong and injury to person and property such as the common law denominates *torts* and regards as inflicted by force, and not the result of voluntary engagements or contracts.

In 1881 Mr. Blaine, Secretary of State of the United States, wrote that a person

voluntarily entering into a contract with the government of a foreign country or with the subjects or citizens of such foreign powers, for any grievance he may have or losses he may suffer resulting from such contract, is remitted to the laws of the country with whose government or citizens the contract is entered into, for redress.

In 1885 Mr. Bayard, then Secretary of State of the United States, wrote in a dispatch on this subject:

All that our government undertakes to do, when the claim is merely contractual, is to interpose its good offices; in other words, to ask the attention of the foreign sovereign to the claim; and that is only done when the claim is one susceptible of strong and clear proof.

President Roosevelt in 1906 expressed himself upon this subject as follows:

It has long been the established policy of the United States not to use its armed forces for the collection of ordinary contract debts due to its citizens by other governments. We have not considered the use of force for such a purpose consistent with that respect for the independent sovereignty of other members of the family of nations which is the most important principle of international law and the chief protection of weak nations against the oppression of the strong. It seems to us that the practice is injurious in its general effect upon the relations of nations and upon the welfare of weak and disordered states, whose development ought to be encouraged in the interests of civilization; that it offers frequent temptation to bullying and oppression and to unnecessary and unjustifiable warfare. We regret that other powers, whose opinions and sense of justice we esteem highly, have at times taken a different view and have permitted themselves, though we believe with reluctance, to collect such debts by force. It is doubtless true that the non-payment of public debts may be accompanied by such circumstances of fraud and wrongdoing or violation of treaties as to justify the use of force. This government would be glad to see an international consideration of the subject which shall discriminate between such cases and the simple nonperformance of a contract with a private person, and a resolution in favor of reliance upon peaceful means in cases of the latter class.

It appears that modern public opinion is decidedly opposed to the collection by force of contractual debts. The *American Journal of International Law,* in its first quarterly number of this year, says, "the tendency among publicists is certainly toward the acceptance of the principle of nonintervention as the correct and normal or everyday rule of international law and practice."

Among modern authorities on international law who either deny the right of intervention or accept the principle of nonintervention with or without exceptions, the following may be cited: de Martens, Bonfils, Heffter, Woolsey, Wilson and Tucker, Walker, de Floecker, Liszt, Despagnet, Rivier, Nys, Mérignhac, and others.

It is not necessary to recall the early consideration and profound study given to this subject by the Argentine Republic, and the exhaustive discussion of the question and of kindred subjects contained in the writings of the former Secretary of State of that country, at present one of our highly esteemed colleagues in this conference.

The view of the majority seems to be that the correct rule of international law is nonintervention, but that intervention is either legally or morally permissible in extreme and exceptional cases.

Debt-collecting expeditions have seldom proved a success. In this age it is assuming a grave responsibility to relegate disputed money claims to the dominion of force instead of law, and substitute the science of destruction for the creative arts of peace.

The principle of nonintervention by force would be of incalculable benefit to all parties concerned.

First, to the nation whose subjects or citizens have become creditors of a foreign government, in that it would be a warning to a class of persons too apt to trade upon the necessities of feeble and embarrassed governments and then expect their government to become responsible for the success of their operations, as it would serve to discourage their transactions. It would enable the government to continue its normal relations with the foreign state, avoid incurring its ill will and suffering perhaps a loss of its commerce. Such an attitude would also save it from all risk of complications with neutral powers.

Secondly, the recognition of this principle would be a substantial relief to neutrals, the interruption to whose commerce by blockades and hostile operations becomes a serious menace to their foreign trade.

Thirdly, it would be of advantage to the debtor states, as it would be an announcement to the lenders of money that they would have to base their operations solely upon considerations of the good faith of the government, the national credit, the justice of local courts, and the economy practiced in the administration of public affairs. This would relieve such states from the importunities of the speculative adventurer who tempts them with the proffer of large loans, which may lead to national extravagance and in the end threaten the seizure of their property and the violation of their sovereignty. The knowledge that all disputed pecuniary claims would be subject to adjudication by an impartial tribunal would be apt to lead prominent bankers and contractors to feel that such claims would be settled promptly without serious disturbance to the administration of the country's public affairs, and without the necessity of assuming the task of prevailing upon their government to undertake the collection of their claims by force of arms. In such case responsible financial men and institutions abroad would be more likely to negotiate loans and make their terms fair and reasonable. The Permanent Court of Arbitration at The Hague would naturally be given the preference in selecting for the settlement of such claims an impartial tribunal.

One significant feature of this conference is that for the first time in history the creditor and the debtor nations of the world are brought together in friendly council, and it seems a singularly appropriate occasion for an earnest endeavor to agree upon some rule concerning the treatment of contractual debts which may commend itself to all here assembled and result in a general treaty on the subject among the nations represented.

No experienced statesman can doubt that a question which, if left open, may work so much evil in exciting and disturbing the commonwealth of nations by threats, rumors, and declarations of war, will some day be removed from the causes of armed conflicts; and if the present conference, from which so much is expected by the onlooking world, neglects this proffered opportunity of accomplishing such a beneficent result, it will record a regrettable failure and lose the credit of having performed a far-reaching act in the true interests of the world's peace.

NOTES

NOTES

INTRODUCTION: FATHER AND DAUGHTER

1. The picture and the bust are now in the library of the Naval Academy at Annapolis.

2. This chair was one of the few pieces of furniture which he took with him from home when he went to France as Ambassador.

3. At that time the claimant to the French throne.

4. The pencil is now in the museum at the Grant Monument.

CHAPTER I: ANCESTRY, BOYHOOD, YOUTH

Pages 3-18

1. Of Andrew Porter's five children by his first wife, the second, Elizabeth, married Robert Parker, who moved to Lexington, Kentucky, and became a planter of considerable means. Their granddaughter, Mary Todd, married Abraham Lincoln.

2. The account of Andrew and David Porter is based on the article on Governor Porter in *Lives of the Governors of Pennsylvania,* by W. C. Armor, pp. 379-391.

3. When Governor Porter was in Texas he met Mary Todd's brother Edward and discovered how bitterly her family resented the marriage. "It was the darkest day of my life," declared Dr. Todd, "when she married that damned 'Black Republican,' Abraham Lincoln."

4. William Augustus Porter, 1821-1886, became a distinguished citizen of Pennsylvania. From 1858 he was judge of the Supreme Court of the State, and in 1874 was appointed judge of the Court of Alabama Claims in Washington. His son William was judge of the Supreme Court of Pennsylvania from 1897 to 1903. Andrew, the Governor's second son, who was considered the handsomest and most gifted member of the family, died at the age of twenty-five. George, the third son, became a prominent physician in Harrisburg and died at an advanced age. Four other sons died in childhood or infancy. The only daughter was Elizabeth, who married James Wheeler and died in 1925 at the age of ninety-two. It was she who told me many of the incidents of my father's childhood.

5. General Alfred Alexander Woodhull was born in Princeton, April 13, 1837. After graduating at Princeton College, he took the medical course at the University of Pennsylvania, and during the Civil War was a medical officer in the regular army. After the close of the war, in which he rendered distinguished services, he continued in the Army, retiring in 1904 with

the rank of brigadier-general. He was a devoted son of Princeton, which in 1894 awarded him the degree of LL.D.

6. Porter's "conditional appointment" was dated February 19, 1855; after passing his examination six months later he received his warrant as cadet with the date of July 1, 1855.

7. Porter's class was composed at first of 83 men, which number dwindled to 41. It was one of the only two classes which spent five years at West Point.

8. Compare Clara Louise Kellogg's *Memories*, pp. 19, 20, 57. She speaks of meeting General Porter again years later, and finding it difficult to recognize in the dignified general the ardent young adjutant of West Point days.

9. On one occasion he succeeded in hitting, at the distance of a mile, a target which had not been hit at that range in five years.

CHAPTER II: FIRST YEAR OF THE CIVIL WAR

Pages 19-35

1. This account is taken, with some direct quotations, from a paper prepared by Gen. Porter in later years, entitled A BEARER OF DESPATCHES.

2. *Battles and Leaders of the Civil War*, vol. ii, p. 8.

3. *Ibid.*, vol. ii, pp. 6, 7.

4. Gen. Gillmore's reports (*Official Records of the War of the Rebellion*, Series I, vol. vi, pp. 144-165), containing full technical details, were translated into several languages.

5. The sword bears his name and the inscription "For gallant and meritorious services."

"Lieutenant Horace Porter of the Ordnance Department has rendered signal, important, and indispensable services. Besides discharging most faithfully the special duties of ordnance officer, he directed in person the transportation of the heaviest ordnance, and drilled and instructed the men in their use, laboring indefatigably night and day. He was actively engaged among the batteries during the action." (Gen. Gillmore's report; *Official Records of the War of the Rebellion*, Series I, vol. vi, p. 146.)

6. Gen. R. B. Marcy, McClellan's chief of staff and also his father-in-law. At this time he was fifty years old. Halleck was General-in-Chief of the Army at Washington.

CHAPTER III: CHICKAMAUGA

Pages 36-42

1. 66,000 effectives. *Numbers and Losses in the Civil War*, Livermore, p. 106.

2. 58,000 effectives. *Ibid.*, p. 105.

3. In describing this council at the Widow Glenn's, Charles A. Dana concludes as follows: "Finally, after everything had been said, hot coffee

was brought in, and then, McCook was called upon to sing the Hebrew Maiden. McCook sang the song, and then the council broke up and the generals went away. This was about midnight, and as I was very tired, I lay down on the floor to sleep, beside Captain Horace Porter, who was at the time Rosecrans' chief of ordnance. There were cracks in the floor of the Widow Glenn's house, and the wind blew up under us. We would go to sleep, and then the wind would come up so cold through the cracks that it would wake us up, and we would turn over together to keep warm." *Recollections of the Civil War,* p. 114.

4. During the battle he was frequently employed by General Rosecrans in guiding troops into position. He had made a careful study of the roads leading to the field in order to give proper directions for the bringing up of the ammunition trains. General Rosecrans, in his report of the battle also commends him for his "wise system of arming each regiment with arms of the same calibre and having the ammunition wagons properly marked, by which most of the difficulties of supplying ammunition where the troops had exhausted it in battle were obviated." (*Official Records of the War of the Rebellion,* Series I, vol. xxx, pt. i; p. 62.)

5. The immediate cause of the disaster was an order given by Gen. Rosecrans himself to Gen. Wood, a division commander, the execution of which left a gap in the Union center just at the place where the Confederates attacked.

6. The quotation is from a speech made to the members of the Lotos Club in New York, Jan. 16, 1896. *Speeches at the Lotos Club,* p. 136.

CHAPTER IV: GRANT'S AIDE

Pages 43-51

1. *Campaigning with Grant,* by Horace Porter, p. 8. From this point on through the remaining chapters dealing with the Civil War, I have made free use of my father's book. For the circumstances connected with his writing it, see p. 150.

2. Headquarters, Department of the Cumberland, Chattanooga, Tenn., Nov. 5, 1863. General Orders, No. 261.

Captain Thomas G. Baylor, ordnance corps, having, pursuant to orders from the Secretary of War, relieved Captain Horace Porter from duty at these headquarters, is announced as chief of ordnance for this army, and will at once enter upon the discharge of his duties.

The general commanding takes this occasion to express his appreciation of the valuable service rendered by Captain Porter during his connection with this army. His thorough knowledge of the duties of his position, his good judgment and untiring industry, have increased the efficiency of the army, and entitle him to the thanks of the general commanding. . . .

By command of Major-General George H. Thomas.

C. Goddard, Asst. Adj.-General.

3. *Campaigning with Grant,* pp. 11-13.

4. *Ibid.,* p. 18.

5. Grant's staff was organized as follows:
   Chief of Staff, Brig.-Gen. John A. Rawlins.
   Aides-de-Camp:
      Lt. Col. C. B. Comstock.
      Lt. Col. Horace Porter.
      Lt. Col. O. E. Babcock.
      Lt. Col. F. T. Dent (a classmate of Grant's and his brother-in-law).
      These four aides were graduates of West Point.
   Military Secretary: Lt. Col. Adam Badeau.
   Military Secretary: Lt. Col. W. R. Rawley.
   Asst. Adjt. Gen.: Lt. Col. T. S. Bowers.
   Asst. Inspector Gen.: Lt. Col. W. L. Duff.
   Asst. Adjt. Gen.: Captain E. S. Parker.
   Asst. Adjt. Gen.: Captain G. K. Leet.
   Asst. Quartermaster: Captain H. W. James.
   Aide-de-Camp: Captain P. T. Hudson.
   Aide to Gen. Rawlins: Lt. W. McK. Dunn, Jr.
6. *Campaigning with Grant*, p. 38.

CHAPTER V: THE BATTLES OF 1864

Pages 52-66

1. *Numbers and Losses in the Civil War*, p. 110.

2. The material in this chapter which has been drawn from *Campaigning with Grant* may be found on pp. 69-210 of that book.

3. Rienzi carried his master through all the hard work of this spring: he shared with Sheridan the honors of the famous Winchester ride and the battle of Five Forks. After his death in 1878, his body was stuffed and put in the museum at Governor's Island, and there my father took me to see him when I was a little girl. His black, shiny coat had turned to a dull brown, his brilliant eyes to lifeless glass; but even stuffed and brown he was still a noble-looking animal. A wreath of faded flowers was lying at his feet, put there by some old soldier as a tribute to a gallant horse who, according to the soldiers, could do everything but speak. (See *Campaigning with Grant*, p. 438.)

4. "I had a great mess finding General Warren. First I went, by the road leading through the woods, to Bethesda Church. There were his aides and his flag: but the General had 'ridden out along the lines'—confound that expression! That is the luck of a Headquarters aide. You say: 'Is the General here?' 'No, sir, he has gone, I believe, along the line.' 'Do you know where?' 'Well, Colonel, he did not say exactly; but, if you will follow down the breastworks, I think you will find him.' (Delightful vision of a line of two miles or so of breastworks with the infantry safely crouched behind, and you perched on a horse, riding down, taking the chance of stray shot, canister, and minié balls, looking for a general who probably is not there.) The greatest piece of coolness is when you are

advised to make a short cut by the picket line!" *Meade's Headquarters,* by Col. Theodore Lyman, p. 146.

5. This man was the late W. R. Thraxton, of Macon, Ga. See *Campaigning with Grant,* p. 118.

6. *Official Records of the War of the Rebellion,* Series I, vol. xxxvi, pt. i, p. 9.

7. *Numbers and Losses in the Civil War,* p. 114.

8. *Official Records of the War of the Rebellion,* Series I, vol. xl, pt. ii, p. 157.

9. *Numbers and Losses in the Civil War,* pp. 110-115.

CHAPTER VI: AT CITY POINT

Pages 67-76

1. The cabin used by Grant is now in Fairmount Park in Philadelphia.

2. The material in this chapter which has been drawn from *Campaigning with Grant* may be found on pp. 215-385 of that book.

3. *Around the World with Grant,* by John Russell Young, vol. ii, p. 301.

4. The investigation of this explosion made at the time led to nothing, and the subject was finally dropped. After the war, while serving as secretary to President Grant at the White House, General Porter received a call from a Virginian, who came to complain of not being fairly treated about some of his patents. He went on to tell General Porter, in order to show his skill as an inventor, that during the war he had invented an infernal machine with a clock-work attachment. He once passed himself off as a workman, went on board a boat to help unload ammunition, hid his infernal machine in the boat, and then departed, after setting the clock-work for the explosion to occur within half an hour. So after seven years the mystery was revealed. *Campaigning with Grant,* p. 274.

5. *Official Records,* vol. xxxix, pt. ii, p. 413.

CHAPTER VII: APPOMATTOX

Pages 77-95

1. From the manuscript of a lecture on Lee's surrender, delivered at Union College, March 3, 1893.

2. Robert, the President's eldest son, who had been graduated at Harvard in 1864, had repeatedly urged his father to let him see active service. Porter speaks of him as being exceedingly popular and as having inherited many of the genial traits of his father.

3. The material in this chapter which has been drawn from *Campaigning with Grant* may be found on p. 220 and on pp. 408-494.

4. My father always claimed that Rienzi distinctly knew the difference in color between the uniforms of the Federal and those of the Confederate troops.

5. *Military History of Ulysses S. Grant,* by Adam Badeau, vol. iii, p. 501.

6. Campbell, at that time only a youth of nineteen, remained in the army after the war. My father's estimate of the value of his services appears in a letter written in 1894 to Daniel Lamont, then Secretary of War. He writes: "He is really a very historical character. He was constantly sent into the enemy's lines by General Sheridan and General Grant and by his tact and superb courage performed services of inestimable value on a great many occasions and constantly risked his life when there was scarcely any hope of escape. . . . His services were absolutely indispensable and Grant and Sheridan always manifested a peculiar personal interest in his welfare."

7. *Personal Memoirs of U. S. Grant,* vol. ii, p. 481.

8. "The march was begun early and was forced all day. The enemy had vanished in the night; the two corps in the rear, like the column south of the Appomattox, pressed on without a sight of the enemy. The country, hitherto untouched by war, was tinged with the early hues of spring. Not a shot was fired, and the straining hosts, pursued and pursuers, rushed through it as if strange to the peace and charm of the land." On this day Lee's army made thirty-five miles. (*The Generalship of the Appomattox Campaign,* by Col. Thomas L. Livermore. *Papers of the Massachusetts Military Historical Society,* vol. vi, p. 501.)

9.   April 8, 1865.

General: I received at a late hour your note of to-day. In mine of yesterday I did not intend to propose the surrender of the Army of Northern Virginia, but to ask the terms of your proposition. To be frank, I do not think the emergency has arisen to call for the surrender of this army; but as the restoration of peace should be the sole object of all, I desired to know whether your proposals would lead to that end. I cannot, therefore, meet you with a view to surrender the Army of Northern Virginia; but as far as your proposal may affect the Confederate States forces under my command, and tend to the restoration of peace, I shall be pleased to meet you at 10 a. m. to-morrow on the old stage-road to Richmond, between the picket-lines of the two armies.

                                                         R. E. Lee, General.

10. In the famous document that follows, the sentence next the last is what Grant wrote after my father saw him hesitate and look at Lee's sword.

                                      Appomattox Court-house, Va., April 9, 1865.

General R. E. Lee, Commanding C. S. A.

General: In accordance with the substance of my letter to you of the 8th inst., I propose to receive the surrender of the Army of Northern Virginia on the following terms, to wit: Rolls of all the officers and men to be made in duplicate, one copy to be given to an officer to be designated by me, the other to be retained by such officer or officers as you may designate. The officers to give their individual paroles not to take up arms against the Government of the United States until properly [exchanged], and each company or regimental commander to sign a like parole for the men of their commands. The arms, artillery, and public property to be parked and stacked and turned over to the officers appointed by me to receive them. This will not embrace the side-arms of the officers nor their private horses or baggage. This done, each officer and man will be allowed to return to their homes, not to be disturbed by United States authority so long as they observe their paroles and the laws in force where they may reside.

Very respectfully,

U. S. Grant, Lieutenant-general.

11. Most of the Confederate soldiers, unlike those fighting on the Union side, owned their horses. This is also often the case among the rich peasants' sons in the Swiss army.

12. This flag is now in the museum at Grant's Tomb.

CHAPTER VIII: AT THE WAR DEPARTMENT

Pages 99-107

1. Badeau's *Grant in Peace*, p. 31.

2. Later, when he was President, Grant refused to allow a painting of Lee's surrender to be made for the Capitol. When my father was in Europe in after years, he was impressed by the fact that Europeans declared that, great as Grant was in war, he would be "best remembered as a peace-maker." "Many foreigners believe that it is owing largely to his guidance in the path of peace and reconciliation that while belligerents in Europe cannot forgive, our people were able to forget." Letter to Grenville M. Dodge, April 12, 1901.

3. When the conspirators implicated in the assassination of Lincoln and the attack on Seward and other members of the Cabinet were brought to trial before a military court, Porter was appointed one of the judges. But since he belonged to the military family of Grant, who had been one of the intended victims of the assassins, he was objected to, and so was spared the necessity of being anything more than an observer at the trial.

4. Official Correspondence, War Department.

CHAPTER IX: SECRETARY TO THE PRESIDENT

Pages 108-125

1. Adam Badeau also served at the White House for a short time. Another appointee from the staff was Grant's brother-in-law, Frederick T. Dent.

2. A relative of Sir Esmé Howard, present British Ambassador in Washington. He was British Minister to the Netherlands and afterwards Ambassador to the Papal Court.

3. "How Judge Hoar Ceased to be Attorney-General," by J. D. Cox, *Atlantic Monthly* for August, 1895, p. 173.

4. When I was in Washington in 1899 and went to the White House to see Mr. and Mrs. McKinley, the President himself took me upstairs and showed me the rooms in which my father had worked, especially that one, now a guest room, in which he had written this memorandum.

5. *North American Review* for June, 1890, p. 767. The article was one of a group written by different people in reply to an article by Goldwin Smith on *Hatred of England*.

6. Testimony of George S. Boutwell before the committee appointed to investigate the gold panic, *Report no. 31, House of Representatives, 41st Congress, 2d session,* p. 358.

7. Testimony of Horace Porter, p. 447.

8. Porter's testimony, p. 445.

9. Porter's testimony, p. 447.

10. Corbin's testimony, p. 267.

11. Corbin's testimony, p. 266.

12. Mr. Louis A. Coolidge, Grant's biographer, once told me that my father's service to Grant at the time of the gold scandal was even greater than anything he did for him during the war.

13. *Senate Report, no. 227, 42d Congress, 2d session,* vol. iii, p. 122

14. Porter's testimony, *ibid.,* p. 123.

15.   Executive Mansion,
Washington, D. C., July 13, 1870.

Dear Sir: You are about to enter upon the duties of collector of customs in New York. Many persons in seeking office may use the President's name or mine, in urging their claims. I wish to state to you distinctly, at the outset, that *no one is authorized to do so*.

Many friends of mine whom I should be very glad to oblige have importuned me to write you letters in their behalf, but I have persistently refused to add to your present embarrassment by so doing.

You will never hear from me on the subject of office. My only desire is to see you so distribute the patronage of your office as to render the most efficient service to the country and the cause of the administration.

Yours, very truly,

HORACE PORTER.

Hon. Thomas Murphy,
    Collector of Customs, New York.

Senate Report no. 227, 42d Congress, 2d session, vol. iii, p. 130. Babcock wrote a similar letter.

16. Testimony of Inspector Horton, *Senate report no. 380, 41st Congress, 3rd session,* pp. 31, 32.

17.   Executive Mansion,
Washington, D. C.
October 31, 1870.

Dear Sir: I am directed by the President to forward to you the marked portion of the inclosed newspaper article.

While the President does not for a moment suppose that you ever uttered the language it imputes to you, he deems it well to take this opportunity to say that if any persons have been employed in the custom-house upon representations that they are his particular friends or favorites, he hopes they may be discharged, and that if any persons ever apply for positions under you upon such a pretense, he requests that they may not be employed.

I am, sir, respectfully yours,

HORACE PORTER.

Hon. Thos. Murphy,

Collector of Customs, New York City.

Senate Report no. 227, 42d Congress, 2d session, vol. iii, p. 130.

18. New York *Nation,* May 21, 1872.

19. *Senate Report no. 227, 42d Congress, 2d session,* vol. i, pp. xii-xvi.

20. In later years Porter was fond of quoting the remark of the Democratic Governor of North Carolina in explanation of this singular alliance: "Well, the fact is our political wagon's got stuck pretty deep in the mud and we don't care a damn who's hitched to it, a race-horse or a mustang, just so he pulls it out."

21. *Sumner's Works,* vol. xv, pp. 131, 133.

22. "He is one of the most suppressive men I ever knew," so testified one of the physicians in attendance on him in his last illness. "What has been called imperturbability in him is simply introversion of his feelings." *Ulysses S. Grant,* by Hamlin Garland, p. 512.

CHAPTER X: BUSINESS

Pages 126-136

1. This extract, and those that follow in this chapter, are taken from Porter's letters to George M. Pullman.

2. The scale of prices which my father found prevailing in Europe appears in the old bills which I discovered among his papers. A night at the Kaiserhof Hotel in Berlin cost him 4.30 marks; five days at the Grand Hotel, Paris, 46 francs; ten days at the Hotel de Rome, in Rome, 49 lire; and a pair of dress boots, bought in London, 1£ 12s!

3. An invention of his in which he always took great satisfaction was that of the ticket-chopper. The company had incurred losses from the not infrequent practice of using the same ticket twice over; his suggestion was a box at the gate, with a large opening and provided with a sharp knife. The inventor used to say that the device was as simple as the guillotine and worked as well!

4. Soon raised to $17,000,000. It was taken at about 50 and the subscribers received a 50 per cent stock bonus.

5. The antagonism between Vanderbilt and Pullman was of long standing. The support given by the New York Central to the Wagner Car Company led to acts of aggression which resulted in frequent litigation with the Pullman Company. Proposals for consolidation made from time

to time came to nothing, and it was not till 1899 that the purchase of the Wagner property by the Pullman Company was effected.

6.   *Horace Porter to L. J. Seargeant*

New York, February 20, 1884.

. . . We have never opened negotiations with Mr. Vanderbilt, or any one connected with him, directly or indirectly, in regard to placing the West Shore Road under his control, or the control of any of his Companies; and speaking for myself, and my immediate friends, there is nothing we would more regret than to see the control of the West Shore Road go in that direction.

While there are various rumors in regard to Mr. Vanderbilt's people owning our securities, we have no evidence that he has been purchasing. The control is so held at the present time, as you know, that no one could purchase it in the market. It would have to be obtained by purchasing a large block, over Twenty Millions of Dollars in amount, of the stock of the West Shore Company, which is now held by the North River Construction Company.

The street rumors that are put forth, and find their way into newspapers are created either for speculative purposes, or because this new enterprise evidently occupies a good deal of Mr. Vanderbilt's attention, as shown by his prepared interviews in the public press, trying to belittle it, and by other acts said to be attributable to him or his people. In fact we have entirely dismissed from our minds the probability of having our property placed under the control of the New York Central, and are making our traffic arrangements with a view to permanency, and looking to the entire independence of the West Shore Line.

Our traffic, even at this dull season, is increasing very rapidly, and it looks as if the first year's business would prove as satisfactory as had been expected.

Horace Porter to J. H. Cornell

January 9, 1885.

I received your letter of the 8th inst. enquiring about the prospects of the North River Construction Company.

That Company built the West Shore Road in a first class manner, making it superior in every respect and furnishing it with every facility for the most economical operation of business. It underwent many unexpected vicissitudes. The unforeseen engineering difficulties; the exactions of the State authorities, requiring about $1,000,000 to be spent in protecting the canal; the excess over estimates of purchase of real estate etc., ran the Construction Company in debt. The hard times came on and in the panicky condition of the markets it had to sell its securities at a much lower

price than any one could have expected. When the railway, whose stock was largely held by the Construction Company, began operations, stagnation in traffic and a desperate railroad war, which has looked like a war of extermination by the New York Central Company, have kept the earnings very light upon the Road and reduced its securities to a very low price. The Construction Company has what it considers just claims against the Railroad Company for a large amount of money, and these claims will be pressed for settlement when the Railway Company is reorganized. I suppose some plan of reorganization will be proposed by the parties largest in interest before long.

There are so many legal questions involved as to the priority of claims and what shape a settlement will take between the Railway Company, the Construction Company and the creditors of the latter that it is hard to make a prediction as to what the Construction stock will be worth.

Though not an officer or director of the Construction Company I took a large amount of the Construction stock and hold it still.

I will be glad to give you any information I can at any time in regard to it, but I cannot say more than I have at present in regard to giving a forecast of its future value.

In a letter dated Nov. 7, 1883, and addressed to the Superintendent of Public Works at Albany, General Porter had written: "I can assure you that it is the wish and intention of this Company to fully carry out the terms of its agreement with the State with all practicable expedition. I am sure you will regard the employment of the large body of men and the expenditure of the vast sum of money during the last two years in the widening and improving of the canal as an earnest of the Company's intentions to comply with all the demands which were made upon it by the State."

7. Shortly after this, as a result of the reorganization of the St. Louis and San Francisco Railroad, Porter became chairman of its board of directors. The service that he expected to render here, however, was interrupted by his participation in the presidential campaign, and terminated by his departure for France.

CHAPTER XI: THE CHIEF

Pages 137-151

1. The men who contributed $5,000 were John D. Rockefeller, Cornelius Vanderbilt, W. K. Vanderbilt, W. W. Astor, H. McK. Twombley, Andrew Carnegie, George M. Pullman, C. P. Huntington, Theo. Havemeyer, L. Z. Lester, a Friend, John Mackay, J. J. Astor, and H. M. Flagler. It was estimated that the number of people who made contributions during the drive was over 64,000. Adding to these the number who contributed to the $155,000 originally raised, the grand total is 90,000.

The story of the drive is told in detail by Porter himself in an article entitled, "The Tomb of General Grant," in the *Century* for April, 1897.

2. For instances see Gen. J. H. Wilson's *Life of Rawlins, passim.*

CHAPTER XII: CITIZEN OF NEW YORK

Pages 152-160

1. New York *Tribune,* June 11, 1892.

CHAPTER XIII: THE CAMPAIGN OF 1896

Pages 161-171

1. Only one man, who collected about $700, received a commission, at the rate of 10 per cent.

2. Of the total sum raised for the Republican campaign, $3,500,000, over $3,000,000 was collected in New York. Not all of this sum was spent. (Croly's *Life of Hanna,* p. 220.) The duty of Porter's committee, as has been said, was to obtain contributions from as many people as possible, representing all business and professional groups. The large sums contributed by individuals and corporations were obtained in other ways.

3. Four years before, plans for a similar parade, of which Gen. Porter was to be grand marshal, were abandoned on account of the death of President Harrison's wife. *The Great Sound Money Parade in New York,* p. 14.

4. To E. F. Winslow, April 2, 1897.

5. In his will my father left the sum of $10,000 to constitute a fund for the care of the monument. He was also largely responsible for raising the money for the Sherman statue; he had much to do with St. Gaudens during the execution of the work, and contributed his influence in settling the question of the suitable site where it now stands, on 59th Street, at the entrance to Central Park.

CHAPTER XIV: GETTING ESTABLISHED

Pages 175-190

1. See the *Century Magazine,* March, 1909, p. 782. "Should the Government Own Its Embassies?" by Horace Porter. This article deals in vigorous fashion with the ignorant and parsimonious policy of the Government in maintaining its diplomatic service, and pays a handsome tribute to Secretary Root for his work in bringing to pass a better state of things.

2. His salary was that of a Minister of the first rank, $17,500; no allowance was made for traveling expenses.

3. *Instructions to Diplomatic Officers of the United States* (1897), p. 5.

4. "Soon after my arrival in Paris," he wrote to the State Department, "upon the occasion of my being escorted officially to the Palace of the Elysée for the purpose of presenting my credentials to the President, I found myself obliged to pay the sum of Frs. 500.00 to the persons who participated in the duty of escorting me. This is the usual amount paid by Ambassadors at this Capital and as it was incurred for a public ceremony, I would request that I be reimbursed for the expenditure. I understand that this has been allowed in the case of other of our diplomatic representatives abroad. Of course no formal vouchers can be furnished."

5. Diplomatic Correspondence, State Department, filed under General Porter's name.

6. *Century* article, March, 1909, p. 784. Thanks to the energy of our present Ambassador to France, Hon. Myron T. Herrick, the American Embassy, at 2 Avenue d'Iena, is the property of the United States. The first reception in it was held on July 4, 1925.

7. *Century* article, March, 1909, p. 783.

8. Diplomatic Correspondence, State Department. To John Hay, May 6, 1903. This letter, which contains a full account of the introduction of an Ambassador at Paris, was written by my father at the request of Hay, who enclosed to him a copy of a similar letter from Bellamy Storer, describing the procedure at Vienna. There every detail of the event was in charge of a court official: the Ambassador's sole duties were to be present and to pay the bills.

9. Private Letter File.

CHAPTER XV: AT THE CHANCERY

Pages 191-196

1. He was first engaged as the Ambassador's private secretary. On the retirement of Vignaud he became first secretary; after valuable services in other diplomatic positions he died in 1925.

2. It was not till April, 1904, that the State Department authorized the use of the typewriter for official correspondence.

3. Letter from Peter Augustus Jay, January, 1924.

4. No counsellor was attached to the Embassy to furnish legal advice; the usual practice was to obtain the services of a lawyer by allowing him to put on his professional card the title—"Counsellor to the American Embassy."

5. Private Letter File.

6. *Ibid.* This extract is a part of the letter to McKinley quoted on p. 186.

CHAPTER XVI: FRANCO-AMERICAN CRISIS

Pages 197-223

1. Colonial expansion formed an important element in French policy at this time. Madagascar had become a colony in 1896, after some years

of fighting; in 1897 Captain Marchand had been sent from French West Africa to penetrate as far as possible into the Anglo-Egyptian Soudan. His expedition brought about the Fashoda crisis with England in the summer of 1898. In the Far East, France followed the example of other powers in obtaining leased territory and "spheres of interest" at the expense of China. The dates of these acquisitions, extremely significant in connection with the events of the Spanish-American War, are as follows:

Acquisition of Kiaochow by Germany, Nov., 1897.
Acquisition of Port Arthur by Russia, Mar., 1898.
Acquisition of Wei-hai-wei by England, Apr., 1898.
Acquisition of Kwangchow Bay by France, Apr., 1898.

2. Diplomatic Correspondence, State Department.

3. Aug. 10, 1897. Private letter file.

4. Since 1898 M. Hanotaux has not been in office, but has devoted himself to literary and historical work. He is a member of the Académie Française, author of *Histoire de la France Contemporaine, Études Diplomatiques,* and many other works, and editor of *Histoire de la Nation Française.*

5. Vol. 15, p. 33, fol'g.

6. "Die anregung wegen die Ubergabe von Manila ist, wie mir Herr Hanotaux sagte, auch hier erfolgt, aber mit Hinweis auf Neutralität sofort und entschieden abgelehnt worden." *Die Grosse Politik,* vol. 15, p. 43. From von Bülow, Secretary of State for Foreign Affairs, to the Kaiser (21 June, '98), quoting a telegram from Prince Münster.

7. "The newspapers of America and of France have had quite a scrap, but it was without just cause. The press here does not represent the Government nor the people at large." Porter to G. M. Dodge, June 22, 1898.

8. "The Government has observed a strict neutrality and has been frank with me from the start and has been prompt to do almost anything I requested." Porter to G. M. Dodge, June 22, 1898.

9. War was declared on April 25.

10. John Sherman had been succeeded, as Secretary of State, by William R. Day.

11. Admiral Dewey entered Manila Bay and overcame the resistance of the Spanish fleet and the arsenal on May 1.

12. Private letter file.

13. The Spanish fleet had been blockaded in Santiago Harbor since the end of May.

14. As Secretary of State; announced on Aug. 7. Secretary Day became one of the Peace Commissioners. Associated with him were Cushman K. Davis, William P. Frye, George Gray, and Whitelaw Reid. The treaty of peace between Spain and the United States was signed on Dec. 10, 1898.

15. Dated Aug. 24; a striking illustration of the effect of the Spanish-American War on the international situation in Europe.

CHAPTER XVII: FRANCO-AMERICAN ENTENTE

Pages 224-237

1. *Instructions to Diplomatic Officers of the United States,* 1897, p. 26. Speeches were to be made only on "exceptional festal occasions."

2. In spite of occasional infelicities such as this, the part played by our country at the Exposition was highly creditable. Our exhibits were everywhere, the United States having the largest display of any foreign country; they were also the earliest in place and the most orderly in arrangement. And at the end we received the highest total of awards of any country outside France.

3. Among the first contributors were Mr. Edward Tuck, the late Mr. John Harjes, and Gen. E. F. Winslow.

4. Presented to the City of Paris by American school-children.

5. Porter had first known Ireland as a young priest indefatigable on the battle-field, saying the Lord's Prayer in Latin or in English, to Catholic and Protestant alike.

6. "Recently America has again captured all Paris, almost as effectually as on the Fourth of July of the Exhibition year, through Barnum and Bailey's 'Show.' After some pains there was secured for its representatives the great Salle des Fêtes which still stands as a souvenir of the Exposition. It certainly is the most magnificent hall in the world, and seats over 8,000 people comfortably. On the opening night, by arrangement with the management, I had a hundred boxes secured for official guests. I sent invitations to the President, Cabinet Ministers, and all the French high public functionaries and the whole diplomatic corps. Nearly all attended, and the representation, with its one thousand selected artists and employees and startling effects, created a sensation, and the success since is the town talk. So America is still ahead, even on the sawdust." Porter to Hay, Dec. 9, 1901. (Private letter file.)

CHAPTER XVIII: KINGS AND COURTS

Pages 238-252

1. The Castle, of which a great part is still in existence, was built in the eleventh century as a fortress against the Norsemen; it had dungeons, and its ghost; King Christopher had been imprisoned and beheaded there.

2. Compare Anna Bowman Dodd's account of these experiences as given in her book, *In the Palaces of the Sultan.*

3. In spite of General Porter's refusal, the Sultan later sent to him through the Turkish Ambassador in Paris, "la Médaille d'or du Liakat"— "Gold medal of patriotism."

4. Afterwards the wife of Senator Albert J. Beveridge.

5. Andrew D. White, who had been Ambassador to Germany since 1897.

6. She had spent most of her life in trying to alleviate the sufferings of

the poor in Moscow, where her husband was governor; she established an order of sisters who were trained as nurses. She was brutally murdered by the Bolsheviks by being thrown down the shaft of a mine.

7. One was Baron Fredericks, afterwards murdered by the Bolsheviks.

CHAPTER XIX: "THE FLOUNDERING EUROPEAN POWERS"

Pages 253-278

1. *Foreign Relations of the United States,* 1899, p. 129 ff.

2. Théophile Delcassé (1852-1923) became Minister of Foreign Affairs in the summer of 1898, succeeding Hanotaux. His effort to establish good relations with Great Britain resulted in the *entente cordiale,* accomplished by the convention of April 8, 1904. The aggressive attitude of France in Morocco provoked active hostility in Germany, and the Kaiser, taking advantage of Russia's weakness as the Russo-Japanese war drew to an end in the spring of 1905, forced the resignation of Delcassé.

3. Diplomatic Correspondence, State Department.

4. *Foreign Relations of the U. S.,* 1899, p. 142.

5. McKinley's annual message, *Foreign Relations of the U. S.,* 1900, p. x.

6. *Foreign Relations of the U. S.,* 1900, p. 311.

7. *Ibid.,* p. 312.

8. *Ibid.,* p. 299.

9. June 10. *Foreign Relations of the U. S.,* 1900, p. 143

10. So the Kaiser stated in a telegram to President Loubet; in point of fact the Kaiser suggested Waldersee to the Tsar. The notes on pp. 82, 83 of *Die Grosse Politik,* vol. 16, call attention to the Kaiser's interference with the procedure of the Foreign Office.

11. Private letter file. In a letter to Whitelaw Reid, Sept. 20, Hay wrote: "About China, it is the devil's own mess. We cannot possibly publish all the facts without breaking off relations with several Powers. We shall have to do the best we can, and take the consequences,—which will be pretty serious, I do not doubt." *Life of John Hay,* by W. R. Thayer, vol. ii, p. 247. It is probably for this same reason that the dispatches announcing the decision which Porter comments on are not printed in *Foreign Relations.* The telegrams on pp. 341-343 (1901, Appendix, *Affairs in China*) throw some light on the subject, as does Commissioner Rockhill's report on p. 5 of the same volume.

12. Private letter file.

13. *Foreign Relations of the U. S.,* 1902, p. 408.

14. "March 28, 1902. Prince Münster died to-day after a short sickness . . . Unfortunately Münster let slip the right moment to resign. To be sure, he was fully equal to his position in Paris and was very highly regarded there; nevertheless, his bodily strength had begun to leave him; his power of work began to decline, as was natural enough at the age of eighty. He was compelled to resign, and in the most unkind manner imaginable. His resentment was directed primarily against the Chancellor and then against Holstein, in whom he rightly saw the originator of it.

To his last breath he never recovered from the pain of this incident." Waldersee's *Denkwürdigkeiten,* vol. iii, p. 183.

15. His agitation is reflected in his dispatches to Berlin. See *Die Grosse Politik,* vol. 20, part ii, pp. 316 ff.

16. *Foreign Relations of the U. S.,* 1904, p. 301.

17. *Ibid.*

18. "Like the Government of the United States, the Government of the French Republic thinks it very desirable that the neutrality of China be respected. But Manchuria, field of military operations, ought to be excepted. Chinese neutrality ought to include leased territories and foreign concessions." Feb. 13. *Foreign Relations of the U. S.,* 1904, p. 302.

19. This is again a case in which a newspaper campaign of propaganda carried on in England, as during the Spanish War (*see* p. 202), had for its object the making of trouble between the United States and a European nation.

20. In the following months Delcassé negotiated four other similar treaties.

21. In the years 1903-1905 the nations of Europe ratified with each other and with the nations of the New World over sixty arbitration treaties; (*The Hague Peace Conferences of 1899 and 1907,* vol. i, pp. 813-815.) The epidemic did not reach the United States till 1908 when, in the course of a few weeks, the Senate ratified twelve treaties, of which the first was with France. Except for a treaty with Great Britain (July, 1904), and one with the United States which was not ratified by the Senate, Germany proved immune.

CHAPTER XX: AN AMERICAN IN EXILE

Pages 279-292

1. Private letter file.

2. Diplomatic Correspondence, State Department.

3. My mother's body was taken to New York, and my brother Clarence and his wife buried her, beside her two sons, in the quiet shaded cemetery of West Long Branch.

4. After being minister to several countries, Jackson gave up his diplomatic career. In 1914 he volunteered his services at our Embassy in Berlin, where his former experience and his knowledge of German made him immensely valuable. In Germany he also looked after the welfare of the English prisoners, a work of untiring devotion and expenditure of strength. Broken in health, he died at Montreux in 1921.

5. *Private Letters of John Hay,* vol. ii, p. 348.

CHAPTER XXI: JOHN PAUL JONES

Pages 293-307

1. a. The *Century Magazine,* October, 1905: "The Recovery of the Body of John Paul Jones," by Horace Porter.

b. John Paul Jones Commemoration at Annapolis, 1907.

c. *John Paul Jones:* Supplement to Report of the Committee on Correspondence of the Grand Lodge F.A.A.M., of the District of Columbia, 1907.

d. Unveiling of the Statue of John Paul Jones, Washington, April 17, 1912.

e. *Foreign Relations of the United States,* 1905, pp. 417-445.

2. In his report Admiral Sigsbee wrote: "I am informed that this is the only occasion when a large body of foreign armed men has been permitted to parade in the streets of Paris in time of peace—that is to say, when not active allies engaged in war." See *John Paul Jones:* Supplement to Report of the Committee on Correspondence, Grand Lodge F.A.A.M., p. 622.

3. The new Ambassador, Robert C. McCormick, and the two special ambassadors designated for the occasion, Gen. Porter and Mr. Loomis, first assistant secretary of state.

CHAPTER XXII: PEACE OR WAR?

Pages 311-332

1. Of the $135,000 appropriated by Congress for the purpose $35,000 represents the sum that Porter expended in France in connection with the recovery of the body. He refused to be reimbursed for this expenditure, and asked that the amount be added to the appropriation for the crypt.

2. *Texts of the Peace Conferences at The Hague,* J. B. Scott, p. 95.

3. Choate had been Ambassador to Great Britain from 1899 to 1905.

4. "Her First Delegate was made President of the Conference and it was he who, after consulting with the representatives of other nations, appointed the presidents of the several commissions among which the business of the Conference was distributed, and it was he, a skilled and experienced diplomatist, who, as President of the Conference, was authorized to appear and take part in the proceedings of any committee or subcommittee, and who, on all critical and important occasions, availed himself of that privilege. Besides this, as before, the State of Montenegro made the delegates of Russia its own, and thus Russia had two votes on every question that came up, instead of the one of every other nation." *The Two Hague Conferences,* by Joseph H. Choate, p. 54.

5. See Secretary Root's instructions, *Foreign Relations of the United States* (1907), pp. 1128-1139.

6. Interview with James Brown Scott.

7. *The Two Hague Conferences,* by Joseph H. Choate, pp. 61, 62.

8. *Ibid.,* pp. 64, 65.

9. The claim against Paraguay (see Moore's *Digest of International Arbitrations,* vol. 2, pp. 1485-1549).

10. Introduction to Scott's *Texts of the Peace Conferences,* p. xxii.

11. *The Two Hague Conferences,* p. 61. The states not voting were Belgium, Roumania, Sweden, Switzerland, and Venezuela. In the final form

the convention provided that armed force should not be used unless "the debtor state refuses or neglects to reply to an offer of arbitration, or after accepting the offer, prevents any *compromis* [formulation of terms] from being agreed on, or, after the arbitration fails to submit to the award." Scott's *Texts of the Peace Conferences,* p. 194.

12. The Swiss army is a national militia, its only permanent forces being the corps of instructors and the fortress guards. Liability to service extends from the twentieth to the forty-eighth year; the term for the first year is from sixty to ninety days according to the arm of service. For the remaining eleven years of the Élite, the term is from eleven to fourteen days annually. For the next eight years in the Landwehr there is a two weeks' course every four years. Candidates for commissions and for further promotion take special courses in the school for officers.

13. New York *American,* April 22, 1909. Carnegie's address on the occasion dealt with the danger to world peace from the naval rivalry of Germany and Great Britain.

14. Union College had similarly honored him in 1894.

INDEX

INDEX